LIBRARY SCIENCE TEXT SERIES

Introduction to Public Services for Library Technicians. 3rd ed. By Marty Bloomberg.

Introduction to Technical Services for Library Technicians. 4th ed. By Marty Bloomberg and G. Edward Evans.

Immroth's Guide to the Library of Congress Classification. 3rd ed. By Lois Mai Chan.

Science and Engineering Literature: A Guide to Reference Sources. 3rd ed. By H. Robert Malinowsky, and Jeanne M. Richardson.

The Vertical File and Its Satellites: A Handbook of Acquisition, Processing, and Organization. 2nd ed. By Shirley Miller.

Introduction to United States Public Documents. 2nd ed. By Joe Morehead.

The School Library Media Center. 2nd ed. By Emanuel T. Prostano and Joyce S. Prostano.

The Humanities: A Selective Guide to Information Sources. 2nd ed. By A. Robert Rogers.

Introduction to Library Science: Basic Elements of Library Service. By Jesse H. Shera.

The School Librarian as Educator. By Lillian Biermann Wehmeyer.

Introduction to Cataloging and Classification. 6th ed. By Bohdan S. Wynar, with the assistance of Arlene Taylor Dowell and Jeanne Osborn.

Library Management. 2nd ed. By Robert D. Stueart and John Taylor Eastlick.

An Introduction to Classification and Number Building in Dewey. By Marty Bloomberg and Hans Weber.

Map Librarianship: An Introduction. By Mary Larsgaard.

Micrographics. By William Saffady.

Developing Library Collections. By G. Edward Evans.

Problems in Library Management. By A. J. Anderson.

Introduction to AV for Technical Assistants. By Albert J. Casciero and Raymond G. Roney.

Introduction to
Library Services
for
Library Technicians

Introduction to
LIBRARY SERVICES
for
LIBRARY TECHNICIANS

By
BARBARA E. CHERNIK

1982
LIBRARIES UNLIMITED, INC.
Littleton, Colorado

Copyright © 1982 Libraries Unlimited, Inc.
All Rights Reserved
Printed in the United States of America

No part of this publication may be reproduced, stored in a retrieval
system, or transmitted, in any form or by any means, electronic,
mechanical, photocopying, recording, or otherwise, without the prior
written permission of the publisher.

LIBRARIES UNLIMITED, INC.
P.O. Box 263
Littleton, Colorado 80160

Library of Congress Cataloging in Publication Data

Chernik, Barbara E., 1938-
    Introduction to library services for library
technicians.

    (Library science text series)
    Includes index.
    1. Library technicians--United States.
2. Library administration--United States.
I. Title. II. Series.
Z682.C534   023'.3   81-15663
ISBN 0-87287-275-0   AACR2
ISBN 0-87287-282-3 (pbk.)

Libraries Unlimited books are bound with Type II nonwoven material that meets
and exceeds National Association of State Textbook Administrators' Type II
nonwoven material specifications Class A through E.

This book is dedicated
with deep affection
to my family, my students, and my colleagues.

PREFACE

Introduction to Library Services for Library Technicians is written for persons who want to work in libraries or who presently are working in libraries. It is also written for persons who have wondered why communities have so many libraries and why and how these libraries differ from one another. Designed to be used in an introductory course in a Library Media Technical Assistant program, this text will approach library services both in general terms and specific terms that focus upon individual types of libraries so as to familiarize the student with the role of the LMTA in a variety of library settings. It will explain the historical development and definition of library philosophy as well as the practical results of the service imperative in public, school, academic, and special libraries. In addition, the levels of personnel that have been established in the organization of these libraries will be outlined in order that the student will know of the various roles today's library technicians may be asked to play. Each type of library will also be explained in terms of its collection and of the relationship between the materials a library holds and its stated goals and objectives. Finally, the reader will be introduced to the changing technology of the library world and to the increasingly important position this technology creates for the technician.

A study of the major types of libraries and their differing objectives should help the reader to understand why libraries are so similar in some areas and yet so different in others. The directions a new LMTA may take are many, and it is hoped this book will give context to the career of library technician. The specific means of executing library procedures and library operations will not be discussed here, because this will vary greatly from institution to institution. Instead, *Introduction to Library Services* will concentrate on the objectives and policies that determine a library's procedures and operations. An LMTA program should train future technicians to become integral parts of the services libraries provide. This text is designed to introduce those services and to describe the technician's place in library operations.

TABLE OF CONTENTS

LIST OF FIGURES

1
THE DEVELOPMENT OF LIBRARIES

WHAT IS A LIBRARY?

Libraries are probably as old as writing itself, which began in 3500-3000 B.C. And yet, if the question "What is a library?" were asked of a group of people on the street, the answers would probably be as varied as the people themselves. Many people would probably simply define a library as a building that has a lot of books. Other persons might go one step further and describe those books — ones read for pleasure or for study — and a few persons might even comment that the books are organized in some manner. However, probably very few persons would think of the library as a collection of materials organized for use — the definition librarians prefer to use.

Even to librarians, however, this definition is not quite adequate. It does not include the fundamental functions of a library: the acquisition, preservation, and dissemination of information in all its graphic forms. To some librarians, this means that the library is part of society's educational and informational system. To them, a library helps educate citizens and exerts a cultural influence on society. To other librarians, this means that the library should make information and graphic materials available and should not be an arbiter of culture. Finally, for some librarians, the library should be a free institution, open to all and serving the needs of every age and every group.

This difference of opinion about what a library really is results from the many different kinds of libraries that have been developed to serve the needs of particular groups of people or segments of our society. For example, school libraries have been developed to provide materials that support the school curriculum. College and university libraries, or "academic libraries," not only support the curriculum but also provide and preserve information and resources for projects ranging from term papers to original research. Other libraries may be devoted to supporting research in companies or industries. These latter libraries are often called "special libraries" because they serve the needs of special groups of people.

The type of library which, however, is probably most familiar to the majority of American readers is the public library. Yet even this institution has developed many different forms to satisfy a variety of needs or purposes. Public libraries are used for leisure reading, for answering questions, to complete class assignments, for self-improvement, for enjoyment, and for learning in general. These various public needs — libraries' various objectives — have been identified as educational, informational, cultural (or aesthetic appreciation), recreational, and research objectives. These basic objectives, combined with the additional needs of social responsibility and the preservation of ideas, have seemed to guide the development of libraries throughout history.

THE NEEDS AND CONDITIONS OF
LIBRARY DEVELOPMENT

This variety of libraries—public, school, academic, and special—did not spring up full blown overnight. Instead, libraries have developed over the thousands of years since writing began in order to meet certain needs and conditions of the societies in which they existed.[1] Though societies throughout history have developed differently, their information needs have remained surprisingly similar. Societies need to preserve governmental and other archival documents for future generations. They also need to support general education as well as religious and moral instruction. Educated and cultured people need literature and information for self-education and self-improvement; they may also have a general interest in scholarly research and in the exploration of new fields of knowledge. In addition, many cultured people have shown an aesthetic need for collecting and possessing books just for the beauty and pleasure they give. These societal needs have influenced the growth of libraries, and libraries in turn have influenced the growth of the societies in which they prospered. However, since not all societies developed strong libraries, it is important to look at the conditions that tended to foster library growth.

Libraries tend to prosper when a combination of certain social, political, and economic conditions exists in a society. Libraries develop during stable social climates when there are periods of relative peace and tranquility that enable individuals to pursue leisure activities. They also prosper wherever a literate population places emphasis on the arts and culture, on self-improvement, and on intellectual creativity. Societies with large urban areas usually stimulate scientific discovery and technological advancement, which encourages the use and growth of libraries. When society's institutions—its schools and government—need to educate and inform the citizenry, libraries also become important. Finally, economic prosperity and a surplus of wealth are needed to provide the financial support for library growth. This economic support is a very important factor in library development because without it the other conditions of society may not provide enough support for library development.

When all of these conditions combine favorably in a society, a flourishing culture develops which can influence the course of history. The following discussion of the history of libraries will review those societies in which these conditions combined to produce both flourishing cultures and flourishing libraries.

THE DEVELOPMENT OF WESTERN LIBRARIES

Although the different types of libraries developed to meet similar needs, the form and function of each library have been largely determined by the society it served. The most striking difference between these societies is in the formats of their written materials. Records were first made on clay tablets, then on rolls of papyrus or parchment, and finally on materials fastened together in a format similar to that of our present book. Despite these differences, libraries could not have flourished unless the raw materials were easily and cheaply available and a book trade was well-established.

Writing and the history of Western libraries began around 3000 B.C. in an area around the Tigris and Euphrates Rivers called the Fertile Crescent.[2] (*See*

Fig. 1-1, page 20, for historical library sites.) Between 3000-650 B.C. this area saw the development of three civilizations — Sumer, Babylonia, and Assyria. The Sumerian and Babylonian civilizations developed libraries of clay tablets which consisted of archives or government and tax records. By contrast, the Assyrians established libraries that were large and well-organized and covered many subject areas; they were not just archives. But these libraries were destroyed later by Roman conquerors.

All of the conditions necessary for library development seem to have existed in Greece around 600 B.C.: a literate population enjoyed peace and tranquility and the economic ability to pursue intellectual creativity and scientific inquiry. Little concrete evidence of Greek libraries has remained thanks to the Roman invaders, but it is assumed that libraries had to exist to support the achievements of the Greek civilization. It is known that public libraries existed and that the Athens public library stored original copies of the Greek plays so that persons could read or copy from them. The major Greek libraries, however, seemed to have been the private libraries of Greek citizens. Plato had a large library, and Aristotle collected one of the largest libraries in Greece, which has been called the greatest library of the ancient world. These private libraries supported self-education rather than just providing aesthetic pleasure for their owners. When the Roman generals invaded Greece in 86 B.C., they captured these magnificent libraries and took them back to Rome as trophies. In Rome, the private libraries seem to have become status symbols rather than libraries for the edification of their owners.

Greek libraries were not the only libraries destroyed by conquerors. The Egyptian library at Alexandria eventually met a similar fate. This great library was founded in 290 B.C. by descendants of Alexander the Great and became one of the most important libraries of its time. Its collection was enormous — 700,000 papyrus rolls, covered every subject, and contained almost all of the literature of the ancient world. The collection was developed by gathering written materials throughout the world. All ships and travelers who came to Egypt had to surrender any manuscripts they possessed. These were copied, the originals placed in the library, and the copies returned to the original owners. Alexandria's library was rivaled only by the great library at Pergamum. In fact, such a great rivalry between the two developed that Alexandria refused to export the papyrus reeds needed to make writing material. In defense, Pergamum developed the process of curing lamb and kid hides to make parchment for their rolls. The Pergamum library supposedly was brought to Cleopatra by Mark Antony in 43 B.C. However, the Alexandria library itself was slowly dismantled, beginning in 47 B.C. with the siege of Julius Caesar and ending with its complete destruction by the Muslims in A.D. 642.

Parts of the Alexandria library were probably added to the spoils of the private libraries of the Roman conquerors. However, the conditions in Roman civilization were also very favorable for the development of all kinds of libraries. A.D. 96-180 was a time of peace, prosperity, and order, which allowed public libraries to prosper. The demand for books stimulated a book trade, and the codex or book form replaced papyrus and parchment rolls. Besides private and public libraries, early Christian libraries were developed, which set the pattern for later monastic libraries. Roman libraries were themselves threatened and destroyed by the time Rome fell in the fifth century.

The fall of Rome would have been disastrous for the history of libraries if the Roman Emperor Constantine had not moved his capital to Byzantium, or

Figure 1-1
Famous library sites in the development of libraries

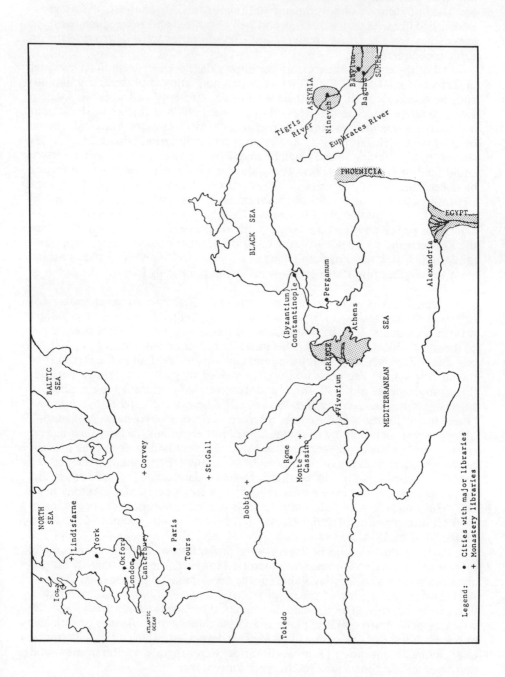

Constantinople as he renamed it, in A.D. 325. Many Roman libraries were moved to this new capital, and the remains of Aristotle's library seem to have also found a new home in this growing civilization. The Byzantine empire flourished from the seventh to the eleventh century, and it preserved the works of both the Greek and the Roman culture. This became important because the conditions in Europe were so chaotic that library development practically came to a standstill there for many centuries.

The sixth to the tenth centuries in Europe became known as the Dark Ages because Europe had been invaded by peoples who were interested neither in culture nor in writings. Also, the social, political, and economic conditions necessary for a society to flourish were not present. This was generally a time when the most dominant need for libraries was the need to preserve ideas for future generations. During these centuries, writings and ideas were preserved in monasteries and monastery libraries because the clergy formed the only literate class. These havens of learning began to loan their copies of Greek and Latin manuscripts back and forth and to make catalogs of their collections. When the political and social climates began to change in the twelfth through the fourteenth century, these libraries were ready to provide a basis for learning.

In contrast to those in Europe during these centuries, the libraries in the Middle East were flourishing. Besides the Byzantine culture, an Islamic empire was established by the Muslims and centered in Baghdad from 750-1050. This society emphasized literacy and encouraged the establishment of schools. Learning was encouraged, and medical and scientific advancements were made. Paper was used as a writing material and books were highly prized. The power and influence of the Islamic culture stretched from Persia around Northern Africa to Spain. In fact, many manuscripts were taken to Spain where they were translated into Latin and passed into the universities of Europe. In the eleventh, twelfth, and thirteenth centuries, this Muslim culture was finally destroyed from without by the crusades and the Mongols and from within by civil wars and religious dissension. The Christian crusaders conquered parts of both Byzantium and Islam and brought back many of the library treasures which had been preserved by these Middle Eastern libraries. Aristotle's library was even returned. A brisk trade developed in classical manuscripts which contained ideas that encouraged the beginning of the Renaissance.

Europe during the thirteenth, fourteenth, and fifteenth centuries began to stabilize. Societies became more secure, and economic trade between countries developed. Persons other than clerics began to read and to feel a need for learning. New ideas were generated based on the classical writings returned from the East. Students who had travelled around following their teachers from city to city began to settle down and establish universities. The Renaissance, or rebirth of learning, and a renewed interest in the humanities and arts flourished from the fourteenth through the sixteenth century. All of the conditions seemed to be favorable for the development of libraries. There was enough wealth to begin large libraries such as the Vatican Library, the Sorbonne Library at the University of Paris, and state and royal libraries. In fact, many of Europe's great libraries were founded during this time.[3]

In the 1400s, the development of printing coincided with a strong growth in nationalism. This meant that books could be written in the vernacular or local language and that many copies could be made available. The Reformation also encouraged the growth of national religions which needed religious materials for everyone to read. These needs helped encourage the spread of literacy and the production of new literature.

From 1500-1800 there was a spread of literacy and libraries throughout Western Europe. Town libraries sprang up in Germany, and circulating or lending libraries provided popular reading. Great Britain founded municipal libraries in the 1600s, and when the British Parliament passed the first Public Libraries Act in 1850, there were already 800 small libraries in Britain. University libraries began to expand during this time. At first, universities had relied upon book stores to supply students with copies of the needed texts. But as the universities grew, libraries soon developed because there were not enough books for the students to use. Private donations such as that of Thomas Bodley to Oxford University provided the bases for the development of great university collections as well as the expansion of national libraries. The British Museum was based on the donation of private collections, and the Bibliotheque Nationale in Paris was based on royal libraries confiscated in the French Revolution. National and state libraries became depositories for the written productions of a country. At the end of the 1800s, the library had been firmly established as an institution which satisfied the needs of the Western European societies.

THE DEVELOPMENT OF AMERICAN LIBRARIES

The development of American libraries paralleled the growth of European libraries from 1500-1800.[4] During this period, not only were private library collections developed, but many became the basis for great university libraries. One private library even became the basis for the United States' national library, The Library of Congress. The first important American libraries were private collections gathered by Colonial leaders such as Thomas Jefferson and William Byrd, both of Virginia, and Governor John Winthrop, Jr. of Connecticut. The subject content of these collections ranged from theology to law, farming, and science, and the volumes were shared with friends and neighbors. These libraries were important because, early in the history of the United States, it was recognized that ideas and education were needed if new colonies and a new nation were to survive.

To satisfy these needs, colleges and universities were quickly established in the new colonies. John Harvard gave his collection of 300 books to help the founding of Harvard University in 1638, and a group of ministers gave some of their own books to found the Yale University library. However, among the early colleges there was a protective attitude toward these library collections, and as in Europe, students' access to them was limited. As late as the 1850s, some libraries were only open one or two hours a week. To enrich themselves in spite of this attitude, students formed literary societies and developed their own libraries. These were later incorporated into the college libraries when educators realized that students needed access to the library's great store of knowledge. In fact, this need for information eventually caused universities and colleges to develop some of the best and largest library collections in the world.

The early colonists believed in the freedom of ideas, the freedom of religion, and the right of people to pursue knowledge. Many brought books with them from Europe and shared them among their friends. In 1731, Benjamin Franklin and some of his friends started the first subscription library in Philadelphia. This library was the forerunner of the many subscription or social libraries that developed in the United States before 1850. These voluntary association libraries were supported by dues, which were used to buy books everyone could use. The subscription libraries fulfilled the needs of the people for self-improvement and self-education – self-improvement so that they could become more cultured and perhaps move upward in society, and self-education so that they could get better vocational training. There were subscription libraries for the general public, merchant's apprentice libraries for those learning trades, mercantile libraries for clerks in the new businesses, and libraries for the factory and labor towns. Often, these libraries were begun by persons who wanted to upgrade the young people and to keep them out of trouble during their leisure hours in the teeming mill towns and urban centers. These social libraries were the true forerunners of the American public library.

In 1800 the Library of Congress was founded to give the members of Congress access to the information they needed. When the Capitol building was built, space was made available for a library to serve the needs of legislators. This library was destroyed when the capitol was burned by the British in the War of 1812.[5] To replace the library's collection, Congress purchased Thomas Jefferson's private collection of 6,700 volumes for $25,000. Since Jefferson's collection covered a wide subject range, this purchase changed the course of the library's development. Instead of remaining a small library to serve legislators' needs, the Library of Congress began to develop into the great national library that it has become today.

The first American public libraries were begun in 1803 in Salisbury, Connecticut, and in 1833 in Peterborough, New Hampshire, but it was not until the Boston Public Library was begun in the 1850s that the publicly supported library we know today became a part of the American scene. This is probably because the conditions necessary for developing strong libraries came together at that time. Public library development follows public education, and by the middle of the nineteenth century formal systems of education had been accepted as important to the American way of life. Many people recognized that learning should continue after formal education. The development of the American Lyceum and Chautauqua movements enhanced education, encouraged continuing education by adults, and helped awaken an interest in the arts, literature, and science.

The social, economic and cultural conditions were all favorable to library development in the latter half of the 1800s. Urban areas were growing; a dynamic nation needed trained persons to work in new occupations; and a democratic nation needed an informed citizenry. Most importantly, a surplus of wealth was available to provide for the establishment and support of libraries. The Boston Public Library and the New York Public Library were begun by donations from wealthy businessmen and philanthropists. All over the country, libraries in colleges and towns were begun and named after alumni or citizens who took great pride in establishing libraries. The steel magnate, Andrew Carnegie, gave over 40 million dollars to public libraries throughout the United States. The only stipulation made by most of these donors was that local communities had to agree to provide continued support for the libraries through public taxation. Beginning with the last quarter of the nineteenth century, public libraries became an important educational and social agency in communities all over the United States.

The century of library development from 1876 to 1976 began with several important library events. In 1876, the American Library Association was founded, and *Library Journal* began publication. Both of these helped to promote the dissemination of information about library services. In this same year, Melvil Dewey published his classification system, which was designed to be used by all libraries to organize their collections. Several years later, Dewey opened the first library school at Columbia University for training professional librarians. Thus, professional staffs, associations, and publications were combined with the right social, political, and economic conditions to encourage the development of strong American libraries.

In addition to the tremendous growth and expansion of academic and public libraries, the twentieth century also brought the establishment of libraries in the public schools.[6] Growth of school libraries has depended upon the educational philosophy of the school systems of which they were a part. Although school libraries had begun in the 1800s, it was not until the educational philosophy of study and inquiry became prevalent in the 1900s that school libraries became important. This change in philosophy encouraged high schools to develop libraries that supported students' inquiries into classroom subjects and that would meet their needs for college preparation. Since this latter incentive was a negligible one for elementary and junior high schools and since the spirit of inquiry there was less pronounced, library development at these levels was also less widespread. Although libraries in elementary and junior high schools did develop in large metropolitan areas, they were often few and far between in rural areas. In fact, the country's need for libraries in elementary and junior high schools was not fully recognized until the Soviet Union launched the first space satellite, Sputnik, in 1957.

This event emphasized a need for teaching science, mathematics, and modern foreign languages at all levels and thrust the United States into a technological and scientific race for national supremacy. Since most educational institutions were unprepared for this, the federal government stepped in and provided federal monies to help schools, colleges, and libraries to prepare people to acquire the technological skills and retraining needed in this society. In 1958, the National Defense Education Act was passed to provide monies for school resources and was followed by such acts as the Library Services and Construction Act, the Elementary and Secondary Education Act and the Higher Education Act. A new technological science, Information Science, was also founded and integrated into the library's information resources as libraries tried to meet the technological needs of their society.

These technological needs also brought into being the fourth major type of library—the special library. These libraries were primarily developed in the twentieth century to satisfy needs for research and access to information. They are found in businesses, industries, organizations, institutions, and government agencies. Special library collections may be in-depth subject collections, extensive collections of specific types of materials (e.g., maps, music), collections of an organization's historical records and documents. However, it is not the content of their collections which sets special libraries apart, it is their emphasis on providing information for the members of their parent institutions or organizations. No matter whether special libraries are large or small, they generally serve the same objective—to provide the needed information to the patron as quickly as possible. For this reason, these libraries have filled the important need for specialized knowledge which a technical society has and which other libraries could not afford to meet.

To be sure that all of these types of libraries were meeting the needs of all of the American people, a National Commission on Libraries and Information Science (NCLIS) was established in the sixties. The purpose of this commission was to investigate the nation's library and information services to determine whether national policies and national programs should be established. After a decade of study, NCLIS identified a number of major problems facing U.S. libraries in the seventies.[7] Primarily, their growth had been fragmented and uneven, and the libraries in well-financed areas had developed better services than those in poorer sections of the country. Library collections in colleges and schools were too small to meet the demands of the post-Sputnik society, and funding was inadequate at every level. The tremendous growth in the twentieth century in the amount of materials being produced and information being made available made it impossible for every library to purchase all the information it needed. Special libraries only served the needs of a limited clientele, and their information was not accessible enough to others who could use it. Finally, there was a critical need to address the problems of those people who were without basic library service.

The commission has recommended a national program to attempt to solve these problems and to ensure basic minimums of library and information services for all of the American people. This program is based on the principle that "information is a national resource" and as such is as important as are the natural resources. Among other things, it encourages the strengthening of existing library systems and the development of a national information network. It also recognizes that the problems identified by NCLIS could best be remedied by providing leadership and funds on a national, federal level.

Whether this ambitious program will succeed or not will probably depend upon the economic conditions of American society in the 1980s. The national program was stymied by the economic recessions of the 1970s. Libraries were hit doubly hard by a reduction of federal funds without a corresponding increase of revenue-sharing funds from the states and cities. Many libraries had to curtail their programs and activities. Not only were outreach programs, which had been initiated under federal monies, curtailed, but some libraries had to cut such basic services as branch libraries and to shorten library hours. The surplus of wealth needed to finance dynamic library services seems to have dried up for a while. If libraries are to overcome this handicap in the 1980s and the 1990s, society must be convinced that strong library and information centers are needed to satisfy important needs of society that other agencies cannot fulfill.

REVIEW QUESTIONS

1. Use the definitions preferred by librarians to define a library.

2. Identify the major needs or conditions that encouraged the development of the following libraries: Renaissance libraries, college and university libraries, subscription or social libraries, school libraries, special libraries.

3. Identify the major needs and conditions that encouraged American library development in the twentieth century.

4.   Briefly state your own concept of library service based on your definition of a library and the major objectives a library should fulfill.

5.   Choose a local library and identify the needs or conditions that encouraged this library's establishment.

SELECTED READINGS

Armour, Richard. *The Happy Bookers: A Playful History of Librarians and Their World from the Stone Age to the Distant Future*. New York: McGraw-Hill, c1976.

Estabrook, Leigh. *Libraries in Post-Industrial Society*. Phoenix, AZ: Oryx Press, 1977.

Hessel, A. *A History of Libraries*. 2nd ed. Translated by Reuben Peiss. New Brunswick, NJ: Scarecrow, 1955.

Hobson, Anthony. *Great Libraries*. New York: Putnam's, c1970.

Jackson, Sidney L. *Libraries and Librarianship in the West: A Brief History*. New York: McGraw-Hill, c1974.

Johnson, Elmer D. *Communication: An Introduction to the History of Writing, Printing, Books and Libraries*. 3rd ed. New York: Scarecrow, 1966.

Johnson, Elmer D. *History of Libraries in the Western World*. 3rd ed. Completely revised by Elmer D. Johnson and Michael H. Harris. Metuchen, NJ: Scarecrow, 1976.

Kent, A., and H. Lancour, eds. *Encyclopedia of Library and Information Science*. New York: Dekker, 1968- .

Knight, Douglas M., ed. *Libraries at Large: Tradition, Innovation and the National Interest*. Ed. by Douglas M. Knight and E. Shepley Nourse. New York: Bowker, 1969.

Shera, Jesse. *Foundations of the Public Library: The Origins of the Public Library Movement in New England, 1624-1855*. Hamden, CT: Shoe String, 1965.

U.S. National Commission on Libraries and Information Science. *Toward a National Program for Library and Information Services: Goals for Action*. Washington, DC: GPO, 1975.

NOTES

[1]Jean Key Gates, *Introduction to Librarianship* (New York: McGraw-Hill, c1968), p. 89-94; Elmer D. Johnson, *History of Libraries in the Western World*, 3rd ed. (Metuchen, NJ: Scarecrow, 1976), pp. 4-5.

[2]For more information on the history of libraries, consult the Selected Readings at the end of this chapter.

[3]*Great Libraries*, by Anthony Hobson (New York: Putnam, c1970), is a beautifully illustrated book that describes these libraries.

[4]For more information on the development of American libraries, consult the Selected Readings at the end of this chapter.

[5]In 1978, the Oxford University Press paid the Library of Congress with contemporary five pound and one pound notes, and with 14 rare antique shillings (about $13.00). This served as repayment for the three Oxford University Press books burned.

[6]For further discussion of this development *see* chapters 5-8.

[7]U.S. National Commission on Libraries and Information Science, *Toward a National Program for Library and Information Services: Goals for Action* (Washington, DC: GPO, 1975), pp. 23-24.

2
LIBRARY AND MEDIA PERSONNEL

In order to run today's complicated libraries, many different types of library personnel are needed. These types of personnel range from head librarians or library directors to librarians, library technicians, clerks, aides, pages, and even bookkeepers and custodians. Each category requires specific job knowledge and experience, and is defined by specific duties which separate it from the next position in the career lattice. For example, library media technical assistants (LMTAs) require some general education background and library knowledge in order to assist librarians in running the internal operations of the library. Librarians require a broad general education background and a foundation in the theory of library science in order to direct and organize a library. These personnel are supported by library clerks, aides, and pages who have more limited library knowledge and who perform specific library operations. Together, they all provide the knowledge and skills that the general public has come to consider as library services.

PERSONAL CHARACTERISTICS

In addition to a general education and a knowledge of how a library works, there are other characteristics that are important for library employees. These are personal characteristics and qualities that center on the inner interests and motives of people and that indicate whether or not an individual would be successful in working in a library. Although it would probably be difficult to use one or two adjectives to describe all of the staff members in a large library staff, a number of personal characteristics and qualities have been identified as common to most library staff members. It is not expected that each staff member will possess all of these qualities, but they may serve as useful guidelines for encouraging a staff member to develop such qualities.

Two of the most basic characteristics needed by persons working in libraries are an interest in people and a concern for the accuracy of details. Very few library or media jobs are free from a need for these two characteristics. Contrary to myth, persons in libraries do not have to love books or to love reading books, and they certainly do not spend their working days reading books. Instead, library staff members are involved with bringing people and these materials together. If they do not like being with people or helping people, they will not be successful in fulfilling this library function. The library maxim, "the right material for the right person at the right time," cannot be adhered to if staff members cannot "tune in" to a person's needs.

Part of this "tuning in" involves attending to details. Since a library law seems to be that the requested item has either just been checked in or checked out to someone else, the staff member must be interested enough to remember such details. Much of the work in libraries is similar to detective work in that staff members must often fit the pieces of a puzzle together to solve a problem or answer a difficult question. They must locate details, analyze them, and make decisions based on their findings. It is the interest with which library staff members approach these decisions that forms a common bond among them.

Other important characteristics good library personnel possess are the ability to exercise judgment and the ability to be flexible. Good judgment is the characteristic many employers most often look for, and yet it is often the hardest to develop. A staff member's judgment should be based on realistically applying library rules and procedures so that the spirit of a library's policies and objectives is carried out. It should also involve flexibility, which will help the employee experiment or adapt when changes seem appropriate or necessary. Finally, good judgment includes the ability to admit one's limitations and, if necessary, to turn a question or problem over to someone who is better able to handle it because of training or experience. Staff members who exercise these abilities are those who help defy and destroy the myths and stereotypes surrounding the library profession.

A list of other characteristics desired of library personnel reads more like a job description for "Superperson!" Yet there are personnel who have fulfilled these descriptions and by their examples have inspired many persons to enter the library field. These characteristics include a pleasant and courteous manner, tact, imagination, intelligence, an open mind, considerateness, a good memory, an ability to communicate well, and a good sense of humor. The best library personnel also seem to be aware of the latest trends in culture and ideas. They can be found in today's libraries, surrounded by patrons who are eager to share and discuss their ideas.

LEVELS OF PERSONNEL

Today's libraries have generally grown larger than operations where one person performs all duties from checking out and shelving materials to selecting, ordering, and classifying them. Rather, in all but the smallest library, there are usually several employees who have distinct job functions separated by the level of responsibility required for each function.

These levels of responsibility were first identified in 1933 by Pierce Butler of the University of Chicago Library School. He defined three levels of library classification: professional library worker, technical library worker, and clerical library worker. He used the word "Professional" to describe the librarian because a profession is a vocation with a service orientation that is based on highly specialized knowledge which comes from extensive education. Butler stated that a

professional library worker must possess a scientific, generalized knowledge which will enable him to discover the complex library needs of a mixed community. His primary concern is with the social effect of the institution. A technical library worker must have been vocationally trained to control the apparatus of the library for an effective realization of its prescribed purpose. His concern is internal institutional efficiency. The clerical worker needs operative skill for performing a particular process. His concern is with the operation performed at his desk.[1]

Although Butler identified these three mutually exclusive levels of library responsibility, they were not generally adopted until the 1970s. Until that time, most libraries had two levels of personnel — professional librarians and nonprofessional personnel. The professional librarian usually had a bachelor's degree in a subject field and a master's degree in Library Science (M.L.S.). Often, a school librarian would have a bachelor's degree in education with a minor of 18-24 hours in library science. The only education that was usually required for nonprofessional personnel was that they be high school graduates. However, the education of many of these employees included several years of college, and for some even a doctoral degree in another subject area. The shortage of librarians brought on by the growth of all libraries after Sputnik in 1957 caused many head librarians to reexamine these personnel categories so that they could make maximum use of the librarians who were available.

This reexamination led the American Library Association (ALA) to adopt a Library Education and Personnel Utilization statement in 1970 which identified four categories of library personnel (*see* Fig. 2-1). This statement also identified the titles, basic requirements, and nature of responsibility for both professional and supportive library positions. Thus, the library world officially recognized that different levels of library knowledge and skills existed for the professional librarian and the untrained nonprofessional. This policy statement also recognized other professionals, such as media specialists, information specialists, etc., as having equal professional status with the professional librarian. This became important as school libraries and school audiovisual centers merged their staffs and facilities into school media centers. However, this has also been a major drawback to the adoption of this policy statement, because school librarians with bachelor's degrees have been reluctant to be relegated to Library Associates at a subprofessional level. Also, audiovisual specialists have found it difficult to join with librarians as members of a single profession. For these and other reasons, this statement has not been implemented on a national basis. However, the statement did, among other things, stimulate studies of job classifications by librarians in many different types of libraries.

Job evaluations or task analyses have been undertaken for school libraries by the School Library Manpower Project, for public libraries by the Illinois Library Task Analysis Project, and for special libraries by the Alberta Government Libraries' Council Job Specifications Committee. Some of these analyses have been based on the premise that "analysis of the nature of the work precedes the determination of both the kinds of personnel needed and the kinds of educational preparation they should have. Analysis on a task-by-task basis of the work performed ... reveals more clearly the nature of the work itself in terms of its demands for skills, aptitudes, and knowledge on the part of the worker."[2] Studies of this nature have tended to support the ALA policy statement and its division of duties into professional, technical, and clerical levels.

The different personnel levels identified by the Personnel Utilization statement were based on the principle that the skills, aptitudes and knowledge needed by each level of library worker can be distinguished from each other in several important areas. The technical (paraprofessional) or subprofessional library worker requires specific library or technical skills, which come from

(Text continues on page 38)

Figure 2-1
Categories of library personnel
(Reprinted by permission of the American Library Association)

LIBRARY EDUCATION
AND PERSONNEL UTILIZATION*

A Statement of Policy Adopted by the Council of the American Library Association, June 30, 1970°°

1 The purpose of the policy statement is to recommend categories of library personnel, and levels of training and education appropriate to the preparation of personnel for these categories, which will support the highest standards of library service for all kinds of libraries and the most effective use of the variety of skills and qualifications needed to provide it.

2 Library service as here understood is concerned with knowledge and information in their several forms—their identification, selection, acquisition, preservation, organization, communication and interpretation, and with assistance in their use.

3 To meet the goals of library service, both professional and supportive staff are needed in libraries. Thus the library occupation is much broader than that segment of it which is the library profession, but the library profession has responsibility for defining the training and education required for the preparation of personnel who work in libraries at any level, supportive or professional.

4 Skills other than those of librarianship may also have an important contribution to make to the achievement of superior library service. There should be equal recognition in both the professional and supportive ranks for those individuals whose expertise contributes to the effective performance of the library.

5 A constant effort must be made to promote the most effective utilization of personnel at all levels, both professional and supportive. The tables on page 2 (Figure 1) suggest a set of categories which illustrate a means for achieving this end.

---

*The policy statement adopted by ALA with the title "Library Education and Manpower." In the spring of 1976, the Office for Library Personnel Resources Advisory Committee edited this statement to remove sexist terminology.

**Throughout this statement, wherever the term "librarianship" is used, it is meant to be read in its broadest sense as encompassing the relevant concepts of information science and documentation; wherever the term "libraries" is used, the current models of media centers, learning centers, educational resources centers, information, documentation, and referral centers are also assumed. To avoid the necessity of repeating the entire gamut of variations and expansions, the traditional library terminology is employed in its most inclusive meaning.

Figure 2-1 (cont'd)

FIGURE 1   CATEGORIES OF LIBRARY PERSONNEL—PROFESSIONAL

TITLE FOR POSITIONS REQUIRING:		BASIC REQUIREMENTS	NATURE OF RESPONSIBILITY
LIBRARY-RELATED QUALIFICATIONS	NONLIBRARY-RELATED QUALIFICATIONS		
Senior Librarian	Senior Specialist	In addition to relevant experience, education beyond the M.A. [i.e., a master's degree in any of its variant designations: M.A., M.L.S., M.S.L.S., M.Ed., etc.] as: post-master's degree; Ph.D.; relevant continuing education in many forms	Top-level responsibilities, including but not limited to administration; superior knowledge of some aspect of librarianship, or of other subject fields of value to the library
Librarian	Specialist	Master's degree	Professional responsibilities including those of management, which require independent judgment, interpretation of rules and procedures, analysis of library problems, and formulation of original and creative solutions for them (normally utilizing knowledge of the subject field represented by the academic degree)

CATEGORIES OF LIBRARY PERSONNEL—SUPPORTIVE

TITLE		BASIC REQUIREMENTS	NATURE OF RESPONSIBILITY
Library Associate	Associate Specialist	Bachelor's degree (with or without course work in library science); OR bachelor's degree, plus additional academic work short of the master's degree (in librarianship for the Library Associate; in other relevant subject fields for the Associate Specialist)	Supportive responsibilities at a high level, normally working within the established procedures and techniques, and with some supervision by a professional, but requiring judgment, and subject knowledge such as is represented by a full, four-year college education culminating in the bachelor's degree.
Library Technical Assistant	Technical Assistant	At least two years of college-level study; OR A.A. degree, with or without Library Technical Assistant training; OR postsecondary school training in relevant skills	Tasks performed as supportive staff to Associates and higher ranks, following established rules and procedures, and including, at the top level, supervision of such tasks
	Clerk	Business school or commercial courses, supplemented by in-service training or on-the-job experience	Clerical assignments as required by the individual library

Figure 2-1 (cont'd)

6 The titles recommended here represent categories or broad classifications, within which it is assumed that there will be several levels of promotional steps. Specific job titles may be used within any category: for example, catalogers, reference librarians, children's librarians would be included in either the "Librarian" or (depending upon the level of their responsibilities and qualifications) "Senior Librarian" categories; department heads, the director of the library, and certain specialists would presumably have the additional qualifications and responsibilities which place them in the "Senior Librarian" category.

7 Where specific job titles dictated by local usage and tradition do not make clear the level of the staff member's qualification and responsibility, it is recommended that reference to the ALA category title be used parenthetically to provide the clarification desirable for communication and reciprocity. For example:

REFERENCE ASSISTANT (Librarian)   HEAD CATALOGER (Senior Librarian)

LIBRARY AIDE (Library Technical Assistant)

8 The title "Librarian" carries with it the connotation of "professional" in the sense that professional tasks are those which require a special background and education on the basis of which library needs are identified, problems are analyzed, goals are set, and original and creative solutions are formulated for them, integrating theory into practice, and planning, organizing, communicating, and administering successful programs of service to users of the library's materials and services. In defining services to users, the professional person recognizes potential users as well as current ones, and designs services which will reach all who could benefit from them.

9 The title "Librarian" therefore should be used only to designate positions in libraries which utilize the qualifications and impose the responsibilities suggested above. Positions which are primarily devoted to the routine application of established rules and techniques, however useful and essential to the effective operation of a library's ongoing services, should not carry the word "Librarian" in the job title.

10 It is recognized that every type and size of library may not need staff appointments in each of these categories. It is urged, however, that this basic scheme be introduced wherever possible to permit where needed the necessary flexibility in staffing.

11 The salaries for each category should offer a range of promotional steps sufficient to permit a career-in-rank. The top salary in any category should overlap the beginning salary in the next higher category, in order to give recognition to the value of experience and knowledge gained on the job.

12 Inadequately supported libraries or libraries too small to be able to afford professional staff should nevertheless have access to the services and supervision of a librarian. To obtain the professional guidance that they themselves cannot supply, such libraries should promote cooperative arrangements or join larger systems of cooperating libraries through which supervisory personnel can be supported. Smaller libraries which are part of such a system can often maintain the local service with building staff at the Associate level.

Figure 2-1 (cont'd)

FIGURE 2

If one thinks of Career *Lattices* rather than Career *Ladders*, the flexibility intended by the Policy Statement may be better visualized. The movement among staff responsibilities, for example, is not necessarily directly up, but often may be lateral to increased responsibilities of equal importance. Each category embodies a number of promotional steps within it, as indicated by the gradation markings on each bar. The top of any category overlaps in responsibility and salary the next higher category.

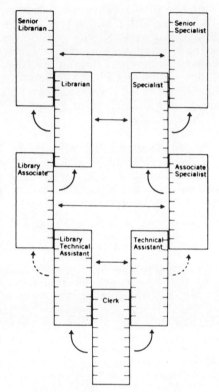

Comments on the Categories

13 The *Clerk* classifications do not require formal academic training in library subjects. The assignments in these categories are based upon general clerical and secretarial proficiencies. Familiarity with basic library terminology and routines necessary to adapt clerical skills to the library's needs is best learned on the job.

14 The *Technical Assistant* categories assume certain kinds of specific "technical" skills; they are not meant simply to accommodate advanced clerks. While clerical skills might well be part of a Technical Assistant's equipment, the emphasis in an assignment should be on the special technical skill. For example, someone who is skilled in handling audiovisual equipment, or at introductory data processing, or in making posters and other displays might well be hired in the Technical Assistant category for these skills, related to librarianship only to the extent that they are employed in a library. A *Library Technical Assistant* is a person with certain specifically library-related skills— in preliminary bibliographic searching for example, or utilization of certain mechanical equipment—the performance of whose duties seldom requires a background in general education.

Figure 2-1 (cont'd)

15 The *Associate* categories assume a need for an educational background like that represented by a bachelor's degree from a good four-year institution of higher education in the United States. Assignments may be such that library knowledge is less important than general education, and whether the title is *Library* Associate or Associate *Specialist* depends upon the nature of the tasks and responsibilities assigned. Persons holding the B.A. degree, with or without a library science minor or practical experience in libraries, are eligible for employment in this category. Titles within the Associate category that are assigned to individuals will depend upon the relevance of their training and background to their specific assignments.

16 The Associate category also provides the opportunity for persons of promise and exceptional talent to begin library employment below the level of professional (as defined in this statement) and thus to combine employment in a library with course work at the graduate level. Where this kind of work/study arrangement is made, the combination of work and formal study should provide 1) increasing responsibility within the Associate ranks as the individual moves through the academic program, and 2) eligibility for promotion, upon completion of the master's degree, to positions of professional responsibility and attendant reclassification to the professional category.

17 The first professional category—*Librarian*, or *Specialist*—assumes responsibilities that are professional in the sense described in paragraph #8 above. A good liberal education plus graduate-level study in the field of specialization (either in librarianship or in a relevant field) are seen as the minimum preparation for the kinds of assignments implied. The title, however, is given for a position entailing professional responsibilities and not automatically upon achievement of the academic degree.

18 The *Senior* categories assume relevant professional experience as well as qualifications beyond those required for admission to the first professional ranks. Normally it is assumed that such advanced qualifications shall be held in some specialty, either in a particular aspect of librarianship or some relevant subject field. Subject specializations are as applicable in the *Senior Librarian* category as they are in the *Senior Specialist* category.

19 Administrative responsibilities entail advanced knowledge and skills comparable to those represented by any other high-level specialty, and appointment to positions in top administration should normally require the qualifications of a *Senior Librarian* with a specialization in administration. This category, however, is not limited to administrators, whose specialty is only one of several specializations of value to the library service. There are many areas of special knowledge within librarianship which are equally important and to which equal recognition in prestige and salary should be given. Highly qualified persons with specialist responsibilities in some aspects of librarianship—archives, bibliography, reference, for example—should be eligible for advanced status and financial rewards without being forced to abandon for administrative responsibilities their areas of major competence.

Figure 2-1 (cont'd)

Implications for Formal Education

20 Until examinations are identified that are valid and reliable tests of equivalent qualifications, the academic degree (or evidence of years of academic work completed) is recommended as the single best means for determining that an applicant has the background recommended for each category.

21 In the selection of applicants for positions at any level, and for admission to library schools, attention should be paid to personal aptitudes and qualifications in addition to academic ones. The nature of the position or specialty, and particularly the degree to which it entails working with others, with the public, or with special audiences or materials should be taken into account in the evaluation of a prospective student or employee.

22 As library services change and expand, as new audiences are reached, as new media take on greater importance in the communication process, and as new approaches to the handling of materials are introduced, the kinds of preparation required of those who will be employed in libraries will become more varied. Degrees in fields other than librarianship will be needed in the Specialist categories. For many Senior Librarian positions, an advanced degree in another subject field rather than an additional degree in librarianship, may be desirable. Previous experience need not always have been in libraries to have pertinence for appointment in a library.

23 Because the principles of librarianship are applied to the materials of information and knowledge broader than any single field, and because they are related to subject matter outside of librarianship itself, responsible education in these principles should be built upon a broad rather than a narrowly specialized background education. To the extent that courses in library science are introduced in the four-year, undergraduate program, they should be concentrated in the last two years and should not constitute a major inroad into course work in the basic disciplines: the humanities, the sciences, and the social sciences.

24 Training courses for Library Technical Assistants at the junior or community college level should be recognized as essentially terminal in intent (or as service courses rather than a formal program of education), designed for the preparation of supportive rather than professional staff. Students interested in librarianship as a career should be counselled to take the general four-year college course rather than the specific two-year program, with its inevitable loss of time and transferable content. Graduates of the two-year programs are not prohibited from taking the additional work leading to the bachelor's and master's degrees, provided they demonstrate the necessary qualifications for admission to the senior college program, but it is an indirect and less desirable way to prepare for a professional career, and the student should be so informed.

25 Emphasis in the two-year Technical Assistant programs should be more on skills training than on general library concepts and procedures. In many cases it would be better from the standpoint of the student to pursue more broadly-based vocational courses which will teach technical skills applicable in a variety of job situations rather than those limited solely to the library setting.

Figure 2-1 (cont'd)

26 Undergraduate instruction in library science other than training courses for Library Technical Assistants should be primarily a contribution to liberal education rather than an opportunity to provide technological and methodological training. This does not preclude the inclusion of course work related to the basic skills of library practice, but it does affect teaching method and approach, and implies an emphasis on the principles that underlie practice rather than how-to-do-it, vocational training.

27 Certain practical skills and procedures at all levels are best learned on the job rather than in the academic classroom. These relate typically to details of operation which may vary from institution to institution, or to routines which require repetition and practice for their mastery. The responsibility for such in-service parts of the total preparation of both librarians and supportive staff rests with libraries and library systems rather than with the library schools.

28 The objective of the master's programs in librarianship should be to prepare librarians capable of anticipating and engineering the change and improvement required to move the profession constantly forward. The curriculum and teaching methods should be designed to serve this kind of education for the future rather than to train for the practice of the present.

29 Certain interdisciplinary concepts (information science is an example) are so intimately related to the basic concepts underlying library service that they properly become a part of the library school curriculum rather than simply an outside specialty. Where such content is introduced into the library school it should be incorporated into the entire curriculum, enriching every course where it is pertinent. The stop-gap addition of individual courses in such a specialty, not integrated into the program as a whole, is an inadequate assimilation of the intellectual contribution of the new concept to library education and thinking.

30 In recognition of the many areas of related subject matter of importance to library service, library schools should make knowledge in other fields readily available to students, either through the appointment of staff members from other disciplines or through permitting students to cross departmental, divisional, and institutional lines in reasoned programs in related fields. Intensive specializations at the graduate level, building upon strengths in the parent institution or the community, are a logical development in professional library education.

31 Library schools should be encouraged to experiment with new teaching methods, new learning devices, different patterns of scheduling and sequence, and other means, both traditional and nontraditional, that may increase the effectiveness of the students' educational experience.

32 Research has an important role to play in the educational process as a source of new knowledge both for the field of librarianship in general and for library education in particular. In its planning, budgeting, and organizational design, the library school should recognize research, both theoretical and applied, as an imperative responsibility.

Figure 2-1 (cont'd)

Continuing Education

33 Continuing Education is essential for all library personnel, professional and supportive, whether they remain within a position category or are preparing to move into a higher one. Continuing education opportunities include both formal and informal learning situations, and need not be limited to library subjects or the offerings of library schools.

34 The "continuing education" which leads to eligibility for Senior Librarian or Specialist positions may take any of the forms suggested directly above so long as the additional education and experience are relevant to the responsibilities of the assignment.

35 Library administrators must accept responsibility for providing support and opportunities (in the form of leaves, sabbaticals, and released time) for the continuing education of their staffs.

---

experience or specialized formal training. These persons need to exercise some judgment in analyzing library information and situations and in comparing them to predetermined guidelines and policies. They are primarily concerned with performing and supervising procedures within the policies of the institution in which they work.

In contrast, the clerical or nonprofessional worker does not require formal academic training because the needed skills are based upon general clerical and secretarial proficiencies.[3] The employee on this level does not exercise judgment or evaluative abilities and is only concerned with specific job duties; he or she is more concerned with *how* to do something than with *why* it is done. The professional librarian or specialist needs the breadth and depth of knowledge that can be gained from extensive education. Second, the professional needs to exercise creative, interpretive, evaluative, and analytical abilities in order to develop library service programs. Finally, the professional needs to apply the philosophy, principles, and theories of library services to developing, assessing, and adapting these programs in response to a community's changing needs.[4] The differences among these levels may be more clearly observed by comparing the example duties and the choice of verbs used for each level in Figure 2-2.

In addition to these levels of employees, libraries also have other positions which require minimal library knowledges and skills. Library pages and student employees usually shelve library materials and keep them in order. These employees may also assist library clerks in other duties such as inventory or serial control. Library secretaries, bookkeepers, and custodians perform duties for the library which are similar to their counterparts in the school or business worlds.

(Text continues on page 40)

Figure 2-2

Examples of personnel duties from task analyses

Reprinted from *Personnel Utilization in Libraries: A Systems Approach.* Prepared for the Illinois Library Task Analysis Project by Myrl Ricking and Robert E. Booth; Published in Cooperation with the Illinois State Library (Chicago: ALA, 1974).

2 COLLECTION ORGANIZATION SUBSYSTEM

P Professional	T Technical	C Clerical
1 Develops and expands classification systems	1 Performs descriptive cataloging of materials for which LC cards or MARC tapes are not available	1 Types cards or inputs data for catalogs, shelf list, and other files from copy provided
2 Establishes, and directs maintenance of, cataloging records	2 Catalogs fiction	2 Reproduces cards in quantity by a variety of processes: tape, photocopy, multigraph, mimeograph
3 Supervises contributions to union catalogs and bibliographic centers and participates in cooperative cataloging arrangements	3 Performs simple classification of materials identified in standard tools	3 Arranges catalog cards in sets, following established procedures

5 CIRCULATION SUBSYSTEM

P Professional	T Technical	C Clerical
		a Registration Module
1 Establishes circulation system for all types of materials	1 Supervises established circulation and registration procedures	1 Explains the library's registration policies and procedures 1.1 Gives applicants any printed information available about the library's services, collections, and procedures
2 Receives and responds to sensitive complaints and inquiries	2 Responds to user complaints, presented in person, by mail, or telephone 2.1 Checks out reasons for problem described 2.2 Interprets policies 2.3 Explains regulations 2.4 Corrects any errors in action or procedure on the part of the library 2.5 Refers to professional staff problems on which assistance is needed	2 Checks to see if applicants have had cards previously

(Table continues on page 40)

Figure 2-2 (cont'd)

5 CIRCULATION SUBSYSTEM (cont'd)

P Professional	T Technical	C Clerical
3 Administers the library's interlibrary loan policy		3 Provides applicants with registration forms and assists as required in their completion
3.1 Coordinates policy with those of neighboring libraries		
3.2 Assists clerical and technical staff with difficult bibliographic searches		
3.3 Exercises final approval on loans		

PERSONNEL CATEGORIES

Most libraries have their employees divided into different personnel categories or classifications. However, there has been very little standardization of the titles of these categories from library to library. Even the title of librarian has been used to apply to any position in the library rather than to refer only to professional positions. The ALA Personnel Utilization statement attempted to define these categories so that a library position in one library could be easily equated to a library position in another library. However, after ten years, there does not seem to be much progress in this area. As of 1979, state civil service categories such as those in Illinois and Wisconsin were the reverse of the personnel categories in the ALA statement. Thus, Library Technical Assistant and Library Technician were used for positions requiring four-year college degrees, and in Wisconsin a Library Assistant was a position for a two-year graduate. *See* Figure 2-3 for a sample representation of the categories some libraries use to indicate positions at the professional, technical, and clerical levels.

LIBRARIAN AND MEDIA SPECIALIST

According to the ALA Personnel Utilization statement, the term "librarian" should only be used to refer to someone with a master's degree in library science because entry-level professional positions require the knowledge and abilities provided by this degree. Advanced professional positions may require further education beyond the master's degree or a degree in a related field. For example, librarians in law libraries might also need to have a law degree, or library administrators often may need to have a doctorate or a master's degree in administration. School media specialists not only need a degree in library or media science, but they must also have education courses and must be certified as teachers. Many standards for school media centers now require a master's degree for district school library media directors. Usually, the master's degree for media specialists should include education in several areas of educational technology, while the specialist degree may be in specialized areas. This specialist degree may be a sixth year degree taken after the master's degree. However, no matter what subject area the master's degree is obtained in, it is required for a person to hold a professional position.

Figure 2-3
Identification of library personnel categories

LEVEL	TITLE	ENTRY LEVEL EDUCATION
PROFESSIONAL	LIBRARIAN Media Specialist Information Specialist Bibliographer Senior Librarian Senior Specialist School Library Media Specialist	MASTER'S DEGREE
SUBPROFESSIONAL	LIBRARY ASSOCIATE	BACHELOR'S DEGREE
TECHNICAL	LIBRARY MEDIA TECHNICAL ASSISTANT	TWO YEARS COLLEGE

Paraprofessional
Supportive
	Assistant Librarian
	Library Assistant II-IV
	Library Technician
	Media Technician
	Senior Library Clerk
	School Library Media
	  Technician
	Library Technician
	  GS 4-7
		Associate Degree
		Post-secondary training

NON-PROFESSIONAL	LIBRARY CLERK	HIGH SCHOOL DIPLOMA
Clerical	Library Aide Library Assistant I Media Aide Library Aide GS 1-3 School Library Media Aide	

A representative sample of position titles used by libraries to indicate categories identified by the ALA *Library Education and Personnel Utilization* statement.

What kinds of duties do these professionals perform which require such advanced knowledge and abilities? Primarily, they analyze the needs of a community, company, or school so that they can develop collections, programs, and services to satisfy these needs. This means that librarians and media specialists are often away from the library attending meetings with city or company officials, citizens, and faculty members to find out what they want the library to provide for them. This also means that professionals are constantly reading current literature to keep abreast of new developments in the field. Librarians and media specialists evaluate and select materials for library collections as well as classify and catalog these materials so that they can be used by the patrons. Media specialists may also design and direct the production of graphics and other audiovisual materials that can be used by teachers. Librarians may conduct classes in the use of libraries as well as develop individualized courses so patrons may use the library by themselves. Librarians may also assist researchers by searching out materials or by developing in-depth bibliographies. Finally, librarians may develop and conduct such programs as outreach services to the aged, the disadvantaged, or the adult learner. The performance of all of these duties requires the application of evaluative and analytical abilities.

LIBRARY ASSOCIATE

Although the Personnel Utilization statement established this category as a subprofessional position for persons having bachelor's degrees, it has not become a widely adopted classification. The task analysis surveys mentioned before did not find enough examples to warrant including this category in their studies. However, some libraries do provide classifications for personnel with bachelor's degrees. These classifications are considered to be either the top subprofessional level (e.g., Library Assistant IV) or at a preprofessional level for those persons planning to attend graduate library school while they are working. In either case, the basic requirements and nature of responsibility for these positions closely follow the ALA statement for library associates.

LIBRARY CLERK

The duties of a library clerk are primarily simple tasks of a clerical or secretarial nature related to some library function or activity. These tasks tend to be repetitious in nature and must be performed by strictly following guidelines which have been established by the supervisor. The library clerk is usually closely supervised in performing these tasks.[5] Typical examples of clerical duties would be checking materials in and out, counting circulation statistics, filing catalog cards, typing catalog cards, processing materials, ordering rental films, and preparing transparencies. Whenever any questions or problems arise, the library clerk should check with the supervisor who would answer the question or determine the solution.

Because many library clerks remain in their jobs for many years, they become very proficient in the performance of their jobs. However, this proficiency is often limited to mastering particular tasks and does not include evaluating whether or not the task should be changed or eliminated. The lack of formal education or exposure to the philosophy and objectives of library service hinders even an experienced clerk from perceiving the relationship of a particular task to the overall objectives of an activity or service. For this reason, the library clerk never has the right to say "no" to a patron or leave a patron dissatisfied. Instead, the clerk has the duty to recognize the limits of his or her authority and to call upon others more qualified by education or experience to handle unusual situations.

LIBRARY MEDIA TECHNICAL ASSISTANT

The Library Media Technical Assistant (LMTA) is a new category established by the ALA statement. This level of employee can perform the tasks of the library clerk, but in addition the LMTA can supervise the performance of these tasks. The LMTA follows established procedures, which have been developed by librarians, and can supervise or be responsible for a service unit in a library or media center. The responsibility an LMTA exercises is based upon reference to staff policy manuals and adherence to established library policies. The LMTA deals with a wide variety of situations which frequently may involve public and personnel contacts. Independent actions and decisions are subject to review because errors in judgment by an LMTA may injure staff and public relations.[6]

The LMTA should have specific library/media-related skills rather than just advanced clerical skills, and it is this distinction which separates a person educated as an LMTA from an advanced clerk. The education and training level of the LMTA have generally come to be accepted as two years of college-level study. This study may or may not include training in a formal library media technical assistant program. However, such two-year programs of study provide the specialized knowledge that many librarians prefer employees in this category to have. That is why over 100 programs throughout the United States and Canada have developed in community colleges. These programs provide the general education and library/media knowledge recommended in the ALA "Criteria for Programs to Prepare Library Technical Assistants." However, in establishing these programs and this new personnel category, ALA has taken great pains to indicate that by gaining more education, persons in these positions should be able to progress upward on a career lattice and move into the next higher career category. (*See* Fig. 2-1, page 34).

What kinds of duties can the LMTA perform with this education?[7] An LMTA may supervise the circulation desk—its procedures and staff, and their contacts with the public. In small libraries, an LMTA may supervise the operations of a branch or community library which is part of a library system. LMTAs may be in charge of interlibrary loans or of reserve room collections at large universities. They also may serve as bibliographic assistants providing preliminary bibliographic searching. In public services, LMTAs may assist patrons in using materials and may give instruction in the use of these materials. In technical services, an LMTA may be an order technician in charge of placing, receiving, and claiming orders. The LMTA may also be a processing technician in charge of the unit that processes all library materials or may be responsible for revising the catalog card filing done by clerks. Other LMTAs may be cataloging technicians who catalog fiction or work with computerized cataloging data bases such as OCLC. Still others may be in charge of particular areas such as serials or pamphlets.

LMTAs also work as media technicians maintaining and repairing audiovisual equipment. They may be responsible for equipment inventories and for the evaluation and selection of audiovisual equipment. Media technicians plan and prepare displays as well as design and prepare audiovisual materials. They can maintain videotape collections as well as assist in the production of in-house video programs. Media technicians with more specialized training can also work as photographic assistants or graphics assistants or as assistants in other specialized media areas.

Before 1970 the LMTA did not exist and these duties were often performed by beginning professionals, library assistants with college degrees, and clerks with years of experience, or they were not performed at all. Although college graduates or experienced clerks may have performed some of these duties, they often did not have the library knowledge needed to perform them well. For this reason, beginning professional librarians often performed many of these quasi-or semi-professional duties. Beginning librarians were assigned to supervise circulation routines, to revise catalog card or shelf-list card filing, and to catalog simple materials or materials using prepared copy. Some librarians performed these duties because it was easier to do them themselves than to train someone else to do them. Other librarians did so because they were afraid that persons who were not professionally trained would fail to recognize the limits of their knowledge and would overstep their job responsibilities. These latter fears have proven to be groundless as graduates of LMTA programs have demonstrated their abilities to recognize their limitations.

What has encouraged librarians to adopt the LMTA positions and revise their personnel categories to include them? One influence has been the task analyses of the 1970s, which showed that many tasks and responsibilities that had been performed by professionals could be performed by trained technical and subprofessional personnel. Another influence has been financial—libraries have found that they can use these task analyses to restructure their jobs and hire less expensive personnel to perform library jobs. A third influence has been the success of civil service staffing categories such as the U.S. government's Library Technician 1411 series (1966), which successfully differentiated the difficulty of assignments, personal contacts, and level of responsibilities among seven levels of Library Aide and Library Technician positions. This standard enumerated the many tasks and areas of responsibility which did not need professional training. The final important influence has been the introduction of the computer into library operations and processes. Computerized processes have eliminated the need for professional decisions from many routine library operations and have substituted a need for technical knowledge which the LMTA can most easily provide. Thus, the librarian has been freed to use his or her evaluative, imaginative, and analytical abilities to develop new library procedures and services and to leave the internal workings of the library to the LMTA's supervision.

That many libraries are reevaluating their staff usage can be seen in the U.S. Department of Labor predictions that requirements for library attendants and assistants are expected to rise sharply by 1985.[8] This is combined with a reduction in the ratio of professional and nonprofessional employees from 3·1 to 1·1. School and special libraries' standards are showing the development of a ratio of one professional to one clerical and one technical employee; "the more rapid rate of growth for attendants and assistants reflects continued attention to task analysis, job redesign and the management of techniques designed to promote effective utilization of staff."[9]

In spite of the body of literature that is developing to support the restructuring of library staffs, many library personnel are wary or strongly opposed to such moves. They see these measures as threats to themselves personally and as a lowering of professional standards. They fear that library administrators will hire subprofessional and technical personnel to fill positions that are truly professional in nature. Other staff members welcome these same measures as natural developments, just as the physician assistant and the legal assistant movements in the medical and legal fields are being accepted as natural developments. These mid-level or paraprofessional positions are recognized by many librarians as positions that can free them from quasi-professional or clerical library work. These librarians look forward to using their scientific and generalized knowledge in developing library policies, services, and systems that trained support staff can carry out.

REVIEW QUESTIONS

1. List the major personal qualities every library staff member should possess.

2. Describe the major differences that distinguish professional level from non-professional level positions.

3. Identify the major categories of personnel by job title, education, and level of classification (professional, clerical, etc.) in the form of a career ladder similar to that in Figure 2-1.

4. Define the position of librarian and identify the most important abilities needed by this level of employee.

5. Define the position of library clerk, including the type of duties the clerk would perform and how he or she is to be supervised.

6. Define a library media technical assistant's position in relation to librarians and library clerks.

7. Describe an LMTA's level of responsibility in following library policies and exercising his or her own judgment.

8. Compare the personnel categories and organizational charts of two local libraries representing any type of library.

SELECTED READINGS

American Library Association. Library Education Division. *Criteria for Programs to Prepare Library/Media Technical Assistants.* Revised edition approved by ALA Council, June 1979. Chicago: ALA, 1979.

American Library Association. Office for Library Education. *Library Education and Personnel Utilization: A Statement of Policy.* Adopted by A.L.A. Council, June 30, 1970. (© 1976). Chicago: ALA, 1970.

American Library Association. "Report of the Interdivisional Ad Hoc Committee of LAD and LED on Subprofessional or Technician Class of Library Employees." Revised by Dorothy Deininger, Chairperson. Chicago: ALA, 1967.

Creth, Sheila. *Personnel Management in Libraries.* New York: Neal-Schuman, 1980.

Moore, N. *Manpower Planning in Libraries.* Phoenix, AZ: Oryx Press, 1980.

Ricking, Myrl, and Robert E. Booth. *Personnel Utilization in Libraries: A Systems Approach.* Prepared for the Illinois Library Task Analysis Project; Published in cooperation with the Illinois State Library. Chicago: ALA, 1974.

United States. Civil Service Commission. *Library Technician Series GS-1411.* Washington, DC: GPO, 1966.

United States. Department of Labor. Bureau of Labor Statistics. *Library Manpower: A Study of Demand and Supply* (Bulletin 1852). Washington, DC: GPO, 1975.

NOTES

[1] Pierce Butler, *Introduction to Library Science* (Chicago: University of Chicago Press, 1933), pp. 111-12.

[2] Myrl Ricking and Robert E. Booth, *Personnel Utilization in Libraries: A Systems Approach*; Prepared for the Illinois Library Task Analysis Project; Published in cooperation with the Illinois State Library (Chicago: ALA, 1974), p. 1.

[3] American Library Association, Office for Library Education, "Library Education and Personnel Utilization: A Statement of Policy Adopted by the Council of American Library Association, June 30, 1970 (Chicago: ALA, 1970), p. 4.

[4] American Library Association, "Report of the Interdivisional Ad Hoc Committee of LAD and LED on Subprofessional or Technician Class of Library Employees," Revised by Dorothy Deininger, Chairperson (Chicago: ALA, 1967), p. 2.

[5] American Library Association, "Report," p. 5.

[6] American Library Association, "Report," p. 8.

[7] The following duties have been extracted from the various documents included in the Selected Readings and Bibliography.

[8] Bureau of Labor Statistics, *Library Manpower: A Study of Demand and Supply* (Bulletin 1852). (Washington, DC: GPO, 1975), p. 35.

[9] Bureau of Labor Statistics, *Library Manpower*, p. 39.

3
LIBRARY MATERIALS AND RESOURCES

The fundamental purpose of a library—to acquire, preserve, and make available information in all its varied forms—has required that today's libraries include a variety of materials and provide depths of information which would have been unheard of only a few decades ago. By expanding their collections beyond the traditional print media to include graphic, audiovisual, and even computer media, libraries now preserve and present information in all its many forms. In addition to books, magazines, newspapers, and pamphlets, library patrons have access to such other media as records, films, filmstrips, audio and videotapes, art prints, games, toys, and even computers. These various media have been included in libraries because their unique characteristics enable each patron to acquire information according to his or her own abilities, interests, or needs. They have also been included because now much of the information in our largely visual and verbal society may only be recorded in these specific forms.

And yet, for many reasons, libraries must choose from the variety and quantity of materials and information available. Since over 35,000 books, 20,000 magazines, thousands of records, and hundreds of films are published or produced each year, no library can afford to buy everything written, printed, or produced. Even if they could afford to do so, very few libraries would want to. In order to serve their patrons effectively, each library must judiciously select those materials which will help fulfill its stated objectives. Thus, the collections and materials from library to library will usually differ by type of media as well as by subject content.

In order for the LMTA to understand why a particular library would include collections of specific media a discussion of the characteristics and definitions of the media most often included in libraries will be presented here. This discussion will also define terms and concepts—such as serial, pamphlet, microform, and COM catalog—which are often referred to without explanation by library staff members. In addition, detailed descriptions and definitions of these media will help the LMTA better understand library instructions and readings which use the technical library names for these various media. By understanding these terms, the LMTA will be better prepared to work in this multi-media world.

BOOKS

The book is still probably the most familiar medium to library users. Several years ago its demise was widely predicted, but economic conditions have slowed this process down so that books will probably remain the major medium in libraries for at least the next decade or two. A book has been defined as a collection of more than 48 pages which has a distinctive title and is fastened together in a binding. However, there are many library terms describing this physical entity which the LMTA should understand.

A book may be called a "volume" in libraries or a "tome" in literature. It is called a "monograph" if it is a complete narrative or treatise on a particular subject written in detail but limited in scope. Monographs that are related to each other may belong to "sets" or "series" (*see* p. 51). Copies of a book which are printed from the same type set up or from the same plates are said to belong to the same "edition." If the content of the book is changed and the type is changed, a new edition of a book is printed. Sometimes the same book content may be published or printed in several different bindings or on different paper and be advertised as different editions. Some publishers print a book in a hardcover binding as well as in a paper binding. Other books may be printed in a "trade edition" intended for sale in bookstores and written for the general reader as well as in a "textbook edition," which has added information (usually study guides and questions) of interest to students and teachers. Some books are even published in a "library binding," which is sturdier than the hardcover of the normal trade edition. "Paperback" books may be published for the mass market or may be "quality paperbacks," often classics or scholarly works, published for colleges and universities. Librarians usually prefer to purchase particular editions of a book. Some libraries will not buy paperback bindings or textbooks; children's libraries often prefer to buy books in library binding editions. Each library's policy is usually based on its budget and the use its collection receives.

PARTS OF A BOOK — PHYSICAL

Each part of the physical book itself usually has a technical term to describe it. The binding of the book is called the "casing" or, more commonly, the "cover" and the back edge with the lettering for the name of the book is called the "spine." The lining papers on the inside of the covers are called "end papers" and may often bear decorative illustrations. The insides of the book are called the "contents" or "text" of the work. The weight and quality of the paper on which the contents are printed may vary greatly from book to book, and older books often have the illustrations printed on one weight of paper and the words printed on a lighter paper. The illustrations themselves often represent various printing techniques and have technical names such as "line," "half-tone," or "color." Selecting the cover, paper, page design, and typefaces to be used in a book is the special art of publishing. The designer or editor in charge of this may be listed at the front of the book, or a statement describing this may be included at the end of a book. This type of editor, however, should not be confused with an editor who contributed to the intellectual content of the book.

The contents of the book are made up of sheets of paper or "leaves'," which are printed on both sides or both "pages." These pages are referred to as the "recto" designating a page on the right side of the open book, and the "verso," which is the page on the back of the same leaf. The text of a book is first printed on large sheets of paper which are then folded and cut to make pages in a book. Sometimes the pages may not be completely cut through in a particular copy of a book so that the library staff must cut them. Each folded sheet of paper is called a "signature," and these signatures are numbered or lettered so that the printer knows in which order to gather them for the book. The number of times a printed sheet of paper is folded will determine the size of the finished book. If the signature is made by folding the paper once to make two leaves or four pages, it is called a "folio." Readers may have heard of Shakespeare's folios, which were named after the printing size rather than the content. A signature folded twice makes four leaves and eight pages and is called a "quarto." Signatures folded three times contain eight leaves or sixteen pages and are called "octavos." The octavo, or 16 page signature, and the 32 page signature are the most commonly found book sizes. In fact, the definition adopted by the United Nations in 1964 designates that a book is made of more than 48 pages, i.e., more than three signatures of 16 pages. Large-sized books may be indicated in libraries by adding the letters Q (for quarto) or FOL (for folio) to the location number of a book so that readers will know that the books are shelved in separate areas of the library.

PARTS OF A BOOK—BIBLIOGRAPHIC

Librarians refer to the description of the contents of a book as bibliographic description. A bibliographic description identifies the title, personal or corporate author, publishing information, and the distinctive characteristics of a book. The "title" or name of a work is the distinctive words or phrases used to identify the work. It may be expanded or further explained by a phrase called a "subtitle," which is often printed in smaller print than the words of the title. The first page of a book usually includes the title, subtitle, any statement of responsibility, and publishing information. It is called the "title page" and is used by libraries to provide the information recorded in library catalogs. (*See* Fig. 3-1, page 50).

The title is usually followed by a "statement of responsibility." This statement may be the "author" of a work, that is, the person or persons responsible for the intellectual content of the book, or it may be an organization, such as the American Library Association, which has issued the work. Any persons who have contributed significantly to the book are also usually mentioned on the title page. Persons such as editors, translators, illustrators, and writers of introductions may also be listed. The last information on the title page usually consists of the publishing information. This information includes the major cities in which the publishing company is located and the name of the publishing company; it may also include the publication date of the book. These three items may be referred to collectively as the "imprint." An edition statement may also be printed on the title page to indicate that a book is an edition other than the first.

The back or verso of the title page also includes important bibliographic information for libraries. Most importantly, it provides the publishing and copyright history of the book. A "copyright" is a legal right to exclusive ownership given by a government to a person or organization for a particular period of time. This is usually indicated by the symbol © followed by the year the copyright was given. Each different edition of a work will have a separate copyright date so that "Copyright © 1981, 1976, 1974, 1971" in Figure 3-1 would indicate that four editions of the work have been published and copyrighted. The publisher might also indicate the number of times a book has been reprinted from the same plates or type, e.g., "Seventh printing." However, librarians are more interested in the copyright date than the printing or publishing date because the copyright date indicates how current the information is—a book listed as the "Seventh printing, 1978" may have a copyright date of "c1959." Besides the publishing date, other information about the publishing history might also be given here, such as any former titles or any other editions that have been published.

Figure 3-1
Sample title page and verso

Copyright © 1981, 1976, 1974, 1971
Marty Bloomberg and G. Edward Evans
All Rights Reserved
Printed in the United States of America

No part of this publication may be reproduced, stored in a retrieval system, or transmitted, in any form or by any means, electronic, mechanical, photocopying, recording or otherwise, without the prior written permission of the publisher.

LIBRARIES UNLIMITED, INC.
P.O. Box 263
Littleton, Colorado 80160

Library of Congress Cataloging in Publication Data

Bloomberg, Marty.
    Introduction to technical services for library technicians.

    (Library science text series)
    Bibliography: p. 343
    Includes index.
    1. Processing (Libraries). I. Evans, G. Edward,
1937-   . II. Title. III. Series.
Z688.5.B5 1981   025'.02   81-798
ISBN 0-87287-228-9   AACR2
ISBN 0-87287-248-3 (pbk.)

Introduction to
TECHNICAL SERVICES
for
LIBRARY TECHNICIANS

Fourth Edition

Marty Bloomberg   G. Edward Evans
Assistant Director of the Library   Professor
California State College   Graduate School of Library Service
San Bernardino   University of California
                                         Los Angeles

1981

LIBRARIES UNLIMITED, INC.
Littleton, Colorado

Several items of principal interest to librarians are often printed on this verso page. The Library of Congress Catalog Card Order Number (e.g., 81-798) is used by libraries to purchase library catalog cards from the Library of Congress. An ISBN (International Standard Book Number) is usually included for books published after 1972. An ISBN is a distinctive number identifying a particular edition of a title by a publisher. Many American books also now include Library of Congress Cataloging-In-Publication (CIP) data; this information is used by libraries to provide cataloging information for library catalogs.

Librarians are also concerned with describing the unique physical characteristics of the book. These characteristics include the number of pages, whether or not the book is illustrated, and the size of the book. All of this information is recorded on the library catalog record. The pages that follow the title page and that precede the first page of the actual text may be numbered in small roman numerals at the bottom of the pages (e.g., "iv, v, vi," etc.). This numbering distinguishes the pages of introductory material from the major content of the book. Literary works often have introductory sections that can run 40-50 pages (or xl-l pages).

The introductory materials following the title page may include a "preface" or the author's statement of the purpose for writing the book. Other materials may include an acknowledgments page, an introduction, or a table of contents. A "table of contents" is a listing of the contents of the book in the order in which they appear in the text. It provides an outline of the book and gives the page numbers for the beginning of each section. The body of the text then follows and is numbered in arabic numbers. It may be followed by "appendices" (or appendixes), which are supplementary material. Common appendices include "glossaries" (definitions of the terms used in a book), "bibliographies" (lists of material on the subject discussed in the book), and an "index." An index is an alphabetical listing of the subjects or items in the book and the page numbers on which they will be found.

The title page or its verso may also indicate that a book belongs to a "series" — notation of which forms the last major element of bibliographic description. A series is the collective title given to a group of separate books or volumes related to one another by subject or purpose. They may also be published in a uniform format having similar bindings and may be issued in succession. Each book in the series is a complete monograph and should not be confused with a serial (*see* below). The publisher determines what books will be published in a series; the series title is then usually included on the half-title page, title page, or cover of the book. A list of the books in a series may also be printed in each book of the series.

SERIALS

The term "serial" refers to publications issued in parts at regular intervals for an indefinite period of time. When a person first hears the term serial, a TV program or story "to be continued ..." may come to mind, but in the library world, "serial" is used as a generic term to include magazines or periodicals (these are synonymous terms), journals, newspapers, annuals, and any publication meant to be published on a continuing basis. The major serial forms are important in libraries because they provide current information on many subjects. Magazines and newspapers contain current or topical information that may not appear in book form for several years — if at all. They also contain short-term information which is of interest this week or month but which may not be needed next year. For this reason, libraries will have varying policies concerning the serials they will buy or retain in their collections. Some serials may be kept forever; others might be thrown out at the end of the year.

The most common serial is a "magazine," or "periodical" as it is referred to in most libraries. In fact, a definition of a periodical and a serial are the same (although not all serials are periodicals). A periodical is issued in parts, which means that it is published or issued at regular intervals, and each issue or part is meant to be read as it is published. Periodicals may be issued at regular intervals — weekly, monthly, quarterly, biweekly, or bimonthly. Each issue is usually dated or numbered (or both), and one complete year of a periodical's issues is called a volume. Often, the pages of each volume are numbered consecutively so that a January issue might start on page 1 and a December issue start on page 1098. Almost every periodical begins publication with volume 1. However, since the first issue of a periodical may have been published at any time of the year, its volume may begin in January, February, June, or October. Periodicals issued on a quarterly basis may be identified by month (January, April, July, and October) or by season (Winter, Spring, Summer, and Fall). Some periodicals may not even publish issues in the summer months so that a monthly periodical may appear to have gaps in its publication issues. As if this variety were not confusing enough for a library staff member to keep track of, periodicals often change their names or cease publication without any warning to the subscribers. Also, periodicals which ceased publication may be revived as new publications, e.g., *The Saturday Evening Post* was originally a weekly and then was revived as a quarterly. It is these characteristics which require many library staff hours to make sure that each issue of every serial is received by the library.

Periodicals contain articles written on general subjects by several contributors and are usually written for the layperson. If the periodical contains in-depth articles on subjects of interest to scholars or subject specialists, it may be called a "journal," e.g., *Library Journal* and the *Journal of Economics.* Journals are often published by institutions, associations, or learned societies and may also contain current news and reports of their activities and work in a particular field.

"Newspapers" are serials that report current events and discuss topics of current public interest. They are most often published daily, but some newspapers are published weekly or even less frequently. Newspapers are excellent sources of local information. Libraries will usually subscribe to national, state, and local newspapers to provide a well-rounded coverage of current events.

"Indexes" are special kinds of serials which provide access to the information found in many of these periodicals and newspapers. Indexes usually provide an author, title, and/or subject access to the articles found in specific periodicals during a specific period of time. They may cover general periodicals, as does the *Readers' Guide to Periodical Literature*, or they may cover specific subjects, as the *Applied Science and Technology Index* does. They may even be indexes for newspapers rather than for periodicals. "Abstracting services" are similar to indexes, but they provide, in addition, brief summaries of the articles or books they index. These services usually cover international publications in specialized subject areas as do *Chemical Abstracts* and *Biological Abstracts*.

OTHER PRINT MEDIA

There are many other important kinds of print media which will be found in libraries. The pamphlet file or vertical file contains much timely information that has not been published in book form. Most of the information is contained in "pamphlets," which are publications of 48 pages or fewer (1-3 signatures) and which are usually paper-covered. Pamphlets provide information which is ephemeral and which fills a library's temporary need. Libraries include them in their collections because they provide information that is often not available in any other form. Also, they are often available either free or very inexpensively. Some typical pamphlets are company annual reports, tourist and travel brochures, and bulletins from companies and government agencies. Some agencies even publish series of pamphlets on particular subjects of interest to them. Libraries have to evaluate pamphlets to be sure that the bias of the issuing agency or company has not influenced the content of the pamphlet. Libraries must also consider the publishing or copyright date of the material and remove pamphlets that have become outdated or have been superseded.

Government documents are not necessarily another form of print media, but they are often treated separately in libraries. A "government document" is a generic term for any publication issued or published at the expense of a governmental agency. Thus, there are local, state, federal, and international government documents. Government documents can include books, pamphlets, serials, and maps, and they are often concerned with many subject areas — not just government or politics. The terms "government document" and "government document collection" are most often used in the United States to refer to U.S. federal documents. Most of these are distributed by the Superintendent of Documents, and many (though by no means all) are printed by the U.S. Government Printing Office (GPO), the official government printer. Libraries may house government documents in separate collections arranged according to the issuing agencies. Libraries like to include government documents from all levels of government in their collections because they are generally objective and reliable sources of information. They also provide current information in useful subject areas at very reasonable costs.

Other forms of print material can also be useful in libraries. Technical reports may be particularly important in special or academic library collections because they report the progress and current status of scientific research and development. In fact, information published in technical reports may never be published in final book form. Some libraries also develop large clipping files of articles relating to local topics or to specific subject areas. Articles usually are clipped from periodicals or newspapers, arranged by subject in envelopes, and kept in the pamphlet files. They are used extensively in newspaper and historical collection libraries.

GRAPHIC MEDIA

Besides print media, libraries have found that various forms of graphic or visual media are needed to support their collections of printed materials and to fulfill their objectives. Pictures, graphs, maps, dioramas, and sculptures are a few of the items included in libraries to support their education and research objectives as well as the cultural or aesthetic appreciation objective. In choosing these materials the library staff should be sure that the information is authentic and that the graphic reproductions are of excellent quality. Also, because these materials may come in varying sizes and shapes, they are usually given special handling and may be kept in special shelving facilities. However, if they are cataloged, they are often cataloged under the artist or photographer's name or under their title if no statement of responsibility can be devised.

Two-dimensional graphic representations may include such forms as paintings, drawings, charts, diagrams, graphs, photographs, and posters. They are used by persons such as artists, historians, sociologists, and theater arts people as well as by teachers and students. Drawings and photographs are particularly useful because one picture can be used by several people for very different purposes, e.g., a picture of Pilgrims at Thanksgiving can be used for a social studies class as well as for costume designs. These materials are often mounted and included in "picture files" or "vertical files." Some libraries may provide pictures solely because they fulfill the aesthetic appreciation objective. These libraries may provide art print reproductions which patrons may borrow to hang on the walls of their homes.

Another two-dimensional graphic form found in libraries is maps. These are flat representations of the earth, the sky, or a celestial body. Library collections usually include physical maps showing geographical features such as rivers and mountains, political maps showing governmental boundaries of states and countries, and thematic or special purpose maps showing subjects such as population, vegetation, or historical developments. Besides maps of the earth's surface, detailed maps of the moon and the universe are also now being published.

Maps are very important in geographic and geological libraries as well as in highway, engineering, history, and other library collections. They may be kept in a library's vertical file, or if a library has many maps, they may be kept as a separate collection in special map cases. Two important items on a map will determine its uses. The scale, or legend, indicates how many miles are represented by one inch of the map. If it is not printed on the map it must be determined and added. Also, the copyright date will indicate how current the information on the map really is. Maps can be obtained from many different sources. Gasoline companies and state governments provide some of the best maps available for individual states. The U.S. Geological Survey, a federal government agency, publishes excellent maps, including quadrangle maps which show very small areas of the United States (15-17 square miles). These maps are so detailed that they even show individual houses in rural areas. It is this detail, currency, and variety which makes maps important in library collections.

Three-dimensional or spherical maps are called "globes." As with maps, globes may be physical, political, or topical; they may also represent the earth's surface or the surface of another celestial body. Many globes may be "relief" globes, which means that the physical features such as mountains are raised on the surface of the globe. The copyright date of a globe is just as important as that of a map. Too many times, libraries buy a globe and keep it for many years forgetting that political boundaries and even the names of nations often change.

Libraries may include many other types of three-dimensional objects. "Models" and "mock-ups" such as those of a volcano or Shakespeare's Globe Theater may be included. "Dioramas" — three-dimensional scenes that use figures and a background to create an illusion of reality — may represent early American Indian life, prehistoric life, or historical battles. "Displays" and "exhibits" may feature special subjects, such as literary authors and their works. Sculpture itself is now also being included in library collections. Both original sculpture (perhaps local in origin) and low-cost reproductions are being checked out to patrons for use in their homes or to teachers to supplement a class unit.

"Realia," or real objects, have become very important in libraries. Some library collections may include specimens of insects, animals, coins, or fabrics. Others may include objects such as clocks, telephones, microscopes, or calculators. Many libraries also include toys, puzzles, and games. These latter materials are made available not only because children might not have the finances to buy such items but also because they are such excellent educational tools. Games such as Scrabble® and Monopoly® can be used to teach students to think, spell, and figure. Libraries may even provide pets which children may check out and take home for several weeks. (Usually pet care instructions and literature are also included.) Some public libraries have provided garden and home care tools in areas where no rental businesses are available. Because they serve such useful purposes, various types of realia will probably be added to libraries as the need for them arises.

AUDIOVISUAL MEDIA

The most common types of audiovisual media found in libraries today are films, slides, filmstrips, records, and tapes. There are many variations of each of these media and sometimes graphic media may be combined with audio or visual media to form instructional packages. If two or more different media are combined in a package, it is called a "kit." Each of these media forms must be used with its own special type of equipment. Not only does a library need film projectors to show moving-picture films, but it must also have the exact type of projector which will show the exact size and type of film the library owns. Each media form added to a library's collection must, therefore, be carefully evaluated to ensure that it can be used on the equipment the library owns or that the necessary equipment can be purchased.

In adding each media form to a library collection, it is also important to identify correctly each media item so that it is distinguished from the same title in other media forms. (It is not uncommon for a library to have a book, film, record, audiotape and videotape for a single work, e.g., *Hamlet*.) Cataloging rules have been established which will bring these similar items together in the catalog by author or by the persons responsible for the performances (e.g., the Beatles) and yet which will distinguish between them by adding a "general material designation." This designation is a term describing the broad class of media to which an item belongs, and it follows the title on a catalog record. The physical description of the item will also usually indicate its characteristics so that the correct type of equipment can be selected for viewing or hearing the item.

Slides and films are among the oldest audiovisual forms in library collections (*see* Fig. 3-2, a and c, page 56). Lantern slides — images printed on 3¼x4-inch glass slides — were in widespread use in libraries during the early part of the twentieth century. They have been largely replaced by 2x2-inch slides made of film or transparent material. The most common film size for slides is 35mm, but 126 film, which is used in Instamatic® cameras, is also used to make slides.

Figure 3-2
Audiovisual media

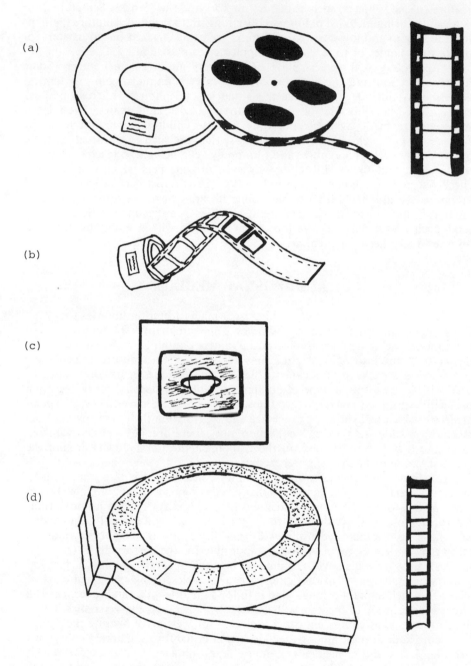

(a)

(b)

(c)

(d)

Slides may be used by themselves or with accompanying audiotapes or records, or they may carry their own sound imprinted on the slide itself. Though most slides are now 2x2 inches, a library must be sure its slides are compatible with the equipment the library owns. Some automatic slide projectors will jam if the slide mount is made of something other than cardboard.

Slides are important in art, architecture, history, and social studies collections. Slides of laboratory specimens or tissue cultures can also be important in scientific and medical collections. Slides are such an important media form in some of the larger U.S. libraries that these libraries have separate slide libraries in which slides are cataloged and filed individually in large slide cabinets. Other libraries and media centers may catalog slides together in sets and store them ready to use in projector trays.

Motion picture films come in many different sizes and shapes and are often found in public libraries, in academic libraries, and in school media centers. They are identified according to the width of the film, whether they are silent or sound, in color or black and white. Libraries most often have 8mm or 16mm films, although some libraries such as motion picture libraries also include feature films in 35mm. These designations indicate the width of the film itself. Most of the films shown to classes or group meetings are 16mm. Their running or showing times vary from 10-30 minutes per film.

8mm films are often used for home movies, but they have become important and useful in library collections as well. These films may come on reels which can be used on 16mm film projectors, or they may be spliced into a continuous loop of film and contained in a cartridge which fits into a special film-loop projector (*see* Fig. 3-2, d). These film loops may run from 3-5 minutes and present one subject or single-concept, or they may run from 8-10 minutes and present a slightly broader coverage of a special topic. Both standard 8mm and Super 8mm film are available in sound or silent forms. Super 8 film allows for an increased picture area, and cannot be used with standard 8mm equipment in either the film or film loop format. It is very important to match carefully the type of film with the projector on which it will be used.

Filmstrips are rolled strips of 35mm film containing from 40-65 frames or images (*see* Fig. 3-2, b). The filmstrips may be silent with captions printed on each frame or accompanied by a script meant to be read as the filmstrip is viewed. Some filmstrips are accompanied by audiotapes or phonorecords and are called sound filmstrips. There is a variety of equipment used to project sound filmstrips, and, unfortunately, this equipment is not yet standardized. Some projectors require that the filmstrip be started from the outer end of the filmstrip. Others, such as the DuKane, require that the filmstrip be rewound and the filmstrip started from the inside end of the filmstrip. This small difference can cause quite a bit of frustration to a speaker or teacher who is using unfamiliar equipment.

Two other forms of projected images are used more often in schools than they are in other situations. Transparencies are usually 8x10-inch images on a transparent material which are projected onto a large screen by an overhead projector. They are excellent teaching or sales aids because they are easy to produce and provide an inexpensive means of presenting visual images of complex concepts. There are many excellent processes by which transparencies can be made, and most school media centers can produce them for the teaching staffs. Materials which are not transparent may be projected through an opaque projector. Pictures from books, posters, etc. can be projected onto a large screen.

However, bulky materials cannot be projected very well and the light bulb lamp tends to overheat the material being shown if it is left under the light too long.

Audiotapes and phonorecords are important forms of audio materials found in library collections. Audiotapes were originally magnetic tape sound recordings which were wound from one reel onto another on bulky tape recorders. These recordings were designated by the speed at which they were recorded, expressed in inches per second (ips). But they have recently been largely replaced in libraries by tapes on cassettes or cartridges, because cassette tapes can be prerecorded, are contained in one unit, and can be less easily erased or damaged by patrons (although they can malfunction). Cassette tapes are available in various lengths ranging from 15 to 120 minutes of recording time. The content of the tapes can range from recorded music of all types to dramatic readings of plays, novels, or poems. Many lectures by prominent people are also available on tapes. Audiotapes are recorded in either monaural, stereophonic, or even quadraphonic sound. They can be recorded as single track tapes so that only one recording is made on a tape, or they can have two, four, or even eight tracks or recordings.

Until cassette audiotapes became commonly available, most libraries had large phonograph record collections of recorded music, poetry, and drama. Records are plastic discs ranging in diameter from 7 inches to 16 inches and are designated by their playback speed expressed in revolutions per minute (rpm). Originally, the only playback speed was 78 rpm, but other speeds such as 16, 33⅓, and 45 rpm were soon developed. The speed most commonly used in libraries is 33⅓. Most record players will play all 4 speeds, but monaural (mono) record players will damage stereo records. The rise in popularity of cassette audiotapes has encouraged the decline of phonorecords in many library collections. This is due partly to the fact that library staffs no longer need to worry that the patrons would get their fingerprints on the records, scratch or break the records, or use them on the wrong type of record player. However, music libraries will probably continue to use phonorecords because they tend to have better audio quality.

Cassette videotapes have also become important in library collections. Videotapes provide the type of picture seen on television and must be viewed on a TV screen. In school media centers, they are used to support education, and in medical libraries, they help provide continuing education for the medical staffs. In public libraries, patrons may check out videocassettes for recreation or self-education to use on their own playback units just as they would check out books or records. The major disadvantage to videocassettes is that standardization has been very slow in coming. Videotapes come in several formats (BETA and VHS) and many widths, and each tape must be used on its own playback equipment. Also, reel-to-reel videotapes and cassette or cartridge tapes require different kinds of playback units. As if this were not enough variety, videodiscs or phonorecord-type visual recordings are also being produced. This variety may cause some confusion, but videotapes will probably become increasingly important in many libraries' collections because they provide important information that is only available in this format.

Libraries are using many aspects of electronic and computer technology wherever it helps them to meet their objectives. Some libraries and media centers are producing radio and TV programs; others are running their own radio or TV stations. Many libraries are providing resources based on new technologies. Teaching machines for programmed instruction and computers for computer-assisted instruction (CAI) are two types of resources for education. Teletype machines and machines that provide electronic transmissions of printed documents support the information objective. Computer data bases also provide information on resources available in many indexes or libraries. Other technical advances are being made every day, and these will surely be added to library collections and resources as they prove their value in acquiring, preserving, and making information available.

MICROFORMS

"Microform" is a generic term used to designate materials that contain micro or small images of printed or graphic material. The most common microforms are produced on rolls or sheets of film. "Microfilms" are rolls of 35mm or 70mm film which contain micro-photo-images of pages which have been reduced up to 1/20th their original size. Many periodicals are filmed on microfilm which is used to replace the paper copies. One microfilm roll can usually contain one year's issues of a monthly magazine or six months' issues of a weekly magazine such as *Time* or *Newsweek*. They not only conserve library space, but also prevent theft of magazine issues. Patrons view the microfilm on microfilm readers which project magnified images onto a small screen equal to or larger than their original size. Reader printers can print the screen image onto a piece of 8½x11-inch paper. Libraries may purchase microfilm which is either negative or positive. Positive microfilm provides an image on the screen of black letters on a white background, and negative microfilm provides an image of white letters on a black background. When a printout is made of these images, they are reversed, so that negative microfilm gives a printout of black letters on a white background.

Another common microform is "microfiche," which was named after the French word for file card. Microfiche are sheets of 3x5-inch or 4x6-inch film, each containing from 60 to 100 images or pages of material. They usually contain the complete text of a report, a pamphlet, or an issue of a periodical. Microfiche require their own reader or reader-printer equipment or attachments. "Microcards" and "microprint" are similar in size to microfiche but they have microimages printed on opaque material and cannot be reproduced. They are not as prevalent in libraries as are the other two microforms.

In the 1970s, a new microform was developed. This form was called "ultrafiche" or "ultra-microfiche" because the reproduction factor is so great that from 1,000 to 3,000 page images can be included on a 4x6-inch fiche. This characteristic has made it possible for collections of rare and difficult-to-obtain material to be filmed and reproduced for purchase by many libraries. One such collection provided 20,000 volumes on American history which could be stored in a space equal to the size of 16 shoe boxes. Ultrafiche readers have been produced in portable sizes so that patrons not only could check out the material but could also check out the equipment to use it on. However, most library patrons have not thrilled to the idea of curling up with a machine rather than with the book itself.

LIBRARY CATALOGS

All of the technology available in libraries has not been limited to the materials. The traditional library resource, the library catalog or index to all of the library's holdings, is also changing its form. The earliest library indexes were in book form. These were replaced by card catalogs of 3x5-inch cards on which information about each item in the library was recorded. The Library of Congress ensured the adoption of the card catalog by reproducing its cataloging information on cards which were sold very reasonably. Now, this library and others have heralded a new era in library cataloging by providing information in machine-readable form or material which can be used by a computer. Libraries all over the world are investigating their cataloging needs and determining what physical form the library catalog should take.

No matter what the format of a library catalog is, its purpose and general characteristics remain the same. Library catalogs provide a record of the books and media contained in a library's collection. The record of each item is called a cataloging record and includes a bibliographic description of each item, a location or call number, and subject headings representing the subject content of the work. Each cataloging record is usually entered in the catalog under three separate headings—those for author, title, and subject. Thus a patron may look for an item by its title, by the name of the persons who wrote or edited it, or by a subject heading (*see* Fig. 3-3).

The basic information for the cataloging record is taken by the cataloger from the item itself. If the item is a book, information from the title page and its verso are recorded in a standard format. Librarians then add physical description information and may add other pertinent notes which will describe the work to the patron. (Compare Figs. 3-1 and 3-3.) Cataloging information for media items is generally taken from any accompanying written material, from a producer's catalog, or from an examination of the work itself. Librarians have attempted to provide all the information they think patrons may wish to know about a work. This is particularly important in libraries that do not allow their patrons to browse or for media items, which cannot be easily examined. Complete cataloging information is provided in card catalogs, but other types of library catalogs may only provide selected information to serve the individual library's needs (*see* Fig. 3-4, page 62).

When librarians first started including audiovisual materials in their collections and recording them in their catalogs, these materials were cataloged and processed differently from the books. Media catalog cards were designated by color-coded bands at the top of each card with a different color representing each media form. The call number for each item usually was a combination media code and accession number (e.g., FS 147 for a filmstrip), and the materials were stored in cabinets or in special shelving areas. Gradually, librarians came to recognize that the information contained in the item was more important than its format. Thus, many libraries now indicate the type of media by a standardized term which follows the title on the catalog record. Call numbers are based on the subject matter rather than on the format, and media materials are intershelved with books on the libraries' shelves. (*See* Fig. 3-5, page 63.)

It is important for the LMTA to understand the variety of library catalogs and their major characteristics. The most visible catalog in the library is called the "public catalog" because it is meant to be used by the patrons as well as by the

Figure 3-3
Sample catalog card set

a) Main entry card   b) Title card   c) Subject heading card

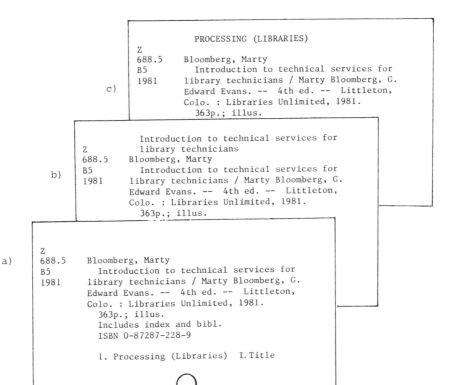

Figure 3-4
Sample book and COM catalog entries

```
        TO   -  TITLES

  910R  TOO LATE THE PHALAROPE
           PATON, ALAN  F P312TO   53

  484J  TOO MANY AMERICANS
           DAY, LINCOLN H   301.329 D274T   64

  887A  TOO MUCH ALONE
           GILLMAN, RICHARD   811.54 G482T   65

  938M  TOOL DESIGN
           COLE, CHARLES BRADFORD   621.9 C689T   41

  687M  TOOL ENGINEERING
           DOYLE, LAWRENCE E   621.7 D754T   50

  912S  TOOL ENGINEERING
           RUSINOFF, SAMUEL EUGENE   658.5 R955T   59
```

```
                          AUTHORS -  COM

  875Q  COLBOURN, H TREVOR   973.311 C684L   65
           LAMP OF EXPERIENCE

  482G  COLBY, FRANK MOORE ED   R 030 N532   32
           NEW INTERNATIONAL YEAR BOOK

 1133L  COLBY, ROBERT A   616.31 C719   61
           COLOR ATLAS OF ORAL PATHOLOGY HISTOLOGY AND EMBRYOLOGY Q

   99J  COLBY, VINETA ED   917.3 C686   64
           AMERICAN CULTURE IN THE SIXTIES

 1114U  COLBY, VINETA JT ED   R 920.04 K96E   67
           EUROPEAN AUTHORS, ONE THOUSAND TO NINETEEN HUNDRED

  248C  COLE, ARTHUR CHARLES   973.6 C689   34
           IRREPRESSIBLE CONFLICT, 1850-1865

  938M  COLE, CHARLES BRADFORD   621.9 C689T   41
           TOOL DESIGN

  120H  COLE, CHARLES WOOLSEY JT AUTH   330.94 C647   52
           ECONOMIC HISTORY OF EUROPE   3D ED
```

```
LAW ENF          BIBLIOGRAPHY BY DEPARTMENT          5/19/76


   KF   4558.1     J2.
 OBSCENITY AND PORNOGRAPHY

   PV   7399.      P5.
 POLICE POWER IN OUR DEMOCRACY:

   HV   6033.      P7.
 PRIVATE WORLD OF A CONVICT

   HV   6033.      P7.          C'
 PRIVATE WORLD OF A CONVICT

   KF   9646.      T3.          R-
 RIGHT TO COUNSEL
```

Figure 3-5
Sample audiovisual media cards

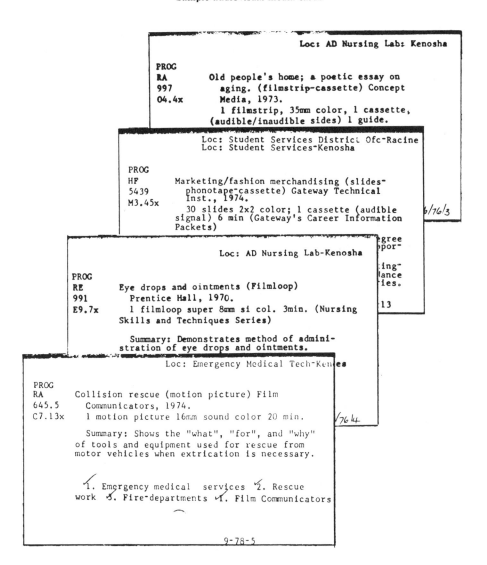

Loc: AD Nursing Lab: Kenosha

PROG
RA
997
04.4x

Old people's home; a poetic essay on aging. (filmstrip-cassette) Concept Media, 1973.
1 filmstrip, 35mm color, 1 cassette, (audible/inaudible sides) 1 guide.

Loc: Student Services District Ofc-Racine
Loc: Student Services-Kenosha

PROG
HF
5439
M3.45x

Marketing/fashion merchandising (slides-phonotape-cassette) Gateway Technical Inst., 1974.
30 slides 2x2 color; 1 cassette (audible signal) 6 min (Gateway's Career Information Packets)

6/76/3

Loc: AD Nursing Lab-Kenosha

PROG
RE
991
E9.7x

Eye drops and ointments (Filmloop) Prentice Hall, 1970.
1 filmloop super 8mm si col. 3min. (Nursing Skills and Techniques Series)

Summary: Demonstrates method of administration of eye drops and ointments.

Loc: Emergency Medical Tech-Kenea

PROG
RA
645.5
C7.13x

Collision rescue (motion picture) Film Communicators, 1974.
1 motion picture 16mm sound color 20 min.

/76 4

Summary: Shows the "what", "for", and "why" of tools and equipment used for rescue from motor vehicles when extrication is necessary.

1. Emergency medical services 2. Rescue work 3. Fire-departments 4. Film Communicators

9-78-5

staff. Another important catalog is the "shelflist," a record of all the items cataloged in the library arranged in the order the items appear on the shelf. The shelflist is most often kept in the staff area and restricted to staff use. If these catalogs contain records of materials in more than one library or collection, they are called "union catalogs." As library systems develop, more and more union catalogs are also being developed. These basic catalogs are now being provided by libraries in several formats. "Card catalogs" are still found in many libraries and will probably not be totally replaced for many years. "Book catalogs" are being produced from computer-generated information, and microform or "COM catalogs" (Computer-Output Microform catalogs) are being produced on microfilm or microfiche. Some libraries are even providing catalogs that are connected directly, or online, to a computer. In evaluating the usefulness of each type of catalog, their major characteristics should be studied carefully.

Card catalogs consist of 3x5-inch catalog cards filed in cabinets of drawers. These catalogs became very popular for a number of reasons. First, the complete cataloging information for an item could usually be easily accommodated on one catalog card. Second, the cards could be filed and removed easily as materials were added or withdrawn from a library's collection. Finally, several persons could use different drawers of the catalog at the same time. A major disadvantage of the card catalog, however, is that people must file the cards in the catalog and this can be a very time-consuming as well as error-prone operation. It also takes up a great deal of space and is difficult to duplicate.

The availability of reasonably-priced computer-output catalogs, whether in book or COM form, has encouraged many libraries to convert their public catalogs to these new forms. (However, most libraries still maintain their shelflists in card format as the master file.) These catalogs have several characteristics which may be more advantageous than the card catalog. First, many copies can be made available to several departments, branches, or libraries within a system because they can be produced at fairly reasonable costs. Second, it is easier to scan a page of catalog entries than to flip through 10-20 catalog cards. This is particularly helpful if the patron has a slightly incorrect spelling or heading. Finally, they are usually updated with periodic supplements. This latter, however, may also be a *dis*advantage in that the patron must look in several places, the main catalog and its supplements, to find information. Another characteristic that could be a disadvantage is that these types of catalogs often do not provide complete cataloging entries. In the future, online computer catalogs could eliminate these disadvantages.

A major advantage to the computer-produced catalogs is that they may be changed in format, style, or arrangement very easily. Most library catalogs were originally arranged in one alphabetical sequence and were called dictionary catalogs. As library collections and catalogs grew, librarians divided the catalogs into several alphabetical sequences to produce separate author, title, and subject catalogs. This division process is very time-consuming when done by hand, but the computer can be programmed to perform this task very easily. Cataloging information that is computer based may also be manipulated to produce special subject or media catalogs or bibliographies of a library's collection. For these reasons, computer-based catalogs will probably become more common in the future.

COMMUNITY RESOURCES

Libraries fulfill a unique function in the communities they serve by providing information about and access to the local natural, human, industrial, and social resources. Libraries can provide information about the unique natural features of the region as well as about its historical development. Many libraries maintain local history collections; these originally included only print materials, but now oral history (audiorecordings) and videotape collections may also be included. Local authors may be highlighted in author collections, and pamphlet files usually contain information about famous personages related to the area. Information on local industries, including their annual statements and the names of their officers and products, is often made available. Providing organization files which give the purposes, officers, and directory-type information for community organizations and businesses has become a standard library service. Cultural calendars of events in the region may also be published and distributed in the community. These are but a few of the services now being provided in many libraries and particularly in public libraries.

During the activist years of the late sixties and seventies, public libraries recognized that they can perform one more service in their local communities: they are often the only place where citizens can find out about local laws and government or learn which agencies can help them out of a dilemma. As a result of this recognition, some libraries are moving into community advocacy, which means they are actively bringing their patrons and community agencies together. They are advertising these agencies' services, participating in community activities, and providing meeting places for these activities. They have taken the major function of a library one step further by "acquiring, preserving, and making available information in *all* of its forms."

REVIEW QUESTIONS

1.   Define the following parts of a book and identify the information included in each: title page, imprint, copyright date, edition, preface, table of contents, index, appendix, bibliography.

2.   Identify the major characteristics of each of the major print media: monograph, series, serial, periodical, newspaper, pamphlet, government document.

3.   Identify the major characteristics of the following graphic and audiovisual media: maps, globes, realia, kits, slides, films, film loops, filmstrips, records, audiotapes, videotapes, microforms.

4.   State the major purpose of a library's catalog and identify the following types of library catalogs: public catalog, shelflist, union catalog, card catalog, book catalog, COM catalog.

5.   Give three examples of the kinds of community resource information a library might provide.

6. Briefly describe why media in all their forms are being included in today's libraries.

7. Visit two local libraries and identify the types of media each has in its collection.

SELECTED READINGS

Brown, James W. *AV Instruction Technology, Media and Methods.* 5th ed. New York: McGraw-Hill, 1977.

Brown, James W. *New Media in Public Libraries: A Survey of Current Practices.* Syracuse, NY: Jeffrey Norton/Gaylord Bros., c1976.

Harrod, Leonard M. *The Librarians' Glossary of Terms Used in Librarianship, Documentation, and the Book Crafts, and Reference Book.* 4th rev. ed. Boulder, CO: Westview, c1977.

Hicks, Warren B., and Alma M. Tillin. *Developing Multi-media Libraries.* New York: Bowker, c1970.

Kemp, Jerrold E. *Planning and Producing Audiovisual Materials.* 3rd ed. New York: Harper and Row, 1975.

Marshall, Lee. *Bookmaking.* 2nd ed. New York: Bowker, 1979.

Miller, Shirley. *Vertical File and Its Satellites.* 2nd ed. Littleton, CO: Libraries Unlimited, 1979.

Morehead, Joe. *Introduction to United States Public Documents.* 2nd ed. Littleton, CO: Libraries Unlimited, 1978.

Saffady, William. *Micrographics.* Littleton, CO: Libraries Unlimited, 1978.

4
LIBRARY ORGANIZATION

Libraries basically develop to serve their functions of building collections, making them accessible, and satisfying their users' needs. In carrying out these functions, libraries have developed certain principles, procedures, and activities common to all libraries. Such areas as administration, finances, governing bodies, and internal organizational patterns are very similar in all libraries, regardless of an individual library's objectives or the type of library it may be. A discussion of the similarities among these principles and patterns will serve as a useful background for the variations that occur among the major types of libraries.

When libraries are organized to provide these activities and to serve these functions, their objectives should first be reviewed so that the pattern for the structure of the organization may be set. Too many times, the library organizational structure has grown by leaps as the staff increased from one person to two, and then from two people to four or more. At other times, the organizational structure has developed as a direct result of the personalities and preferences of the people on the staff. For example, rather than develop a single school media center to serve a school's objectives, some school library and audiovisual departments have remained apart because the librarian or audiovisual specialist did not like working with different materials or equipment. Libraries should base their organization, not on such accidents, but upon well-thought-out objectives.

In addition to defined objectives, a library's organizational structure should be based upon sound administrative principles. One of the most important administrative principles requires that one person be made responsible for leading and directing the library's operations. Although the person in this position may be called librarian, media specialist, head librarian, or library director, the title is not as important as the fact that responsibility for directing the library is vested in one person who guides the formulation of library objectives, establishes policies and programs to carry them out, and recommends their adoption by a governing authority. A library administrator also engages in activities common to all administrators such as preparing a budget, supervising buildings and equipment, developing personnel classification and salary schedules, making recommendations regarding personnel appointments, and engaging in public relations.

In order to fulfill these functions, a library administrator should follow several important administrative principles. One principle is that the head librarian or library director should delegate as many responsibilities as possible to subordinates. In addition, the number of employees reporting directly to the library director should be limited to a small number of people. This allows members of the organization to have an immediate supervisor to whom they have easy accessibility and who will in turn represent their views to a higher supervisor.

Another administrative principle is that the organizational structure should be clearly charted and verbalized so that the relationships among all departments can easily be seen. However, all library staff should realize that an organizational structure is not permanent and may be changed in response to important factors. New library building programs or technologies might necessitate a library's reevaluating its structure. Changes in institutional organization or financial support could also eliminate positions and force a library to reorganize. When such changes do occur, a library should design the best structure for its new needs rather than persist in using an outdated or outmoded one.

VARIETY AND CHANGE IN LIBRARY ORGANIZATION

Generally, libraries have been very flexible in designing their organizational structures and patterns to suit their purposes. Libraries were originally organized into many departments based upon the specific duties and activities performed by the personnel in each of these categories (*see* Figs. 4-1 and 4-2). However, as library staffs grew and employed more and more people, it became poor administrative policy for the department heads of many departments to report directly to the library director. Therefore, in recent years many departments whose activities were related – such as ordering, cataloging, and processing – have been reorganized into larger departments. In fact, one trend today is to divide the library into two large departments that direct the majority of the library's activities. These departments are public services and technical services (*see* Fig. 4-3).

Figure 4-1
Public library organization chart

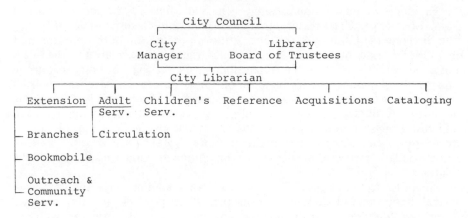

Figure 4-2
Academic library organization chart

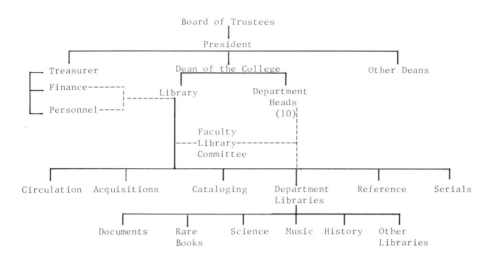

Legend: Solid lines indicate line supervisors; broken lines indicate advisory capacity.

Figure 4-3
Public library organization chart

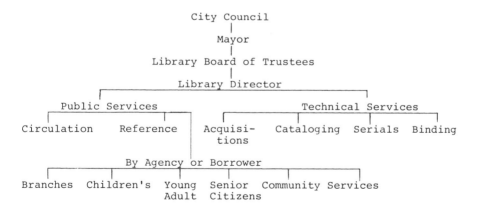

The major function of Public Services is to provide the best possible service to the user. For this reason, Public Services provides the most important contact with the public. This department usually combines such formerly separate functions as circulation (the loan and return of materials) and reference (assisting the patron to find information), and may also include service to special clientele such as children, young adults, and senior citizens. The director of outreach programs and the extension department (which directs branches or bookmobiles) may also be included in this department. Another major purpose Public Services shares jointly with Technical Services is the selection and acquisition of materials to support the library programs.

Although Technical Services shares with Public Services the purpose of selecting and acquiring materials, its major purpose is to make the collection available for the user. This means that the department is primarily concerned with procuring and organizing materials after they have been selected. Technical Services usually combines the formerly separate functions of acquisitions or ordering, cataloging or organizing the materials, processing materials for use, receipt and maintenance of serials, and binding books and serials. It is also concerned with the conservation of materials and may supervise their repair or preservation. Technical Services also shares a responsibility with Public Services for developing library policies and procedures which will enable "the right patron to receive the right material at the right time."

Although Public and Technical Services have become the two most common departments in today's libraries, several other patterns of organization are also important. Libraries may divide their organization into departments based upon several different categories. Public and technical service departments are excellent examples of departments arranged by function. However, libraries may also be arranged according to territory or location, clientele or patron, subject matter, or form of resources. Many libraries have departments such as branches or bookmobiles which are based on location or territory. Academic and school libraries may have resource centers which are both territory and subject departments, such as branch engineering or history libraries. Sometimes the administration of these libraries may even be shared with the subject departments (*see* Fig. 4-2 and Fig. 4-5). Public libraries also sometimes divide their main collections and staffs into subject departments such as the fine arts or business departments. Some libraries have departments based on the form of the resources, such as film departments, map departments, serials departments, or government document departments. Special libraries may have library services based upon the user or patron. For example, a hospital may have a medical library for its medical staff as well as a patients' library. Finally, many libraries have found that basing their organizational structure upon a combination of these categories can provide them with an organization which can best serve their objectives and best suit their needs.

Library organizational patterns have also changed in recent years to reflect changes in the theories of administrative management. The library director who used to make all major decisions alone is now often joined by management-level department heads who help direct and shape the library's operations. These department heads in turn rely upon their supervisors for providing input into the decision-making process. This process has become more complicated as libraries have increased in size and activity. In fact, decisions made in one department can have such a far-reaching effect in other areas that many libraries have adopted group-directed problem-solving techniques. These group-directed efforts may be

Figure 4-4
School media center organization chart

```
                                    Principal
                                       |
                            Media Center Director
    ┌──────────────┬────────────┬───────────────────┬──────────────┬──────────────┐
Technical        Public      Instructional        Broadcast        Media
Services         Services       Services           Services       Operations

 └ Acquisitions   └ Reference   └ Classroom         └ Radio         └ Maintenance
                                  Instruction
 └ Cataloging     └ Circulation                     └ TV            └ Production
                               ┌ Resource
                                 Center-Math &
                                 Science

                               └ Resource
                                 Center-English &
                                 History
```

called task forces, ad hoc committees, or interdepartmental committees, but they have all arisen to provide a team approach to solving library-wide problems.

Another type of management practice can be seen in the development of several parallel supervisory channels. Many libraries have designated some of their department heads and supervisors as "line" administrators who have direct responsibility for the personnel, operations and materials under them. In addition, these libraries may also have "staff" administrators who provide subject expertise or specialized knowledge and serve in an advisory capacity. These "staff" personnel do not have any authority over the actual library operations of a department but do provide facts and information that can be used by the line supervisors to make decisions. Typical staff supervisors in libraries would be personnel officers, automation specialists, and school library supervisors, while line supervisors would be circulation supervisors, public services librarians, and principals.

These line and staff supervisors can be found in libraries representing all of the major types of libraries. Public libraries often have "line" branch librarians who supervise branch operations as well as coordinators of children or young adult services who supervise or coordinate such services for the entire library system. Special libraries may rely on subject specialists within the organization for advice in specific subject areas (*see* Fig. 4-5, page 72). In school media centers, the line supervisor of a school media specialist or school librarian is the principal of the school to whom the librarian reports for the running of the library. If a school system employs a school library supervisor, this person serves in the capacity of a staff position. This staff supervisor may provide assistance, support services, and advice to the school media specialist and the principal (*see* Fig. 4-6, page 72). Usually, the school library supervisor would also advise on the hiring of library personnel, but the principal, as line supervisor, would be responsible for hiring and firing personnel in an individual library. Academic libraries often have Faculty Library Committees which serve in this "staff" capacity (*see* Fig. 4-2). Such a committee can be very helpful to the library staff by serving as an advisory board on library policies and collection development and as a communications link between the faculty and the library. However, sometimes faculty library committees overstep this "staff" function and try to assume the "line" function. When this happens the authority and autonomy of the academic library are seriously threatened.

Figure 4-5
Special library organization chart

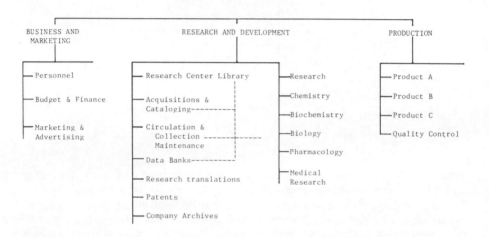

Figure 4-6
School library organization chart

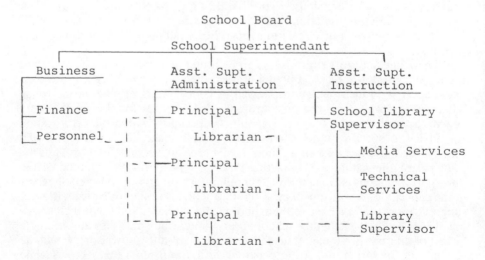

Legend: Solid lines indicate line supervisors; broken lines indicate staff supervisors.

GOVERNING AUTHORITY

In addition to having their own administrations and organizations, libraries are also usually responsible to the administration of other institutions or to elected governmental bodies. Sometimes a library may be an entity in itself, such as the John Crerar Library or a public library district, but even then the autonomous library is governed by a board of trustees or directors. This governing authority is legally responsible to the public or the stockholders for the efficient fiscal and administrative operation of the library. The governing authority usually approves the financial budget and appoints the members of the administrative hierarchy (city manager, school superintendent, or board of trustees) who will hire the library director and staff. Most often, the library is a department of a local government, school district, or academic institution and fits into the structure of this governing body for administration, finances, and personnel selection (*see* Fig. 4-7, page 74).

Governing authorities may differ in the administrative structure of their libraries, but they generally perform the same administrative functions. A governing authority is responsible for determining and adopting the objectives and written policies of its library. It is also responsible for hiring a qualified and competent professional library or media administrator to direct the operations of the library. The library administrator then hires a library staff that is legally accountable to this authority for carrying out the library objectives, policies, and services within the limits set by the authority. This means that the library director does not "run" the library alone, but works with higher administrators or with a library board to develop library objectives and policies and to define the library budget. In turn, the governing body should not get involved in "running the library" or in making decisions about daily operations of the library; it should allow its professional staff to carry out its policies. The concern of the governing authority should be to represent the library in the institution or community to which it belongs and to communicate and interpret the library's objectives, services, and problems to that community.

The manner in which the various governing authorities direct or control libraries under their jurisdiction can differ by type of library. Public libraries often are governed by state library laws which require governing bodies to appoint separate library boards of trustees. These boards of trustees represent citizen interest or control of the library and are often appointed by a mayor or county board chairman and approved by the elected body. Thus, the appointment to these boards may be governed by political considerations rather than by what is best for library services in a particular community. Often these public libraries are also considered to be departments within the city or county government and the library director may also be a department head reporting to a chief administrator, such as a mayor or city or county manager (*see* Fig. 4-1 and Fig. 4-3). Some public libraries are truly departments within a government, and the librarian is appointed by and reports to an administrator rather than to a board of trustees.

Libraries within schools and academic institutions are ultimately controlled by a school board or governing board of trustees which designates responsibility for running the institution to the superintendent of schools or the president of the college or university. Usually, this individual delegates responsibility for the library or media department to one of the subordinate administrators such as an assistant superintendent, dean of the college, or administrator or dean of

Figure 4-7
Types of libraries

LIBRARY	PURPOSES OR OBJECTIVES	CLIENTELE	FINANCIAL SUPPORT	GOVERNING AUTHORITY
PUBLIC: local county multi-county	Recreation Information Self-education Culture Social Responsibility	Free to all residents of a community or district	Public tax funds	Local government's elected body appoints Library Board of Trustees OR Department of local govt. OR elected Board of Trustees
SCHOOL: elementary secondary	Education Self-enrichment	Students and teachers of a school	Public schools – public taxes Private schools – tuition, endowments	School board, School administration
ACADEMIC: colleges universities post-secondary schools	Education Research Information Preservation	Students, faculty, alumni. Also, general public in publicly supported insts.	Public tax funds Tuition Endowment	Board of Trustees, Administration
SPECIAL: (Selective in clientele, subject coverage, materials or format)				
Industry Business	Research Information	Specialized staff and clientele	Within budget of a business operating for profit	Board of Directors, Administrative officers of staff
Organization Association	Research Information Preservation	Membership of the organization or association	Within budget of a nonprofit organization	Board of Directors, Administrative staff
Institution	Recreation Information	Patients, inmates, etc.	Institution budget	Institution administration
Federal	All objectives	Specialized staff & clientele Tax-paying citizens	Federal tax funds	U.S. federal government

instruction. The library director reports to this individual, and the library itself fits into the administrative pattern of the school or university. As a school or university department, the library works with the personnel department, business office, maintenance department and other departments to conduct its operations. The library staff fits into the staffing patterns of the parent institution as well, so that professional librarians may be a part of the faculty, and the clerical and technical staffs may be hired by the business or personnel offices with consultation from the librarians.

Special libraries usually are part of the administrative structure of their corporations, institutions, or governing bodies. In many companies they may be part of the research and development divisions and report to the director of research or to a high ranking officer or administrator. Special libraries that are also academic department libraries usually report to the library director. Other libraries may report to the chief administrator of a hospital, the executive secretary or director of an association, or, for libraries in small organizations, even to the president of the company.

FINANCES

The finances of the library may come from the governing authority in a variety of ways. Public libraries often will draw up a proposed budget, and submit it to the governing authority for approval. When the budget is approved, the governing body will prorate the budgeted amount among the taxpayers and collect the taxes to fund the budget. School libraries usually receive their finances as part of the school budget adopted by the school board at the request of the school superintendent. Public school taxes are then collected from citizens based on a tax levy. Private schools get their operating funds from tuition, endowments, and gifts. Academic libraries usually request a budget from the university administration, which receives its funds from public taxes, tuition, student fees, or endowments. However, this budget may be based upon the prorated needs of the various university departments. In other words, the library may ask for a specific amount of money to support the English department or the science department.

Special libraries may carry this method one step further and develop their budget based on a departmental charge system. This means that the engineering department or the chemistry department, for instance, would have to pay a percentage of the special library's budget for the information and support the library will provide to that department in the coming year. Other special libraries may simply submit a budget to the business office to be approved and included in the total institution budget. The funds for this budget in special libraries come from drastically different sources than those for other types of libraries. Many special libraries are part of companies and businesses which operate for profit, and company profits will determine the company's budget. Other library budgets are dependent upon membership dues in associations and organizations. The special library must prove that it contributes to the profits or the organization as a whole in order to get a workable budget. However, libraries of all types have almost always found that the governing authority questions and changes the library's submitted budget to correspond with the objectives and budget of the institution as a whole.

CLIENTELE

If there are so many different libraries governed by so many governing authorities, how are these libraries distinguished from each other and how do they keep from providing duplicate services and resources? Primarily, each library develops along individual lines to satisfy an established objective or purpose which differs from the objective or purpose of any other library. This objective is determined by the particular needs of the individuals or patrons the library serves. Because these patrons may have many different needs, they may depend upon several libraries to satisfy these needs.

In order to determine these needs and the resources and services that should be provided to satisfy them, libraries may use a variety of techniques. They may conduct surveys of their patrons and of potential patrons. Libraries may also study and evaluate library statistics and usage patterns. Finally, they will try to learn as much as possible about the community or institution they serve in order to coordinate their services with other agencies or departments.

Libraries have usually evaluated their community of patrons so well that several libraries can successfully serve differing needs of the same patron. These library needs are so varied because, as children and adults grow, their interests and needs grow and change in many ways. When children first begin using a library, they usually want to look at picture books and listen to stories. As they learn to read, they will usually read fictional stories for pleasure and nonfiction books on subjects that especially interest them. For all of these needs, children will usually be served by a public library. However, as they enter school and need access to books and information for classes, they will usually find that school libraries provide more material to support these class assignments than do public libraries.

Adults also find that different libraries serve different needs. Students going to college turn to the college or academic library to provide information and resources for course assignments as well as for research projects. However, these same students may visit the public library for leisure reading or for information on subjects of personal interest to them. In addition, both adults and children may enjoy the activities and programs that the public library may offer for pleasure and entertainment.

Often, patrons may turn to special libraries to fulfill their needs for special subject information, for their hobbies or for their work. These patrons may seek out genealogy or local history information in special collections in public libraries. They may also use the special libraries at their places of business, and some may even write to special libraries of professional associations or national organizations for information which may interest them. Thus, throughout their lives, patrons will usually turn to different types of libraries to satisfy their different needs.

THE MAJOR TYPES OF LIBRARIES

Each library usually serves the needs of a specific group of patrons or public based upon its objectives and its political and financial support (*see* Fig. 4-8). Public libraries are financed by public funds from a particular governing unit or tax base, be it city, county, district, or regional. Therefore, every individual who lives within the jurisdiction of the governing body is able to use the public library free of charge. The strength of the public library has been that it has been freely available to all (though, in fact, until the 1960s and 1970s, many public libraries did not permit black Americans to use their libraries). The public library's mission has been to satisfy the needs of all people for education, information, aesthetic appreciation or culture, and recreation. Public libraries all over the country, both large and small, have attempted to fill these needs by establishing specific objectives. A public library might develop a library collection of "quality" as well as of popular materials to meet its patrons' reading needs, or it might provide reference services to satisfy its patrons' informational needs.

Figure 4-8
The major types of libraries and their objectives

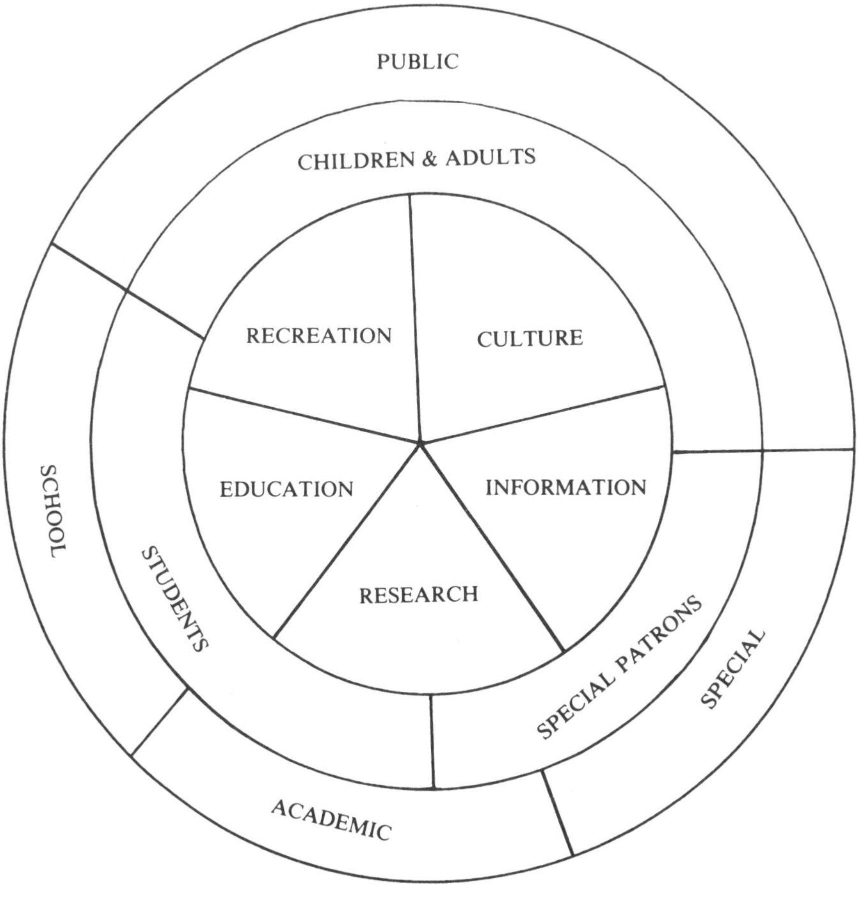

Some public libraries are so small that they are only open a few hours a week, while other public libraries are among the largest libraries in the world. Public library materials collections can range from just 5,000-10,000 books to millions of books plus records, films, audio and videotapes, maps, etc. The size of library staffs can also vary from one or two people to 15-20, or even 50-100, depending upon the size of the community served and the importance of the library in the community. This latter factor is usually directly proportional to the educational level of the community. The higher the average citizen's level of schooling is, the better developed the library services tend to be. Also, public libraries that are well supported tend to pay better salaries and to provide more levels of staffing than other libraries do. Finally, some very large cities such as Detroit and Tulsa have even been able to develop pioneer library services such as Information and Referral Services and Community Advocacy in response to a new recognized need or objective — that of social responsibility.

School libraries or media centers are part of educational institutions and their objective is to support the curricula of their schools. Because they are parts of larger institutions, their clientele is restricted to the students and staff of a particular school. School media centers are distinguished from academic libraries in that schools are defined as educational institutions serving kindergarten through high school grades. Thus, school media centers serve both elementary (K-6) and secondary (7-12) schools.

In recent years, many of these schools have combined their libraries and audiovisual centers into media centers housing all types of print and AV materials. However, the size and scope of these media centers can vary greatly depending upon the size of the school district they are in. Small school districts serving small population areas may staff their media centers or libraries with aides, clerks, or technicians who are supervised by a librarian or media specialist at the district level. Medium-sized school systems may have both a librarian or media specialist and support staff at the building level. Large school systems may often have several professionals, specializing in different areas, who are supported by both technical and clerical staff. These large school systems may also provide collections of many varied types of media backed up by a centralized processing center.

The growth of these media centers also enabled libraries to expand their objective beyond that of solely supporting the curriculum. In recent years, another objective developed as educators came to realize they were educating a whole child. Librarians recognized that this child had interests that were outside of the class curriculum or that needed more depth than the curriculum could provide. For this reason, whenever possible, school media centers accepted the objective of providing self-enrichment for their students. However, this objective was soon hampered by the decrease of funds to school media centers in the 1970s. Also, many people believed that it should be the public library's objective to fulfill the self-enrichment and recreational needs of the child outside of the classroom.

Academic libraries serve institutions of higher education or post-secondary education, that is, schools beyond the high-school level. Because these libraries are part of an educational institution, one of their objectives is to serve the educational needs of the members of their parent institutions. These institutions range from two-year and four-year schools, such as community and junior colleges, vocational and technical institutions, and colleges and universities, to graduate and professional schools, such as law schools and medical colleges. However, these varying school levels require varying levels of library collections and services to support each type of education.

Academic libraries in small junior colleges or four-year colleges tend to have library collections that mainly contain books and magazines. These collections may range from 20,000-50,000 volumes and may have library staffs with a few professional librarians, a few clerks, and a number of college students. Larger academic libraries may have collections of 100,000-200,000 volumes as well as other media such as maps, films, and records. Their staffs might have four or five librarians or as many as ten, depending upon the services they might offer. Many academic libraries are now providing extensive library instruction programs in order to achieve their educational objectives.

Academic institutions, however, have broader missions than just the education of their students. Often, large colleges and universities are also centers of research which need the latest information and in-depth collections to support student and faculty research projects and reports. Thus, the libraries in these institutions must also support the need for research and information. To this end, our nation's universities have developed some of the largest and finest library collections in the world. Harvard, Princeton, Yale, the University of Illinois, and many others, each have millions of volumes in their collections. In addition, these large collections may be distributed into department or subject libraries that are larger than many collections found in smaller college libraries.

In addition to providing current research materials, many research projects may also depend upon historical and archival materials. Thus, libraries must also fulfill the need for preserving materials from the past to be used by students and faculty in the present and the future. The academic library, therefore, tries to fulfill the following major objectives — education, research, information, and preservation.

Special libraries may differ from one another more than those in any other major type of library. They may be defined as libraries providing special services to special clientele to satisfy special needs which sometimes cover special subject areas. Another definition might almost be that special libraries include libraries which are neither public, school, nor academic libraries, but this would be an erroneous definition. Special libraries do have special characteristics which are common to most of these libraries. First, a special library's governing body or institution most often is an organization, business, industry, association, institution, or government agency which restricts the use of the library to the members or employees of the parent organization. Second, these members and employees have special needs most often related to special subject interests; thus, a special library's collection will often be restricted to major subject areas. Finally, libraries are primarily distinguished as special libraries when their primary objective is to provide special services to the patron. The special library will generally serve its patrons by providing library references, locating the materials, and sending them directly to the patron. This service provides the maximum use of the time and knowledge of its personnel for the parent organization or institution.

Some of the most common types of special subject libraries are law libraries, medical libraries, business or commerce libraries, and scientific and technical libraries. They may range in size and scope from small collections of a few hundred or thousand books and magazines to medium-sized collections of 5,000-10,000 books, magazines, and technical reports. Large special libraries may provide many thousands of books, magazines, technical reports, patents, and microforms as well as automated information data bases. These libraries may belong to independent institutions such as business corporations and manufacturing companies, or they may be part of larger institutions such as hospitals, governments, and universities. Law libraries and medical libraries are not only special libraries, but may also be departmental libraries of an academic institution and, therefore, also academic libraries.

Other typical special libraries are those that serve the needs of special clientele. Thus, there are libraries to serve prisoners or inmates in prisons or institutions, and libraries to serve hospital patients or mental institution patients. The U.S. armed forces have large library systems throughout the world to serve military personnel and their families. These latter types of special libraries may provide services for their clientele which would be similar to services provided by the public libraries for their patrons. However, the majority of special libraries are designed to fulfill the specific need for information which their clients or patrons have.

In order to fulfill this need, many special libraries emphasize subject expertise among their staff members. The special librarian may even have a degree in a subject specialty rather than library science, or sometimes both. Subject specialists contribute to the library's objectives by making translations and doing in-depth research to help locate and provide the exact information a patron may need. In large libraries, they are often backed up by professional librarians and information scientists as well as by technicians, programmers, and clerks. Medium-sized special libraries usually have smaller staffs of just a few people, and the small special libraries may truly be one-person shows.

The staffing of these special libraries is often dependent upon the parent institution or organization's financial ability to support a library as well as upon its commitment to library service. Businesses and industries which are governed by the profit margin (and this includes hospitals) may cut back on library personnel and services when their profits are cut. Even nonprofit institutions and organizations may be forced in times of austerity to reduce their overhead which all too often includes the library staff and services.

STANDARDS

To help librarians in all types of libraries describe their functions to their users, many library associations have adopted national statements of purpose and standards of performance. These statements and standards or guidelines identify recommended or acceptable levels of library service. They can be used as measuring instruments to indicate how well a library compares with those recommended standards which provide quality library service in a particular type of library. Standards have been developed by national associations for such types of libraries as public libraries, school libraries, college libraries, junior college libraries, hospital libraries, and prison libraries. But, it is up to each librarian to determine how to use these standards in developing library services in his or her individual library.

Many factors will influence how well an individual library will measure up to the national standards. (These factors will be discussed in more detail in the following chapters.) Since the standards are meant to be goals a library should strive to reach if it is to provide adequate library service, some libraries may already meet or exceed the goals for their particular type of library. However, these libraries would be the shining examples and exceptions rather than the rule, and most libraries will strive for many years to equal them. Often, just as they are reached, new standards will be published, and libraries will begin to strive again for their achievement, adding dimensions of breadth and depth to their collections and services which they would probably never have reached on their own. Thus, when new standards are published, libraries are usually willing to tackle them and to begin anew to reach these new goals.

REVIEW QUESTIONS

1.   Identify the four major types of libraries and the major purposes or objectives of each.

2.   Identify the clientele served by each type of library, the governing authority, and the source of financial support for each type of library.

3.   Define "line" and "staff" levels of supervision and give examples of each.

4.   Identify the major responsibilities of Public Services and Technical Services and three functions which could be included in each.

5.   Identify the patterns of library organization structure and give an example of each.

6.   Identify the organizational structure of two local libraries, including their place in the parent organization or institution.

SELECTED READINGS

Boaz, Martha. *Current Concepts in Library Management.* Littleton, CO: Libraries Unlimited, 1979.

Christianson, Elin. *New Special Libraries: A Summary of Research.* New York: Special Libraries Association, 1980.

Closurdo, Janette. *Library Management.* New York: Special Libraries Association, 1979.

Gates, Jean Key. *Introduction to Librarianship.* New York: McGraw-Hill, 1968.

Johnson, Robert K. *Organization Charts of Selected Libraries: School, Special, Public and Academic.* Ann Arbor, MI: University Microfilms, c1973.

Lyle, Guy. *Administration of the College Library.* 4th ed. New York: H. W. Wilson, 1974.

Rizzo, John. *Management for Librarians: Fundamentals and Issues.* Westport, CT: Greenwood, 1980.

Stebbins, Kathleen B. *Personnel Administration in Libraries.* 2nd ed. Revised and largely rewritten by Foster E. Mohrhardt. New York: Scarecrow, 1966.

Stueart, Robert D., and John Taylor Eastlick. *Library Management.* 2nd ed. Littleton, CO: Libraries Unlimited, 1981.

5
PUBLIC LIBRARIES

Public libraries are the one major type of library that serves every citizen at every stage of life. Thus, public libraries serve more needs and objectives than other libraries do. They serve the leisure reading needs of persons from preschool age through senior citizen as well as the information needs of either first graders or scholars. Public libraries have even been termed the "people's university" because they can enable persons to pursue their own search for knowledge in the library's treasure-house of literary works and scientific and technical information. Because they are so important in everyone's life, public libraries can be found in every community, both large and small, trying to serve these needs.

OBJECTIVES

As these needs have changed over the years, the American public library objectives have changed to keep up with them. Four phases of public library objectives have been identified by Robert Lee.[1] He describes the first phase, from 1850-1875, as a time when the education objective was foremost in the public library. The second phase covered the last quarter of the nineteenth century to World War I and added recreation and reference as objectives. At first, recreational reading was seen as a way to lead patrons to more serious reading, but this objective soon exceeded the education objective in terms of emphasis. This occurred because libraries were trying to reach the multitudes of people flocking to the cities from the farms and from other countries. To assimilate these peoples, society needed to popularize general knowledge. In order to do this, libraries not only provided reading materials inside the library, but some libraries even took bookwagons into the streets and byways. Other libraries provided books and magazines in languages other than English to provide for their foreign-language-speaking patrons.

After World War I and up to 1957, the third phase identified by Lee found some librarians trying to make education once more the dominant function of the public library. This objective was favored by Franklin Roosevelt and encouraged by New Deal programs. More public libraries offered services and activities related to continuing education and began to function as adult education agencies. In addition to helping individual patrons develop their own reading programs, many libraries sponsored discussion groups and educational programs.

The fourth phase of public library objectives began after the Sputnik scare in 1957 and lasted through the late sixties. During this period there was an increased emphasis on the provision of reference and information services. Less emphasis was placed on the need for providing materials for recreation because of the changes in communications materials. The rise of television, the growth of the news magazines, and the abundance of inexpensive paperbound books released libraries from being the only agency providing this information. Once these technological needs were being met, it became apparent that there were social needs which must also be met.

A new fifth phase of public library objectives began in the late 1960s to meet the needs caused by the growth and changes in the makeup of the American population. The baby boom after World War II produced more adults in the sixties than were needed to run a mechanized American society. The centers of population grew bigger as many people moved from rural areas or from the South to the North and West looking for work in the industrial and economic centers. However, society no longer needed masses of unskilled labor, and these people did not have the technical skills needed to survive in their new environments. Along with this, the anti-war years of the Vietnam era produced social unrest and dissatisfaction with the established order. In response to the social and economic problems caused by this population unheaval, many of the minority and disadvantaged people who had remained outside the mainstream of American life demanded to become a part of it. In this social climate, librarians began to recognize that libraries had to satisfy a new need in society, that of social responsibility, and began to help poor and uneducated people to fit into a highly scientific and technical society.

STANDARDS

The major direction for today's public libraries was given when the American Library Association published its post-war *Standards for Public Libraries* in 1943. These standards emphasized that a public library should provide free library service to the residents of a particular community. It should also satisfy the needs of those residents for education, information, aesthetic appreciation, recreation and research by providing services for adult education and vocational education, as well as services to the citizen, particularly the child and the young adult. This direction was expanded to include the concept that "Service to all" is the reason the library exists with the publication in 1966 of the *Minimum Standards for Public Library Systems*. This expanded concept meant that libraries were looking beyond their typical library patron—the middle class better-educated adult female who only represented a minority of the population. They were looking toward the unserved one-third of the population who had never used a library. They were also looking to the millions of Americans who had no access to free public service because they lived in rural communities. It was recognized that all citizens had the same needs for information and education regardless of where they lived. Thus, the 1966 standards were based on the philosophy that "people need similar library resources whether they live in cities, in suburbs, or in rural areas."[2]

These 1966 standards also identified important functions which the public library should fulfill. In essence, the public library has the function of providing materials and services 1) to facilitate informal self-education of all people in the community, 2) to enrich and further develop the subjects on which the individuals are undertaking formal education, 3) to meet the informational needs of all, 4) to support the educational, civic, and cultural activities of groups and organizations, and 5) to encourage wholesome recreation and constructive use of leisure time.[3] These functions and the underlying philosophy of service to all seemed to be fulfilled best by developing library systems based upon a population base that was broad enough to support financially the type of library that was needed.

The 1966 standards suggested that library systems be developed which would serve at least 150,000 people. This was felt to be the minimum population base which could support resources and staff financially and effectively and provide quality library service for the American public. The system was to be made up of levels of service that would provide services within easy access of all persons and that would be backed up by a pool of in-depth resources and services. The local or community level could be provided by branch libraries, small town libraries, bookmobiles, etc., which could work jointly with schools and colleges to share resources. This level would be backed up by a systems center or headquarters library, which would serve the entire region. This headquarters library would provide a comprehensive collection of materials which could be loaned to units at the local level when needed. It would also provide specialized staff and services to help the local units. These services could include centralized ordering, cataloging, and processing; reference library staff to provide reference support (perhaps via telephone); staff specialists in children's and young adult work; public relations; administrative support; and guidance in developing community services. The headquarters library would also provide any guidance and direction the local library staff might ask for and would provide in-service education for system staff members as needed.

The next level of library service would be the state library agency, which would provide resources, personnel, and support for the library systems. Many state agencies had already developed resource personnel and strong state programs as a result of the federal Library Services Act (1956) and the Library Services and Construction Act (1964). Through these acts, state libraries had developed state plans for library service and distributed federal funds to support library systems. Most state libraries had used these funds to develop and support those programs which would benefit the largest number of their citizens. Such programs as demonstration or model library services, statewide interlibrary loan networks, and contracts with large libraries to share their resources with other libraries were initiated in many states. The 1966 standards recommended that a state library agency not only continue in these roles, but also assume the leadership for library development, coordination, and research within each state.

The emphasis in these standards for library systems was upon the quality of library service provided rather than upon the quantity of library materials. In order to fulfill its functions, the public library should develop written selection policies and choose materials that are accurate, that include opposing views, and that appeal to all members of the community. Materials should be purchased and discarded on a planned basis. Services and programs should be developed to satisfy the needs of all individuals and groups. Services to many groups, such as children, young adults (persons aged 14-21), and blind and physically handicapped persons, have been identified in separate standards by divisions of the American Library Association.

Although library systems are based on qualitative standards, librarians often find it useful to state these in quantitative terms for public relations purposes. Librarians have found it very useful to say that "so much money per capita should be spent to support library services." Thus, the 1966 standards also included quantitative standards for such areas as services, materials, and staffing.[4] For services, it is recommended that the local community library be open at least six days a week and that bookmobile services be provided to areas without libraries. The minimum provision for staff should be one full-time staff member for every 2,000 people in the system area, and the staff should be one-third professional and subprofessional and two-thirds supportive staff. For materials, the total system should provide at least two to four volumes per capita and add one volume a year for every six persons in the system. The headquarters library should have at least 100,000 adult nonfiction titles and a comprehensive collection of older and current fiction. One-third of the book collection should be for children and at least five percent for young adults. Magazines should be kept for 10-15 years as a back-up resource at the headquarters library and the system should have at least one magazine title for each 250 persons.

In 1970, the ALA established quantitative guidelines for AV materials and services.[5] For a system with 150,000 population, no less than 20% of the materials budget should be spent on audiovisual materials. Minimum standards which covered materials and staff were established for even the smallest regional systems. A minimum collection of 300 16mm films was recommended as well as one sound recording for 50 people or not less than 5,000 sound recordings for a system. The audiovisual collection should also include other media such as audiotapes, 8mm films, filmstrips, framed art collections, discs, slides, and videotapes. An audiovisual staff of one librarian, one assistant, and one technician should be hired to work with the audiovisual media which should be integrated into the total library program rather than be an adjunct to it. These numerical or quantitative standards were not meant to be definitive quantities but guidelines which libraries should strive to meet.

All of these standards were not met with equal levels of acceptance by librarians, community leaders, and state legislators. Many people felt threatened by the systems concept and feared they would lose their local autonomy and control. Others enthusiastically endorsed them and developed statewide regional library systems. The quantitative standards were considered to be too low and short-sighted by librarians in metropolitan and progressive libraries and too high and impossible to achieve by others. Although some libraries quickly and easily reached the standards, many took 5-10 years, and others still had not achieved them by 1980. That they were achieved in any measure was probably due to the perseverance and farsightedness of many librarians and to the guidance and pressure of state library agencies, which often used state and federal funds as "the carrot" for incentive.

As librarians were striving to meet these quantitative standards, they also began to recognize that each library had its own unique characteristics, which sometimes did not fit into any standard formula. Therefore, librarians began to look at the quality of services an individual library could provide. The Public Library Association encouraged such an approach when its mission statement for public libraries, published in the 1970s, focused on a library's formulation of its own objectives. Further emphasis was given to this individual approach with the publication in 1980 of *A Planning Process for Public Libraries*. This process stressed that an analysis of the library and its community by community members, library staff, and library board members could help identify library needs and set directions for library services. Although this process was not new to libraries, its strong emphasis on community involvement came at a time of financial retrenchment when librarians needed to enlist as much community support as possible.

LIBRARY SERVICES

Libraries have used the standards as guidelines not only in developing their collections but also in developing services and programs for their communities. Most public libraries in the 1960s developed collections, programming, and staff for childrens' services, and programs such as story hours, puppet shows, drama groups, and reading clubs were common. Collections, programming, and staff for young adult services were often provided for persons aged 14-21. The young adult collections consisted of adult books which were of interest to young people, and programming often consisted of film programs, discussion groups, or specialized activities. Some libraries also provided adult education programming, which included book discussion groups, music appreciation groups, art or craft groups, film programs, and many programs and discussion groups on special topics for adults in their communities.

Other libraries also provided programming and services for persons with special needs. Some of these services included foreign language collections for the foreign-speaking populations, programs for senior citizens, and access to talking-books (books recorded on records for blind persons), braille materials and large print books for blind and visually handicapped individuals. Services were also provided which were based on the various uses of media. As well as using audiovisual collections to support library programming, some libraries produced their own radio and TV programs to reach all segments of their populations. The majority of libraries built in the 1960s and 1970s included meeting rooms that could house library programs and also be made available for community organizations to use. Many libraries also included housing for bookmobiles which took programming and collections to persons who could not get to the main or branch libraries. All of these services were provided in addition to the traditional library functions of circulating library materials and providing reference service. Together, they helped libraries strive to meet the goals set by the 1966 standards.

The guidelines or standards adopted in 1966 by the Public Library Association were further expanded in 1972 by Allie Beth Martin in response to the question, "What is the unique role of the public library?" Using survey responses to this question, Martin identified four basic functions of the public library for the future.[6] They are: to provide free service to all without question of user purpose; to provide the widest possible range of resources for information and for decision making; to serve as a repository of the recorded past; and to provide resources for educational purposes. Other functions mentioned were recreation and group services, motivation of patrons and interpretation of the use of materials, and service to adults. These functions seem to be supported by the goals, which were identified as follows: to provide service to all, to provide information services, to provide for adult and continuing education, to collect and disseminate all kinds of informational, educational, and cultural materials, to support education, both formal and informal, and to serve as a cultural center.[7] These goals and functions seemed to recognize that libraries were dealing with changing environments — socially, economically, and intellectually. The library could no longer afford to serve only the middle class educated adult, but must now reach out into the community to prove to all the other citizens that it had a *raison d'être*.

This need to reach out was felt most strongly by libraries in the late 1960s and 1970s. The social upheaval in the cities, caused by the influx of poor, uneducated people and followed by the flight to the suburbs of the middle classes, presented new problems and dilemmas for public libraries. In response, librarians began to develop programs and services to reach the formerly unserved populations. They encouraged integration of the segregated libraries that still existed in the South. They developed programs of action, or outreach programs, which took library services outside the library building to the community centers and streets where the people gathered. Libraries were even combined with community action centers to serve all peoples within their jurisdictions better. The term "community advocacy" was used to describe this role of the public library as it went out, psychologically and physically, into the community to meet society's changing needs.

Many libraries responded by designing "outreach" programs and services which they hoped would meet the needs of these disadvantaged peoples. Bookmobiles were repainted in bright, attractive designs and were restocked with lower level reading materials, paperbacks, and magazines. Mediamobiles were instituted which toured the inner city areas bringing library programs to children and young adults on their own street corners. Libraries began to take their services to the people rather than waiting for the people to come to them! Many libraries established storefront branches or placed materials collections in urban housing developments or local black, Latino or senior citizen community centers. New staff members were hired who had similar ethnic backgrounds to the population being served, and many Spanish-speaking centers were established. Many libraries began to realize the importance of providing various media forms for patrons who could not use the traditional print materials, and audiovisual departments became important in the library organizational structure. The type of services offered by libraries is probably best expressed by the Inglewood, California Public Library as "providing resources, services, and programs to those in the community who are unable to use library service in its traditional form."[8]

INNOVATIONS IN SERVICES

In serving those patrons who could not use the library in its traditional form, libraries experimented with many innovative services and programs. One service initiated by some libraries was a service most often called "Books by Mail," which provided catalogs of paperback books for patrons to choose from and receive by mail from the library. These services seemed to be successful in reaching persons who were unable to use or had no access to traditional library facilities. In some areas, "Books by Mail" even successfully supplanted bookmobile service, and in all of the programs, the service seemed to reach previously unserved populations. Successful programs were developed in rural areas by library systems, in urban areas by city libraries, and on a state-wide basis by state library agencies. Some states even contracted with individual libraries to provide Books by Mail services to persons in rural areas or in prisons who had no access to other library service. The success of these new delivery systems underscored the need for libraries to provide "service to all."

In serving this need, libraries also attempted to reach their unserved populations by serving as centers for independent study. They supported the federal government's concept that every person had the "Right to Read" and encouraged individuals to participate in non-traditional education programs.

Libraries cooperated with educational institutions and community agencies by assisting individual patrons to study for credit courses or to take equivalency tests for high school (GED) or college (CLEP). Some libraries also conducted adult education classes and courses within the library. These classes covered both traditional educational subjects and subjects such as consumer education and family life education which were of importance to the community. However, even these attempts by libraries were not successful in providing "service to all."

Libraries had found that many of their patrons had needs which could best be met by other agencies within the community. Rather than ignore these needs, many progressive libraries accepted this "need to know" as a valid objective for the public library. They began to design Information and Referral Services (I&R) to help the individual get information or services which he or she could not get alone. These I&R services ranged from clearinghouses or data banks of information about community agencies to referral programs which contacted the agency for the patron and followed-up to see that the patron's need was satisfied.

I&R was not a new concept or a library innovation. There were many agencies providing I&R, and national I&R standards had been developed. However, because of their major function as information-gathering sources, libraries were in a unique position to bridge the information gap by helping the patron find the needed information in the right place at the right time. Libraries became partners with other agencies in I&R rather than competitors or sole proprietors.

I&R helped people solve problems dealing with health, housing, and transportation, as well as family problems, legal problems, business, consumer, employment, and personal-social problems. It gathered information about such agencies and organizations as government bureaus, social service agencies, health organizations, educational facilities, crisis centers, and other organized bodies serving the community. Librarians who provided I&R did not serve as counselors but as advocates or ombudsmen who would present to the patron the alternatives available, bring the patron and agency of his or her choice together, and perhaps serve as interpreter (both literally and figuratively) between the two. For I&R to be successful, the entire library staff, rather than just a few specific people, should be committed to and provide I&R. Libraries that have made such total commitments to I&R as the Detroit and Memphis public libraries have found that I&R services have provided an important new stimulus to library use. This stimulus has made the library visible within the community as a viable and vital institution responding to and satisfying the public's needs. As Clara Jones, Librarian of Detroit Public Library and ALA past-president, said, "By incorporating I&R into its traditional reference service, the public library can become a comprehensive community information center. This expansion into community-based, often 'fugitive,' information is necessary if the public library is to fulfill its claim as an institution basic to civilization."[9]

That the public library as "an institution basic to civilization" is being challenged today, is due to several factors which will affect the survival of the free public library. First and foremost has been the economic recessions of the 1970s which will probably continue into the 1980s. Second, has been the rising functional illiteracy of the adult population that pays the taxes to support public library services they seldom use. Third has been the publication explosion, which is producing more and more materials at a time when shrinking budgets allow libraries less purchasing power. In light of these economic factors, libraries have had to eliminate or drastically reduce many programs and services which were begun with high hopes and funding. Many libraries even had to charge fees for some services, close branches, and lay off staff members. Libraries were forced to reevaluate their objectives and programs to be sure they met their communities' needs.

In reevaluating their objectives, public libraries have recognized that they must also readjust the services and programs they have traditionally offered. No longer can they provide access to all the information needed by their patrons at even a system headquarters library. Instead, many libraries have joined cooperative library networks in order to share their resources and stretch their budgets. These networks have blossomed in the 1970s because the technical capabilities of the computer have made it feasible for libraries to share their cataloging and bibliographic information bases. Now that the technology is available and the cooperative mechanisms have begun, public libraries should work to fulfill their objectives effectively in the 1980s and 1990s.

LIBRARY ADMINISTRATION

In order for public libraries to be able to fulfill their objectives in the next decades effectively, library administrators and staff members will have to develop creative and insightful methods for dealing with a variety of administrative problems. No longer will libraries be able to adopt more objectives and initiate more services without first carefully determining if something else should be let go. In order to stretch their budgets to cover every area adequately and to provide balanced resources, staffing, and programs, all departments and personnel, from the library board and director down to the lowliest library clerk, may become involved in solving these problems.

Several major administrative problems for public libraries stem from their attempts to provide "service to all." Because no public library patron should have more rank or privilege than another patron, administrators and their staffs must design policies and procedures that are equitable for all patrons. This simple premise can become complicated when policies are established to cover both adults and children or residents and non-residents. However, public libraries are probably the only type of library in which procedures are usually based upon equal access to library materials and programs for all library patrons.

By attempting to serve all patrons, public libraries automatically serve a broader range of age groups and interest groups and provide more subjects, materials, and services than do other types of libraries. In addition, some public library departments and personnel have become just as specialized as any found in academic or special libraries. Many public libraries have special subject divisions, local history and rare book divisions, audiovisual services divisions, and computer divisions, as well as the traditional public services, technical services, and children, young adult, and adult services divisions. Balancing the needs of all these areas requires library directors and their staffs to set priorities and establish criteria for performance and evaluation.

One area in which public libraries have had to reevaluate their priorities is in the programs and services they provide for various age groups. For example, in the 1940s and the 1950s, the majority of a library's users were children, and children's rooms, children's librarians, and strong children's programming were common in most libraries. However, in the 1960s and the 1970s, the decline in the birth rate, accent on disadvantaged youth, and the increase in the number of senior citizens left many libraries with unbalanced staffs and collections. Sometimes, administrators and their staffs were faced with infrequently used children's rooms that could not be converted to use for senior citizens because they required patrons to go up or down the stairs. Other libraries found they had an overabundance of personnel who were trained to work with children. Although some of these staff members could be shifted to work with senior citizens or in outreach programs, libraries generally found that they were unprepared for these population shifts.

In addition to having staffing problems in serving different age groups, public libraries usually have more staffing requirements than school libraries and many special libraries do. Public libraries are often open many hours during the week. It is not unusual for a public library to be open from 9-9 Monday through Friday, and 9-5 on Saturday. Some public libraries are also open on Sundays. These 60-80 hour weeks often need the equivalent of 1½-2 separate staffs working 40 hours each to serve the library patrons. Library administrators and supervisors must often do quite a bit of juggling to schedule enough staff members to cover all the hours that a library is open, let alone cover a library's busiest hours.

Besides scheduling staff members so that the library is well-staffed, most supervisors must also take many other factors into account. The staff members' personal preferences for the hours they work cannot usually be ignored. Many people do not like to work more often than every other Saturday, and most staff members only want to work a few nights a week. State labor laws may also restrict the number of hours in a day which personnel can work or the number of hours a person can be scheduled to work without a lunch or dinner break. If staff members belong to a union, there may be special restrictions or requirements pertaining to the work week, such as special provisions for overtime pay on Saturdays or Sundays. If staffs in some library departments work regular daytime hours while staffs in other departments must work irregular hours, there might be some jealousy or antagonism between the staffs. Sometimes there could even be library departments or branches which, for one reason or another, generate more transfer requests than do other areas. These and other staffing complications can combine to make the job of scheduling even a small public library one which requires a considerable amount of thought and planning.

The staff in public libraries can range from a one- or two-person branch to a main library staffed with 50-100 people. In very small libraries and branches, or on bookmobiles, the staff members tend to be generalists and share all the jobs from checking out materials to helping a person find a book. In these libraries, there may not be a great differentiation between library positions. In fact, the person in charge may not have much formal library education.

As libraries grow in size and circulation, the staff members usually become more specialized and job classifications become more distinct. Library staff members tend to have more education although they might not have masters' degrees in library science. Library technicians or high-level library clerks may perform paraprofessional or supportive tasks in such areas as children's services, bookmobiles, or outreach and technical services. When professional librarians work in these libraries, they usually are responsible for administration, reference services, and programming.

Medium-to-large-sized libraries usually have a large range of library positions at all levels filled with appropriately trained personnel. In addition, these libraries may also hire personnel with specialties other than library science.

Graphic artists, TV technicians, computer programmers, and specialists in information science or public relations are just a few of the varied types of personnel found in public libraries today. In these larger library systems, there is also a very definite pattern of departmentalization among library personnel. For instance, in the circulation department, one clerk might be specifically responsible for reserves, one for overdues, and other clerks for charging or discharging materials. These clerks might be supervised by a library technician or librarian and supported by library pages or shelvers. It is not unusual in such libraries for a library employee to work many years in one specialized area of either public or technical services.

Each type of public library, therefore, has its own personnel needs and tends to appeal to particular types of people. If staff members prefer to work in many different areas, they often enjoy the variety of patrons, subjects, and materials found in public libraries. If they prefer to specialize in one library department, they will enjoy being able to work only in that area of larger libraries. This flexibility in selection has been one factor which has kept the library personnel turnover rate in public libraries at such a relatively low level.

REVIEW QUESTIONS

1.   Identify the major purposes of a public library.

2.   Identify some of the major services provided by public libraries.

3.   State the underlying philosophy of library service for the 1966 ALA *Public Library Standards*.

4.   Identify the population base and major levels of service of a library system.

5.   Visit a public library which you have not been to before. Compare the objectives and services of this library with those discussed in the text. Also, compare the quantitative standards with the staff, collection, etc., of the library you visited.

6.   Identify some of the duties of an LMTA (or a similar level employee) in the above local library.

SELECTED READINGS

American Library Association, *Guidelines for Audiovisual Materials and Services for Public Libraries.* Chicago: ALA, 1970.

ALA Yearbook: A Review of Library Events. Chicago: American Library Association, 1976- . Articles on public libraries.

Getz, Malcolm. *Public Library: An Economic View.* Baltimore, MD: Johns Hopkins, 1980.

Jones, Clara Stanton, ed. *Public Library Information and Referral Service.* Syracuse, NY: Gaylord Professional Publications, 1978.

Palmour, Vernon E. *A Planning Process for Public Libraries.* Chicago: American Library Association, 1980.

Public Library Association. *Minimum Standards for Public Library Systems, 1966.* Chicago: American Library Association, 1967.

Public Library Association. Goals, Guidelines and Standards Committee. *Public Library Mission Statement and Its Imperatives for Service.* Chicago: American Library Association, 1979.

Rayward, W. Boyd. *The Public Library: Circumstances and Prospects.* Chicago: University of Chicago, 1979.

Rochell, Carlton. *Wheeler and Goldhor's Administration of Public Libraries.* Rev. ed. Harper-Row, 1981.

Seymour, Whitney. *The Changing Role of Public Libraries: Background Papers from the White House Conference.* Metuchen, NJ: Scarecrow, 1980.

Shera, Jesse. *Foundations of the Public Library: The Origins of the Public Library Movement in New England, 1624-1855.* 1949. Reprint. Hamden, CT: Shoe String, 1974.

Sinclair, Dorothy. *Administration of the Small Public Library.* 2nd ed. Chicago: American Library Association, 1979.

Totterdell, Barry. *Public Library Purpose: A Reader.* Hamden, CT: Shoe String, 1978.

U.S. Commissioner of Education. *Public Libraries in the United States of America: Their History, Condition and Management.* 1876. Reprint in 3 vols. Totowa, NJ: Rowman, 1971.

NOTES

[1]Robert Ellis Lee, *Continuing Education for Adults through the American Public Library, 1833-1964.* (Chicago: American Library Association, 1966), pp. 116-19.

[2]Public Library Association, *Minimum Standards for Public Library Systems, 1966* (Chicago: American Library Association, 1967), p. 10.

[3]Public Library Association, *Minimum Standards*, p. 9.

[4]Public Library Association, *Minimum Standards*, passim.

[5]American Library Association, *Guidelines for Audiovisual Materials and Services for Public Libraries* (Chicago: ALA, 1970).

[6]Allie Beth Martin, *Strategy for Public Library Change: Proposed Public Library Goals – Feasibility Study* (Chicago: American Library Association, 1972), p. 20.

[7]Martin, *Strategy*, p. 46.

⁸Inglewood Public Library, *Library Community Service* (Inglewood, CA: IPL, 1977), p. 6.

⁹Clara Stanton Jones, *Public Library Information and Referral Services* (Syracuse, NY: Gaylord Professional Publications, 1978), p. 22.

6
SCHOOL LIBRARY MEDIA CENTERS

In many of today's schools, a well-run library media center may very well be the most active room in the entire school. Children may come there on an individual basis to choose books, use computers or learning machines, or listen to records and view filmstrips. Entire classes may come to learn how to use the library or to locate information for their reports. Groups of students may come for help in making transparencies or producing videotapes for class projects. All of these students may be assisted by professional librarians or media specialists, media technicians, and library/media clerks, who are often backed up by specialized personnel at district-level media centers. These active media centers have shown how important they can be in a modern educational system. And yet, it is an amazing phenomenon that school libraries have taken so long to become a basic part of the educational institutions of this country.

THE BEGINNINGS

Not until the 1950s did most secondary schools have libraries, and even in the 1970s many elementary school libraries were just getting started. What took the educational systems so long to recognize that libraries were necessary components of the education process? The answer to this question lies in the educational goals and methods of the schools. In the early centuries of our country's history, schooling consisted primarily of the students' memorizing information presented by the teacher. There were few textbooks, and students were not encouraged to question. In the nineteenth century and the early part of the twentieth century, the emphasis was on subject content, which was mainly learned from textbooks. In the 1920s and 1930s, the emphasis shifted to the learner, and finally, in the 1940s, the emphasis was placed on life adjustment and the education of all youth for their future roles.[1]

However, the Sputnik scare of the 1950s placed new emphasis on subject mastery so that our education would be equal to education in the Soviet Union. To achieve this end, the 1960s also emphasized educating the individual student according to his or her needs and abilities in order to prepare each individual for participation in American society. Each of these educational philosophies had its effect on school library services since school libraries always function within the goals and objectives of the school.

The first school library services supported learning that came mainly from textbooks. These libraries tended to be just classroom collections of encyclopedias, older textbooks, and perhaps a few reading books. The major impetus for the development of centralized secondary or high school libraries came from the establishment of educational accreditation associations at the turn of the twentieth century. The purpose of these associations was to rate high schools so that colleges could equate graduates of one high school with another. Libraries were included in the criteria listed by the associations, so that those schools which wanted to become accredited had to develop libraries which met the standards of the accrediting associations.

STANDARDS

In the 1920s, these associations and the American Library Association began to develop standards first for high school libraries and then for elementary school libraries. However, they did not become widely adopted. Instead, the major type of library service provided by the schools (particularly by those below the high school level) consisted of traveling library collections provided by state agencies or services to the schools provided by public libraries. Many public libraries provided school collections to the classrooms and public librarians to visit the schools. Sometimes, the public library was actually part of the school system or housed public library branches in the school buildings. These services seemed to be satisfactory for those school systems which still considered learning to be largely classroom oriented.

As educators in the 1940s began to recognize that the student should be involved in the discovery of learning based on study and inquiry, the school systems began to experiment with new methods of teaching. These methods emphasized the need for library services and materials to support the expanded curriculum. To help identify what these library services and materials should be, the American Library Association published standards for school library service in 1945 entitled *School Libraries for Today and Tomorrow*. These standards emphasized that the school library was an integral part of a quality educational system. They also identified qualitative and quantitative standards for library resources and services which should be provided by a professional staff in a centralized library.

The typical school library that developed at this time was a high school library housed in one room about the size of two classrooms and located in a corner of the school. The collection consisted of books arranged on shelves that stood along the walls, and the staff consisted of one professional librarian (with perhaps a clerk) who only had time to manage the library and its collection. If the schools provided audiovisual films and equipment, they were often housed in a closet near the library or administered by someone else in another part of the school building. Very few elementary school libraries were established, and on the whole, the concept of library services envisioned by the standards were seldom implemented.

To encourage library development, the American Library Association in 1956 published a policy statement identifying the important role the school library should play in the total instructional process of the school. For the first time, the library was envisioned to be a central school library which included all types of learning materials available to both students and teachers. The concepts of this statement were translated into new *Standards for School Library Programs* in 1960. The adoption of these standards was greatly facilitated by the country's interest in the educational system after Sputnik was launched in 1957. In addition, the National Defense Education Act (NDEA) of 1958 provided funds for schools to buy print and nonprint materials and equipment, which funds were used by some states to hire state school library supervisors. The 1960 standards, therefore, coincided with society's need for quality education.

The standards helped usher in a new era for library services. Not only did central libraries containing all types of learning materials develop in elementary, junior, and senior high schools, but educators recognized for the first time that these libraries were an integral part of the educational curriculum. Librarians were recognized as teachers whose subject specialty enabled them to help students and teachers use such materials as books, audiotapes, records, films, filmstrips, transparencies, and programmed instruction. These materials were used equally in either the classroom or the library to help students learn. The concept of a library changed to that of an IMC, Instructional Materials Center, where many learning activities took place. In the IMC, students and teachers could listen to or view the library's media or even produce their own. Here also, students and teachers could work on group projects or hold meetings in the library's conference rooms, or they could still study independently in the library's quiet areas. Library paraprofessional and clerical staffs were hired, which freed librarians to provide instruction in the use of the library and its resources or to help students learn independently. Librarians were also able to perform such professional tasks as offering in-service training to teachers in the use of audiovisual materials and equipment or becoming active members of curriculum committees and teaching teams. The modern school library as perceived by librarians many years before had finally arrived in the 1960s in many school districts.

This phenomenal growth of school libraries in the 1960s was largely due to several important developments. Foremost among these developments was the constant change that took place in educational philosophies and systems. Educators began to recognize that their students had varying educational backgrounds, abilities, and needs and that, in order for these needs to be met, the schools must provide varied educational methods and opportunities for learning. To meet these varied needs, libraries were encouraged by the influx of private funds, which was the second major development that affected school library growth. In the 1960s, the Knapp Foundation funded a school library demonstration project. This project chose demonstration libraries to serve as model school IMCs providing effective library programs in accordance with the new standards. These libraries were visited by librarians and educators from throughout this country and the world. These visits enabled librarians to show their superintendents and school boards how quality library services could be integrated into their own school systems. The Knapp Foundation also sponsored a School Library Manpower Project which delineated and identified the kinds of staffing needed to support such comprehensive library services.

The final major development affecting library growth during this period was the passing of the Elementary and Secondary Education Act (ESEA) in 1965. Title (or chapter) II and later Title IV of this act provided the monies, direction, and impetus to state school library agencies and local schools to develop library services. ESEA funds were used by state agencies to hire state school library consultants, to provide guidelines for local schools, and to direct and consult with them in developing and improving library programs. The state agencies also distributed ESEA monies to local schools to purchase materials, hire staff, and develop innovative and model IMC programs. This influx of monies for school library services, combined with the interest in the community for providing such services, seemed to herald the arrival of quality school library/instructional materials centers.

With school instructional materials centers well on their way to becoming a part of many local school systems, new standards were proposed in 1969 by the American Association of School Librarians (AASL) and the Association of Educational Communications and Technology (AECT), formerly the Department of Audio-Visual Instruction of the National Education Association (DAVI). These *Standards for School Media Centers* carried the IMC concept one step further. They proposed that schools develop media programs and services which integrated all types of media into the curriculum based upon their contributions to the educational program of the school rather than upon their formats. The standards also proposed the replacement of the terms "library," "librarian," "audiovisual center," and "audiovisual specialist" with the new terms "media center" and "media specialist" to identify better the entities that would emerge from fulfilling these new standards.

MEDIA CENTERS

The concept of a "media center" caused great consternation in the educational and library worlds. Many school systems enthusiastically endorsed this concept and combined their library, audiovisual, video, and graphics operations and programs into one media department. Titles for such new departments varied from Media Center and Library Media Center to Learning Resource Center, Instructional Media Center, Instructional Resource Center, or just Resource Center, but they all attempted to provide the media services recommended in the standards. Other librarians and audiovisual specialists had difficulty adjusting to this new concept which required them to alter their thinking and their focus. Often, they, as well as many educators, believed that the quantitative standards were utopian rather than practicable—especially in relation to the 1960 standards (*see* Fig. 6-1, page 98). To add to this confusion, the economic crisis of the 1970s practically wiped out the federal monies which had been used to develop such services. In order to provide direction in this chaotic time, the AASL and AECT published new standards in 1975.

The new standards, *Media Programs, District and School* (*see* Fig. 6-2, page 99), expanded the concept of media programs beyond the individual school to include services and facilities which could be provided at the district level. The standards were based on the principle that media were a central part of the learning process and that if schools were to meet the individual needs of their students, they must provide quality media programs. These programs were seen to be a combination of district-wide and building-level services which would be tailored to fit the educational goals and objectives of each individual school system. Therefore, the qualitative aspect of the standards was stressed rather than the quantitative standards. The adoption of district media programs was given a great boost by many state library agencies. These state agencies often developed their own media standards which schools had to meet if they wanted to receive state or federal monies (*see* Fig. 6-1). Thus, the development of school media programs was continued in spite of the economic setbacks of the seventies.

Figure 6-1

A brief comparison of quantitative standards for school libraries

	1960 A.L.A.	Wisconsin 1968-69 IMC Minimum Stand.	1969 Media Centers A.L.A.	Wisconsin 1972-75 Sch. Library/Med Programs
OBJECTIVES	Support curriculum	Recent books of high quality which suppl. curriculum and provide leisure reading	Unified media program is recommended	Full accessibility to collection of materials that meets standards for variety, breadth & scope. Duplicates to meet curricular needs and student requests for leisure read.
STAFF	.For first 900 stud: 1 libn. for 300, for each add.400 stud. - 1 libn.; .1 clerk for each 600 stud. .AV - partial admin. by lib., increase staff by 25% .AV - full admin. by lib., increase staff by 50%	.0-299 students, at least 1/2 qualified libn. Towards 300, more libn. time. 300-439 studs.,1 libn. .500 or more , 1 libn. add libn.help for one period daily for every 100 studs. over 500. .1 clerk for 500 studs.	.1 media specialist for every 250 studs. .1 media tech. & 1 media aide for spec. in schools of 2000 or less. .1 graphics tech. .over 2000 studs., adjust ratio 2 to 1	.0-299 1/2 libn.; as approaches 300, 1 libn. 300-499 studs., 1 libn. .500 or more, 1 libn. & 1 libn. per period daily for every 100 stud. over 500. .AV: 0-399 stud., 1/2 AV spec.; 400-750, 1 AV spec. 1 add. spec. for each 1000 .1 clerk for 1 prof. .1 AV asst. for each 750
COLLECTION	.Books: Min. size 200-299 studs., 6000-10,000 bks; 1000 stud., 10 bks. per stud. .AV - sufficient for sch., home & classroom use.	.Books: Min.collection 6000 vols. or 10 vol. per stud.,whichever is larger .AV - each type of material enumerated.	.Books: at least 6000-10,000 titles representing 10,000 vol. or 20 vol. per stud. .AV - each type of material enumerated.	.Books: Basic (min.) 8000, or 12 vol. per stud., whichever is greater. .Advanced collection: 10,000 or 15 vol. per stud., whichever is greater .AV - each type of material enumerated.
EXPENDITURES	.200-249 stud.,at least $1000-1500. .250 or more stud. at least $4-6 per stud. .Add. funds for reference, supplies,etc. .AV - not less than 1% instr. cost ($2-6 for AV mats)	.Books: Min. of $5 per stud. or $1000 per school bldg. whichever is greater. .Periodical budget enumerated.	.To maintain an up-to-date collection: NOT LESS than 6% of natl. ave. per pupil operational cost, per year per stud. .Funds used for ind. school & system media center. Flex. is desired. Usually, 1/2 bks.,1/2 AV.	.Basic: Books $7 per stud. or $1000 per bldg. whichever is larger. .AV - $7 per stud. or $1000 per bldg. .Advanced: $10 per stud. or $1500 per bldg. .AV - $10 per stud. or $1500 per bldg.

Figure 6-2
Media programs: District and school. 1975 (A.A.S.L. & A.E.C.T.)*

OBJECTIVES:

1. Meet the needs of students of differing abilities, backgrounds, and interests, enabling them both to adjust to and influence the changing society in which they live.
2. Support and further the purposes formulated by the school or district of which it is an integral part.
3. Media program should be tailored to individual program, district, or school.
4. Program's quality is judged by its effectiveness in achieving program purposes.

STAFF:

(School size)	Professional Head	Additional	Support Staff Media Technicians	Aides	Total
250	1	0	1	1	3
500	1	0-1	1-2	2-3	4-6
1000	1	2-3	3-5	3-5	10-12
1500	1	3-5	4-6	4-6	12-18
2000	1	4-7	5-8	5-8	15-24

1. Staff should be balanced depending on services offered.
2. District services will effect the needs for school level personnel.

COLLECTION:

District

Films: access to at least 3000 titles, 5000 films
Professional library for staff.
Examination collection of new items.
Inexpensive, infrequently used, rare or temporary items.

School

Pupil size 500 or fewer students:
20,000 items or 40 per student
Books: 8000-12,000 or 16-24 per user.
Serials: 50-175 titles
Filmstrips: 500-2000 or 1-4 items per user. (1 viewer per 3 users)
Slides and transparencies: 2000-6000 or 4-12 items per user (1 slide viewer per 50 users)
Graphics: 800-1200
Super 8 films: 500-1000 or 1-2 per user
Tapes, cassettes: 1500-2000 items or 3-4 per user.

EXPENDITURES:

School district should spend for each student 10% of the national "Per Pupil Operational Cost (PPOC)" as outlined by U.S.O.E.

*American Association of School Librarians/Association of Educational Communications Technology. *Media Programs: District and School.* Chicago: American Library Association, 1975.

PROGRAMS

The development of district media programs was as varied as the philosophies and objectives of the individual school systems. Whereas most systems hired district media supervisors to assist the building-level media center personnel, some districts also established district media centers. These district centers provided such varied services as centralized ordering, cataloging, and processing; centralized television or radio production; centralized graphic and duplicating production; and centralized distribution of expensive media collections such as films, kits, and living animal exhibits. The building-level media centers also varied according to the educational goals of each school. Some media centers were centralized in one geographic area while others had a central media center supported by satellite subject resource centers. These satellite centers might be adjacent to the central facility or adjacent to their subject areas in other parts of the building. Some schools adopted an "open concept" of learning which could range from a media center without walls to the integration of the media center resources and activities into every part of the school's curriculum and facilities. However, the pattern of organization did not determine the quality of a media center; the philosophy and goals of the center itself determined how effective its programs would be.

Successful and effective media programs at all levels were based upon stated philosophies and objectives carefully designed by everyone concerned—including media center staffs, administrators, teachers, students, and parents. Students and teachers helped in the evaluation and selection of materials for the media collection as well as in developing media center activities and programs to meet the needs of individual students. These activities were often as varied as the students themselves. Some example activities found in school media centers were: individual learning stations or packages which provided all types of media on specialized subjects for independent study; media productions of class projects; oral history audio or videotapes of local interest (similar to the Foxfire books); games and kits, designed to encourage students to think, which were designed and produced by students or teachers; and group, in-depth research reports on subjects using library and community resources. A few media centers even provided computer/information retrieval systems such as dial-access video or audio programs or computerized educational systems such as PLATO. Others even provided small commercial computers, such as the Apple, which could be used for both recreational and educational purposes.

STAFF

In order to carry out these activities, many media centers had also expanded their staffs beyond one professional and one clerk. Building-level media center staffs often included professionals with varied backgrounds and experiences supported by technical and clerical staffs. They were often backed up by district media staffs, which could provide further professional or technical expertise. These larger staffs often enabled paraprofessionals to assume more direct work with children so that media specialists could assume a more consultant, management role. Among the duties of the media specialist were the following: teaching media courses, helping teachers incorporate media into their curricula, providing in-service training for teachers in using the center's media and equipment, supervising and training student and volunteer personnel, publicizing the media center's services and programs within the school and the community, and coordinating library services with other libraries in the community.

Media specialists were finally able to perform as true professionals within the educational system because the day-to-day operations of the library had been turned over to paraprofessional and clerical staff members. Media technicians supervised clerks, students, and volunteers in checking out materials. Resource centers, which were separated from the main media centers, were often directed by media technicians. Sometimes, media technicians even ran building-level media centers in small schools under the direction of a system-wide media specialist. Although this latter practice was not recommended by library professionals, some school administrators have found it to be a convenient way to satisfy state certification requirements. Also, where the technicians have had any library training, this staffing pattern has provided trained library staff in many schools for the first time.

In larger school systems, technicians supported professionals in specialized areas such as graphics, television, or audiovisual production. These trained personnel usually would be found in district media centers producing resource materials to be used in classrooms and in building-level media centers. District-wide processing centers also required centralized support staff to order and process materials for the individual media centers. Centralized booking services for films and videotapes were usually staffed by clerks and/or technicians.

School librarians/media specialists and their staffs had come a long way toward providing effective services and programs by 1980. However, they still had a long way to go. Many administrators still did not recognize the contributions media centers and their staffs could make to their educational systems. Because of this, many media centers were understaffed, and what staffs they did enjoy were poorly paid. Although media specialists were considered to be teachers and received teachers' salaries, the clerical and technical staffs often received little more than the minimum-wage, regardless of their training. This practice was often encouraged by people willing to work for low wages so that their work hours and vacations coincided with those of their families.

To combat this economic phenomenon, media specialists spent many hours persuading their administrators that trained clerical and paraprofessional staffs were vital to their centers' missions. Sometimes, media specialists even had to educate their school administrators about what the media centers' mission really was. Media specialists had to convince some of these administrators that media specialists could and should be more than babysitters for students so that their teachers could take a break. They sometimes had to fight for budgets, staff, materials, and equipment with building principals who would rather have spent the money elsewhere. In addition, the media specialists often had to educate their teaching colleagues about the contributions the media center could make in each teacher's own area of interest. And, finally, media specialists often had to convince their own staffs, their administrators, and their fellow teachers that the media center should provide access to information and should be free of censorship. Thus, salesmanship became one of the media specialist's most important functions.

It is an unjust irony that just as more and more school administrators and teachers were beginning to accept and depend upon media centers and their staffs, educational establishments themselves began to come under attack. The economic plight of the nation in the late 1970s and 1980s began adversely to affect school systems and, thus, their support of media services. Many of the services and programs started in the 1960s and 1970s had come under fire as libraries were caught in the twin backlashes of the public's outrage at the failure of the schools to educate their children and the taxpayers' revolt at paying high taxes. Declining monies, declining enrollments, and a growing view of media as educational frills forced some school systems to close or consolidate their schools and to reduce or eliminate media staffs and services. Other school systems and communities even investigated the economics of combining their public and school libraries and housing them in school buildings.

To meet such challenges and changes, media specialists began to reevaluate their objectives and their programs and to look for alternative ways to continue providing effective media services. In an economic fight for their lives, they joined forces with public librarians to publicize the community's need for both public and school library services. Many media specialists also joined with other libraries in cooperatives and networks to develop and participate in cooperative library operations and programming. They realized that cooperative efforts might help provide the answer to financial issues which school boards and taxpayers were looking for. Only time will tell whether or not these regrouping and retrenchment efforts have been successful in maintaining effective school media services.

REVIEW QUESTIONS

1. Identify the major objectives of school media centers.

2. Briefly describe school library development from the classroom library to school library to IMC to media center.

3. Identify the major philosophies of the 1969 and 1975 school library standards.

4. Identify the kinds of media which could be found in a school media center.

5. Describe the characteristics for successful media center programs.

6. Identify duties of the professional media specialist in the modern school media center.

7. Visit a school library/media center and compare its objectives, staff, materials, and services with those described in this chapter.

8. Identify some of the duties of a media technician in the above school library/media center.

SELECTED READINGS

AASL/AECT Media Programs: District and School. Chicago: American Library Association, 1975.

AASL/AECT Standards for School Media Cent. Chicago: American Library Association, 1969.

ALA Yearbook: A Review of Library Events. Chicago: American Library Association, 1976- .

American Association of School Librarians. Knapp School Libraries Project. *Realization: The Final Report of the Knapp School Libraries Project.* Edited by Peggy Sullivan. Chicago: American Library Association, 1968.

"At the Center." Washington, DC: Smithsonian Institute, 1970. 16mm film.

Davies, Ruth. *The School Library Media Program: Instructional Force for Excellence.* 3rd ed. New York: Bowker, 1979.

Gillespie, John T. *Model School District Media Program.* Chicago: American Library Association, 1977.

Hicks, Warren B., and Alma M. Tillin, eds. *Managing Multimedia Libraries.* New York: Bowker, 1977.

Marshall, F. *Managing the Modern School Library.* Englewood Cliffs, NJ: Prentice-Hall, 1976.

Peterson, Ralph L. *A Place for Caring and Celebration: The School Media Center.* Chicago: American Library Association, c1979.

Prostano, Emanuel T., and Joyce S. Prostano. *The School Library Media Center.* 2nd ed. Littleton, CO: Libraries Unlimited, 1977.

Standards for School Library Programs. Chicago: American Library Association, 1960.

Toggart, Dorothy T. *Management and Administration of the School Library Media Program.* Hamden, CT: Shoe String, 1980.

Wehmeyer, Lillian Biermann. *The School Librarian as Educator.* Littleton, CO: Libraries Unlimited, 1976.

NOTES

[1]Jean Key Gates, *Introduction to Librarianship* (New York: McGraw-Hill, 1968), pp. 220-21.

7
ACADEMIC LIBRARIES

Just as school media centers met the changing needs of the public schools, so have academic libraries met the changing needs and objectives of their parent institutions. Colleges and universities have changed since the 1700s; they are no longer institutions based primarily on faculty lectures and faculty research. As a result, academic libraries have also changed, from storehouses of books to learning centers providing access to information in all its varied forms. And yet, it is difficult to talk of one type of academic institution or academic library because of the variety of institutions covered by this general term. Instead, we should define these institutions before we discuss their development and characteristics.

KINDS OF ACADEMIC LIBRARIES

The library world defines an academic library as a library in an institution providing education beyond the high school level. This level of education is also called post-secondary or higher education. The most common academic libraries are found in colleges and universities, but community colleges, junior colleges, and technical institutions also have academic libraries. A college is an institution which offers bachelor's degrees, and perhaps master's degrees, in the liberal arts and sciences. On the other hand, a university is an institution which offers doctoral degrees and may contain a number of undergraduate colleges. The distinction between the two types is very important to library development.

College libraries will generally be much smaller in size and scope than university libraries because they are not trying to support graduate education to the extensive degree that the universities attempt to provide. College libraries may have collections ranging in size from 50,000 to 200,000 volumes and are likely staffed by 5-10 professionals who are supported by clerical and student personnel. University libraries may have collections which range from several hundred thousand volumes to millions of volumes. These larger libraries may be staffed by 25-100 professional, associate, paraprofessional, and non-professional personnel who are supported by many student helpers. Also, university libraries will generally have large collections in every subject area, while college libraries tend to concentrate on the general arts and sciences with a strong emphasis on humanities and the social sciences.

In contrast, the university library may provide specialized subject collections to support graduate and faculty education and research to such a great extent that they may become, in essence, research libraries serving primarily the needs of scholars (*see* chapter 8). An example of this objective or function can be seen in the title of the Research Libraries Group, which was formed by Harvard

University, Yale University, Columbia University, and the New York Public Library. This function is also supported by the academic library association, which is an Association of College and Research Libraries rather than of college and university libraries. Although the development of college and university libraries originally followed similar patterns, in recent years their development has begun to diverge.

Other common academic libraries are community college libraries, junior college libraries, and libraries in technical institutes. These similar institutions are primarily products of the twentieth century and primarily serve the same purpose — that of providing academic education equal to the first two years of college. Many also provide vocational or avocational education as well as adult education. Their impact on library development has been tremendous because more than one-third of today's academic libraries can be found in these institutions.

However, the majority of academic libraries generally began as mere adjuncts to the classroom, housed in small rooms and administered by part-time faculty members. They were seen as "collections of books" rather than as part of the education function. As society changed from an agrarian to an industrialized society, colleges and universities began to place more emphasis on research and to offer new programs to meet the need for new occupations. In order to support these programs, collegiate accreditation associations began to emphasize qualitative library collections and staff. Professional library schools graduated librarians to administer and develop these growing libraries. Since many librarians also became subject specialists, faculty departments became willing to give up control and development of their subject department libraries to the college or university library.

Further library development was spurred on by the rapid expansion of the world's known information. By 1950, such knowledge had doubled since the beginnings of the 1900s, and academic libraries expanded their collections accordingly. This expansion of known information helped influence changes in institutional philosophies and methods and helped spark the introduction of electives in academic programs. The large influx of students after World War II also placed heavy demands on libraries to provide materials in great quantities to meet student needs. To help satisfy this demand without bankrupting themselves, academic institutions began to join together in cooperative collection development programs such as the Farmington Plan. Under these programs, each academic library was responsible for collecting all of the published materials from a specific country or in a specific subject area. These materials were then made available for loan to other academic institutions. Thus, by the 1950s the academic library had become an important element in fulfilling the goals of its college or university.

A typical academic library of the 1950s would have contained only print materials — books, serials, and pamphlets — housed in an architectural monument named after some benefactor. In smaller libraries, the books were usually kept on shelves arranged into alcoves where students studied at long reading tables. Separate rooms were available for the reserve book collection, where students read many of their course assignments, and for browsing where students could sit in easy chairs and read leisure materials or perhaps hear a lecture. Separate rooms for rare books and maps might also be available, but these were often only accessible to "serious" students.

Universities often kept most of their collections in closed stack areas to which only graduate students and faculty members gained admittance. Undergraduates had to ask for books at a circulation desk and wait for the materials to be delivered. Many universities attempted to help the first- and second-year students adjust to the wealth of library materials by providing separate "Undergraduate libraries." These libraries contained duplicate materials in open stacks which were particularly useful for students in their general studies during the first two years. The third- and fourth-year students usually had access to departmental libraries scattered throughout the campus next to the subject departments. However, all of the libraries were usually only open during hours that were convenient for library staffing rather than for student studying.

OBJECTIVES OF ACADEMIC LIBRARIES

The primary objective of these libraries was to contribute to the goals and the philosophy of the academic institutions they served. However, since the academic institutions were still largely faculty, graduate student, and research oriented, the objectives of the library also leaned in that direction. Of the functions Guy Lyle identified in 1949 for a college library to fulfill, only two were directly related to the needs of its students.[1] These two functions were to provide study and reference materials for supplementing classroom instruction and to encourage students to use books independently. Even in fulfilling this latter function, libraries were supposed to cooperate with the faculty to develop student interests rather than with the students themselves. Two other functions served the faculty by providing technical and specialized study materials to keep the faculty abreast of their fields and to support the research needs of individual faculty members. Another function was to provide alumni and correspondence students with bibliographies and study materials needed for courses and institutes.

The final function encouraged cooperation with other libraries to strengthen library resources in the local area, but the cooperative efforts that developed up to the 1960s were still often research oriented. Although most academic libraries provided interlibrary loans, these were restricted to faculty and graduate students by the National Interlibrary Loan Code. Undergraduate students did not usually have access to materials which their college or university did not own. These same undergraduate students were also hampered by not knowing how to find materials which the library did own because library instruction was often limited to an orientation tour for freshmen during their first week on campus. By 1960, the academic libraries, as well as the colleges and universities themselves, were generally not meeting the needs of their students, a problem that would increase as students inundated the campuses throughout the sixties.

The 1960s were a time of plenty and a time of crisis for the academic world. The post-Sputnik emphasis on education at all levels and the democratic society's emphasis on "education for all" flooded the colleges and universities with students. However, many of these students had more varied interests, backgrounds and needs than earlier students had ever had. Colleges and universities found that their traditional courses and teaching methods did not serve these new students. At the same time, students were demanding a voice in developing relevant education to meet their needs. In this climate, many educators and progressive librarians began to look for new ways to provide programs, materials, and services that would enable students, many of whom had poor academic backgrounds, to learn.

The passage in 1965 of the Higher Education Act provided funds for institutions and libraries to experiment and develop new materials, new services, and new programs to satisfy these needs. These funds also helped in the development of new philosophies of education and new concepts of what a college or university should be. Comprehensive public community colleges developed all over the country, providing for the academic, technical, vocational, and avocational needs of their local communities. Most importantly, these colleges provided educational opportunities for many persons to learn new skills, get high school diplomas, be exposed to cultural opportunities, and participate in general education activities. Emphasis was placed on each individual's needs, and independent study programs were initiated. Many community colleges and other colleges and universities began to develop new programs that extended beyond the traditional classroom/lecture hall. New terms, such as "external degree programs," "non-traditional study programs," "independent study," "extended education," and the "open university," were used to describe the educational programs which were initiated. Many colleges and universities proved they were equal to meeting the educational crisis.

As their parent institutions changed to meet this crisis, academic libraries also changed to support the new educational programs. Many libraries began to experiment and to expand their library collections beyond the traditional print materials. The media explosion which had hit the elementary and secondary schools expanded to include higher education. Some libraries began to incorporate all types of media into their collections and programs: audiotapes, videotapes, microforms, transparencies, films of all shapes and sizes, filmstrips, slides, programmed learning, and computer-assisted instruction (CAI). The library no longer remained a passive member of the institution but began to reach out beyond its traditional confines to participate in the learning process. Libraries began to provide book stores, media and graphic production facilities, and equipment support for instruction, whether it was listening labs, TV sets and cameras, or overhead projectors. Library staff members began to participate in the teaching process by working with teachers to develop bibliographic units or courses or by developing their own library-oriented units and courses. Some institutions even developed into "library-colleges" in which the library was a prime factor in contributing to a student's education. For some libraries, they had truly become the "heart of the university."

These new libraries developed other new names such as Learning Resource Centers, Media Centers, Learning Centers, and extended libraries, to identify their new functions. Robert Taylor has identified the five functions of these new college libraries as providing direct support to undergraduate instruction, supporting independent student honors work, giving minimal support to faculty and graduate research, providing space where students may study on their own, and providing a context within which the student may browse freely among all subjects and materials.[2] The library had become student oriented rather than faculty and graduate research oriented.

The growth and development of these new types of libraries and library services in the 1960s encouraged the development of new academic library standards in the 1970s. Whereas previous academic standards had emphasized traditional library materials and services, the new standards emphasized quality learning resources programs and student access to all media within the library.

When quantitative standards were stated they were usually based upon formulas rather than upon absolutes. Standards for all types of academic libraries were adopted by library associations in the 1970s: Guidelines for Two-Year College Learning Resources Programs were adopted in 1973 and followed in 1979 by quantitative standards; Standards for College Libraries were adopted in 1975; and Standards for University Libraries were adopted in 1979. However, rather than setting the pace for library services as the school standards had done, the academic standards seemed to be following rather than leading in the development of innovative library services.

By the end of the 1970s, it could no longer be said that there was one typical academic library. University, college, and community college libraries each had distinctive variations designed to meet their institutions' objectives. Perhaps community colleges were the one type of institution in which most libraries resembled each other. Because they were largely developed during the media revolution of the 1960s and 1970s, most community colleges developed learning resources programs which combined all print and media materials and services into one department or organization. Four-year colleges which were founded or expanded during this time also often became learning resources centers or library-colleges. Other college libraries may not have changed their organization, but their objectives changed to serve the student rather than the faculty member. University libraries became the most diverse group of academic libraries; some developed learning resource centers while many others maintained their traditional roles.

However, no matter what form the academic library took in the 1970s, there seemed to be one student-centered philosophy which had developed. Library services and procedures were often changed to match students' needs. Many new university library buildings housed the major book collections in open stacks which were made accessible to undergraduates for the first time. The interiors of these buildings also changed. Books were shelved on free standing stacks in the centers of the rooms, and students found seating at individual study cubicles, or carrels, or relaxed in modern lounging areas. Library hours became long and flexible, with some libraries staying open until midnight or even 24 hours a day. Professional staff was often available for student assistance whenever the library was open. The academic library had finally removed the physical barriers that restricted student access to the collection.

Many libraries began to make their collections more usable by reclassifying them from the Dewey Decimal or other classification systems to the Library of Congress classification system. This reclassification enabled libraries to spread out large subject collections into many class numbers rather than cramming them into a relatively small group of numbers. It also enabled libraries to use one standardized classification number so that they could use established classification numbers and lessen the need for original cataloging. This standardization of classifying materials also paved the way for libraries to adapt Library of Congress cataloging in its many formats and thus reduced the need for large cataloging departments in each individual institution.

These reclassification projects had other benefits as well. They helped make it easier for libraries to organize materials so that they could be located more easily. They also enabled libraries to shift their professional personnel from the technical services department to the public services department. There, professional librarians began to recognize that students must be taught how to find and use these materials. Librarians began to develop extensive library instruction programs. Besides giving orientation tours of the library, they developed media packages explaining parts of the library or individual library resource tools. Both credit and noncredit courses in library instruction and subject bibliographies were taught by librarians. A few institutions even developed competency-based library courses and examinations which students were required to pass in order to become upperclassmen or to graduate. Patron use of the academic library had finally become an important function not only of the library but of the college and university as well.

In order to serve these patrons better, academic libraries recognized many years ago that they must share their resources, both bibliographically and physically. This sharing originally began on an informal basis with academic libraries in the same geographic area sharing materials or allowing reciprocal borrowing among their patrons. As library budgets shrank and the publication explosion produced more materials than one library could buy, these informal arrangements became formal agreements for interlibrary cooperation and networks.

This interlibrary cooperation took many forms and provided many varied services. Some academic institutions joined together in formal consortia to allocate their educational resources and prevent costly duplication of subject specialties. Other universities and colleges actually formed joint libraries which developed one major collection to serve several different institutions. The Joint University Libraries of Nashville and the Atlanta University Libraries are two excellent examples of this type of cooperation. Other libraries formed networks to provide interlibrary loan to undergraduates as the Wisconsin academic libraries did in WILS (Wisconsin Interlibrary Loan Service). The now defunct Farmington Plan was a cooperative project for acquiring foreign publications. The Center for Research Libraries developed cooperative storage facilities, and regional Bibliographic Centers in Denver and Philadelphia provided regional union catalogs for interlibrary loans. The behemoth of all cooperative ventures, the Ohio College Library Center (now OCLC, Inc.) originally began as an Ohio academic library cooperative network established to develop and share a computerized cataloging data base. This network was so successful that it expanded nation-wide and even spawned other networks such as PALINET (Pennsylvania Area Library Network) and SOLINET (Southeastern Library Network). Some other cooperative areas were document delivery services using photocopying, telefacsimiles and mail delivery; cooperative collection development; and the sharing of periodical banks. By 1980 almost every academic library in the country participated in at least one cooperative or network which provided these and other services.

ADMINISTRATION OF ACADEMIC LIBRARIES

All of these cooperative developments and changes in library service also called for changes in library staffing and administration. No longer was the library director usually a professor from another department with a Ph.D. but no library training. The academic library director of the 1970s and 1980s usually had at least one graduate library science degree and perhaps one advanced degree in another subject. The library director was not only administrator of a large department and budget, but he or she was also usually active in the total university administration. This expanded role of the library director strengthened and solidified the library's place in the entire academic institution.

As the library grew in importance to its parent institution, its administration and staffing patterns also changed. Such single purpose library departments as circulation, reference, acquisitions, serials, binding, and cataloging, were combined into public service and technical service areas. In many libraries, circulation became an adjunct of public services and professional circulation librarians were often replaced by library technicians who supervised clerical and student personnel. Some libraries experimented with staffing patterns that included subject bibliographers or specialists who were not only responsible for selecting and cataloging materials in specific subject areas, but who also provided reference and research assistance and formal classroom instruction in their subject specialties.

Staffing patterns were further affected by the introduction of automated library systems. The statistical and clerical capabilities of the automated circulation systems reduced the need for highly trained clerical help in this area. Many libraries found that a few paraprofessionals could supervise many students in these routines. The bibliographic capabilities of the automated cataloging systems also enabled trained paraprofessionals to handle much of the cataloging which was formerly done by professional librarians. However, these professional librarians were then needed to use their expertise in formulating search strategies and in accessing data bases. Thus, the introduction of automated systems did not lessen the need for academic library staff members, it just enabled libraries to assign more staff members to public service areas.

These changes in staffing patterns also enabled academic libraries to support their institutions' missions more effectively. Librarians were freed from in-house library responsibilities so that they could serve on faculty and institution committees and work with their faculty colleagues to develop their libraries' collections. Library budgets also were revamped to support the institution's major objectives rather than to build up the subject collections of senior department chairmen. Library administrators were also usually able to apply modern management techniques to library operations so that library resources and personnel were used as effectively and efficiently as possible.

How much more will these academic libraries change by the year 2000? Librarians differ on the exact form of academic libraries in the future. Many believe they will not be very different from the libraries of the 1960s, and others believe that all academic libraries will become library-colleges. Some see increases in interlibrary cooperation and computer automation as two important methods libraries can use to maximize their resources and increase their efficiency. But, practically everyone agrees that the economic and social factors of the 1970s cannot be ignored in the 1980s and that the "new depression in higher education" will force librarians into reevaluating their programs, maximizing their resources, and increasing their efficiency.

REVIEW QUESTIONS

1. Identify the objectives served by an academic library.

2. Enumerate the functions of a modern college library.

3. Describe the changes in academic library services for college and university undergraduates.

4. Identify some of the major characteristics of the library-college, learning resource center, etc.

5. List some example cooperative efforts which academic libraries have developed.

6. Visit a local academic institution and compare it with the objectives, functions, and services discussed in this chapter. If possible, visit two types of academic institutions such as a community college and a four-year college or university in order to compare and contrast their libraries to each other.

7. Identify some of the duties of the LMTA in the above academic libraries.

SELECTED READINGS

Burlingame, Dwight F., Dennis C. Fields, and Anthony C. Schulzetenberg, *The College Learning Resource Center*. Littleton, CO: Libraries Unlimited, 1978.

Byrd, P. *Guide to Academic Libraries in the U.S.* Englewood Cliffs, NJ: Prentice-Hall, 1981.

"Draft: Statement on Quantitative Standards for Two-Year Learning Resources Programs," *College and Research Library News*, March 1979, pp. 69-73.

Jefferson, G. *The College Library: A Collection of Essays*. Hamden, CT: Shoe String, 1978.

Johnson, Edward. *Organization Development for Academic Libraries: An Evaluation of the Management Review and Analysis Program*. Westport, CT: Greenwood, 1980.

Josey, E. J. *New Dimensions for Academic Library Service*. Metuchen, NJ: Scarecrow, 1975.

"Standards for College Libraries," *College and Research Library News*, October 1975, pp. 277-99.

"Standards for University Libraries," *College and Research Library News*, April 1979, pp. 101-110.

Taylor, Robert S. *The Making of a Library: The Academic Library in Transition*. New York: Becker & Hayes, 1972.

NOTES

[1]Guy Lyle, *The Administration of the College Library* (New York: H. W. Wilson, 1949), pp. 24-25.

[2]Robert S. Taylor, *The Making of a Library: The Academic Library in Transition* (New York: Becker & Hayes, 1972), p. 36.

8
SPECIAL LIBRARIES

From the time that the term "special libraries" was first used, there have been many attempts at defining what special libraries really are. The ALA thought the terms and objectives for these libraries were very vague when the Special Libraries Association was founded in 1909. The library world itself has seemed to be vague when it has used the term special library as an umbrella term to describe many different libraries. What could a large scientific library with thousands of volumes and many paid staff members have in common with a small local historical museum library with 1,000 books cared for by volunteer staff members? What characteristics of these two libraries would enable one term to be used to define them both?

Of the characteristics which are most common to these libraries, the primary one is that their collections include materials relating to specialized subject areas. Second, these libraries gather their collections and design their services to support and further the objectives of a parent organization rather than to support a curriculum as school and academic libraries do. Finally, these libraries are primarily concerned with actively seeking out and providing information which the library's clients or patrons may need rather than just acquiring and preserving the information in a collection. These three characteristics are key elements of any special library and make understandable the definition of a special library as a library which provides special services in a specialized subject area or in a special format for special clientele.

There are many different libraries that fit this definition of a special library. They usually can be identified as libraries devoted to special subject areas such as music and art libraries, libraries devoted to special forms such as map libraries and film libraries, and libraries devoted to special clientele such as hospital patient libraries and prison libraries. Special libraries can also be identified by their parent organizations or institutions such as bank or insurance libraries, church libraries, and federal libraries. However, even these designations do not begin to include all of the different kinds of libraries that are special libraries. If there is an organization, institution, or group of people with a special interest or need for library services, a special library has probably been developed to satisfy this interest and need.

The growth and development of the various kinds of special libraries has been as varied as a patchwork quilt. Some libraries such as independent research libraries began in the 1700s, while other libraries such as map libraries developed primarily in the twentieth century. The growth of some libraries has been encouraged by the development of library standards while others have not developed in spite of such standards. And yet, in spite of these differences, most special libraries share common goals in providing library services and have common needs and problems in carrying out these goals. A brief survey of some of the major kinds of libraries and their services may provide an introduction to this kaleidoscopic field of special libraries.

RESEARCH LIBRARIES

Research libraries are some of our most important special libraries. Since they have been developed to support the subject research needs of the world's scholars, they have traditionally been more allied with academic libraries, and the majority of them are actually part of large universities. Other kinds of research libraries are federal government libraries and independent research libraries which are their own institutions. The New York Public Library even has its own research library as its central library. (The branches are public libraries funded by public taxes.) Most of the research libraries were originally established and endowed by wealthy benefactors, but the financial support for them today often comes from further endowments or from university and public funds. Limited funds have forced most research libraries to limit and refine their subject interests, but by judicious acquisition many libraries have been able to develop definitive collections of the world's knowledge in narrow subject areas.

Independent research libraries are among our oldest and most unique research libraries. They are independent and unique because they do not belong to any other institution but exist for their own sakes. They have generally been established by wealthy benefactors with their own boards of directors and their own facilities and endowment funds. Usually, the board of directors will choose a particular subject interest area in which the library will specialize. These subject areas may be based on the private collection of the library benefactor, such as the Folger Shakespeare Library, or they may be chosen to coordinate with other research libraries. For example, the subjects of the Newberry Library (humanities) and the John Crerar Library (physical and natural sciences) in Chicago were chosen to complement each other and those of the Chicago Public Library.

Some of the earliest research libraries were begun in the 1700s by scientific and historical societies. These libraries helped preserve priceless documentation of an era so that it would be saved for future historians. Each of these libraries has tended to "build on strength" by gaining eminence in particular historical periods or forms of materials.[1] For example, the American Philosophical Society Library contains over one-half of Benjamin Franklin's surviving papers and concentrates on all sciences in the colonies and the United States to 1850. The Boston Atheneum Library holds George Washington's personal library and is recognized for its strength in New England colonial books and pamphlets. It also has purchased and developed a valuable collection of Confederate literature and imprints. By establishing such subject parameters, research libraries have been able to develop coexisting libraries rather than competitive collections.

The independent research libraries often provide similar library services. Like other research libraries, they primarily provide non-circulating subject collections for the use of special clientele who are most often scholars of the world doing research at the post-doctoral level. Besides providing access to the collections and physical facilities for research, some libraries also provide funds to the scholars for such research. Most libraries have publishing programs and some have microfilming programs so that they may share the unique information contained in their collections. In recent years, these independent libraries have received government grants to serve as centers of research for other libraries, and two libraries have become regional medical libraries for the National Library of Medicine. Although these libraries have been called independent research libraries, their services have shown them to be necessary links in the developing network of national information resources.

FEDERAL LIBRARIES

Another important link in our national information resources is the federal government libraries. These libraries represent the most varied kind of special libraries for they include such libraries as national, health, technical, and institution libraries, as well as academic, school, and quasi-public libraries. However, all of the federal libraries are still considered to be special libraries because they serve the goals of their parent institutions and their users are usually members of these institutions. In 1972, there were about 2,300 federal libraries serving the various departments and agencies of the U.S. government;[2] 43% of these libaries were scientific and technical (including health and medical) libraries and served the special library objectives of providing information and supporting research; 37% serve as quasi-public libraries and provide services to persons in Veterans Administration Hospitals, federal prisons, and military installations; 18% serve the educational needs of personnel in the military academies, schools for Native Americans, and military-dependent schools overseas. Although the universe of federal libraries is constantly changing, in 1972 the Department of Defense had 63% of all of the federal libraries, containing 42% of the total collections, and independent agencies supported another 23% of the libraries. The majority of the federal libraries have been identified as having comprehensive research and/or unique collections.[3]

The most unique collections belonging to the federal libraries are contained in the national libraries – the Library of Congress (LC), the National Library of Medicine (NLM), and the National Agriculture Library (NAL). These three libraries not only provide extensive research collections in all forms of media, but they represent ⅓ of the total federal collections, ½ of all expenditures and 2/5 of all the personnel in federal libraries. In 1978, the Library of Congress alone had over 18 million volumes, 75 million pieces of research material, a budget over $150 million, and more than 5,000 employees.[4] These libraries provide library services to the nation and serve as national resource centers. The NLM and the NAL have developed subject collections in medicine and agriculture and their allied fields; LC covers all the other subjects and has become the largest library in the world. In fact, LC provides more national library functions and services than any other national library in the world.

Serving as a national library is still an unofficial function of the Library of Congress, although it has been steered in this direction by two important events. The first was the purchase of Thomas Jefferson's collection by Congress which contained materials on many different subjects rather than just legislative materials. Over the years, Librarians of Congress continued to strengthen these subjects. The passage of the Copyright Law in 1870 ensured this by requiring that two copies of every copyrighted work be given to the Library of Congress. This national library function was further enhanced in the early 1900s when the library began to sell its classification schedules and catalog cards and to provide interlibrary loan privileges. The National Union Catalog (NUC) and the Union

List of Serials (ULS) also enabled libraries to share LC's collection as well as the collections of the largest libraries in the United States. LC began to serve as a national resource for materials for blind and physically handicapped persons and to make its extensive collections available to all citizens.

In spite of these services to the nation, the primary purpose of the Library of Congress is still to serve as a legislative library for Congress. Librarians of Congress have judiciously nourished this relationship, and their skillful public relations have used it to gain unparalleled financial support for the library and its programs. This financial support has enabled LC and the other national libraries to provide national leadership for library cooperation and services.

The financial support has also enabled them to develop library automation programs of international significance. In the late 1960s, LC began providing computerized cataloging for its monographs under the MARC (**MA**chine **R**eadable **C**ataloging) program which has become the basis for many automated data bases. NAL developed CAIN, an online bibliographic data base for agriculture and its related fields. NLM also developed an online bibliographic system (MEDLINE) based on MEDLARS a data base of indexes and abstracts of medical literature. However, NLM also provides document delivery to medical personnel and libraries for items listed in MEDLINE and *Index Medicus*, an indexing service based on MEDLARS. CATLINE provides medical libraries with NLM's computerized cataloging information in the bio-medical areas. NLM has truly become a national library by developing Regional Medical Libraries throughout the country which serve as resource centers between the local library and NLM. These national services were developed in the 1960s and 1970s and will be expanded in the 1980s as libraries with diminishing budgets look to the national scene for leadership.

BUSINESS LIBRARIES

The private world of business and industry has not lagged behind government in developing libraries to support their research needs. Almost every business or industry, be they banks, insurance companies, advertising agencies, chemical companies, or aerospace corporations, have their own libraries. Though the products of the companies may vary considerably, their libraries are similar in that their collections and services are completely identified with the objectives of the parent organization. In fact, not only should the librarians have subject and library expertise, but they must be well-grounded in the company's objectives and organization. The major purpose of these libraries is to collect, organize, and put to use the knowledge of their library collections for the greatest efficiency of the company. Since private companies are profit-oriented, the library must contribute to this profit motive if it is to continue to exist within the company. It is this characteristic which distinguishes business and industrial libraries from other special libraries.

The profit-making motive may be one of the most influential factors in the makeup of a business or industrial library. Some businesses such as newspapers, advertising and marketing firms, insurance companies, and law firms may be so dependent upon the quick retrieval of information in their collections that they would always provide trained staffs in their libraries. Other types of businesses, particularly small businesses and industries, might consider library services as peripheral services and cut their libraries' staffing and funding when profits begin to sag.

In order to contribute to this profit objective, company libraries have attempted to provide all types of information when it is needed or even in anticipation of a need. This information is often contained in externally published materials such as books, microforms, periodicals, and patents, and in internally generated materials such as research and technical reports, correspondence, market surveys, and data compilations. Libraries also usually collect and index everything written or published, either externally or internally, concerning the company and its products. Because their collections are used by every division in the company, they include not only information about the company and its products, but also information about their clients or customers, as well as business management and economic information. To facilitate easy access to these collections, libraries often devise simplified classification and subject heading systems as well as in-depth cataloging for book chapters and periodical issues. Whenever possible, libraries have also computerized this information or provided access to national or commercial subject data bases. In providing this information, libraries never forget that quick access to the most current information is necessary to satisfy their companies' needs.

In fact, it is just this reason which has encouraged many special librarians to develop their libraries into information and research centers. These information centers support other departments which have identified a problem or a need. The information/library staff will not only locate bibliographic citations in a particular area, they will often obtain the documents and read and analyze them. The information may then be synthesized in a written report which is sent to the department that had the original problem or need. Sometimes information specialists even join with departmental teams in working on company projects. Here they may not only provide research background and reports, but they may also take an active part in writing or editing any departmental reports. Such active participation in a company's programs has helped prove the library's worth to many company executives.

In addition to participating in original research projects, special librarians have also been primarily concerned with quickly disseminating all the information available in the library or accessible to it. Most company libraries circulate books, route periodicals, publish and distribute bibliographies and acquisitions lists, provide abstracting and translating services, publish library bulletins, maintain and index special company and product files, search literature, and provide copies of relevant articles or patents. The automated data bases have made this last service more comprehensive and important than it ever was in the past. Through these many services, the company library attempts to improve the company's efficiency and profits by taking an active part in the day-to-day operations of the company to which it belongs.

INSTITUTION LIBRARIES

Other special libraries also take an important part in the day-to-day activities of their parent bodies. Museum libraries, association libraries and organization libraries also organize their collections and provide services that help put information to work. These libraries vary in size from very small to very large and are funded by both private and public agencies. Within each of these areas there are numerous variations based on the subjects or individual organizations or institutions a library serves. About 3,000 libraries can be found in historical museums, art museums, science museums, and other museum-type establishments such as zoos, arboretums and national parks. Although a few of these libraries have large collections and well-trained staffs, most have small collections (1,000-5,000 items) which may or may not be staffed by trained personnel. Museum libraries are primarily open during regular business hours to serve the staff and researchers at the museums.

Professional association libraries also serve the needs of their parent organizations. The American Library Association, the American Dental Association, and the American Medical Association are just a few of the associations which provide libraries for their executive staffs and their members. State and local government agencies also provide libraries to serve their staffs, although these libraries are not as extensive as the federal libraries are. However, law libraries can be found in practically every county courthouse in the United States as well as in municipal city halls and state capitol buildings. All of these libraries serve their organizations and institutions by providing both in-depth research and current information as quickly and efficiently as possible.

One type of institution is unique because it often has two kinds of special libraries or one library which provides two distinct types of services. Hospitals usually provide medical libraries to serve the research needs of the medical staff. Some medical libraries may also support the medical staff's continuing education needs by providing lectures and current medical information on audio and videotapes. Medical libraries may be very extensive and provide access to medical collections through *Index Medicus*, MEDLINE, and other medical data bases, or they may be small and poorly staffed. Although there are standards for medical libraries, the standards set by the Joint Commission on Accreditation of Hospitals are very vague and do not provide many quantitative standards for administrators to use.[5]

The other hospital libraries are patient libraries which provide recreational and leisure reading for the patients. These libraries usually have very flexible circulation routines and services may be provided by volunteer staff rather than by paid or professional staff. Two new interesting services have developed in hospital libraries in recent years which have enabled librarians to become members of the medical teams. "Clinical librarians" make the patient rounds with the doctors so that they may provide them with specific literature or information that may be needed for a patient's care. The other service is "bibliotherapy," which is the use of selected reading materials as therapeutic adjuncts to medicine or psychiatry. A natural extension of bibliotherapy has been for medical libraries to extend their information services to the patients' families and to the community in general. Such community education can often help a patient adjust more easily to a medical condition or disease. After all, the goal of all of these services in hospital libraries is to enable the hospital to provide the best care for the patient.

Prison libraries also have been provided to serve their patrons, but the goals of prison libraries have varied throughout the years as the philosophy of prison reform has changed. The first prison library collections contained moral and religious works to help the prisoners see the error of their ways. Then, prison collections became important in supporting the educational system in the prison, and, finally, the library became a part of the rehabilitative function of the prison. Some librarians have advocated bibliotherapy as a service librarians should perform in the rehabilitative function, while other librarians have advocated supporting libraries because prisoners should have the "right to read." Whatever the function of prison libraries has been, studies have shown that more people in prison read than people who are not in prison, and this occurs in spite of inadequate and poorly staffed collections in most prison libraries. The largest library growth in prisons has been in prison law library services. In the 1970s, federal courts said that prisons must provide adequate law libraries for inmates to research material for drafting legal papers and briefs. Some prisons have developed their own law libraries, while others have contracted with state or local libaries to provide such service. Some of these city and state libraries are also providing deposit collections, books-by-mail, and bookmobile service to serve the informational and recreational needs of these citizens.

About the only major kind of special library that has not been discussed yet is the subject collection libraries. Since many of these are connected with universities and colleges, their subjects can vary as much as academic curricula do, and they can be as numerous as university departments are. Naming a few subject areas which have their own library associations or their own sections in a library association may give a flavor of this variety. There are associations for art, architecture, agriculture, astronomy, documentation, film archives, geography and maps, law, medicine, music, social science, sound archives, and theater. In addition, there are religious library associations such as the Theological, Jewish, Catholic, and Lutheran Church Library Associations. The proliferation of these subject associations lends some credence to the belief that the term "special libraries" was too vague to cover all of these diverse libraries.

ADMINISTRATION AND STAFFING

The administration and staffing of special libraries is probably more varied and distinct than that found in other types of libraries. More often than not, the administrator responsible for the library/information center is probably not a librarian, but is a director or officer of a major department or division. In business and industrial libraries, the directors of research and development or the vice presidents of marketing may be given library administration responsibilities. These administrators usually hire library staffs which indicate and support their conceptions of library services. Thus, if a Research and Development director considers library services important, he or she will provide a sufficient number of well-trained staff members to support the R&D function. Such a library might have a staff of professional librarians supported by technicians and clerks. If another R&D director considers the materials more important than the services, his or her library staff might only consist of clerical workers. If either director were to be replaced, the library services in each of the above libraries might be changed to fit the new director's conceptions of library service.

The personnel working in special libraries usually have more varied backgrounds than staff do in other types of libraries. Sometimes the staff in a special library may only be a secretary who has been put in charge of a collection of books and magazines. In other special libraries, several clerks and technicians may be supervised by a librarian who has a degree in the subject specialty of the parent company or institution rather than in library science. In fact, this subject expertise may be so important to companies and businesses that they may prefer a technician with subject specialization to a librarian with a master's degree in library science.

Ideally, a special library should be staffed with personnel who have both library and subject expertise. However, the reality is that many special libraries cannot hire such people because they do not pay very well. Clerical and technical staff members may be paid clerk-typist or secretarial wages without taking into account the subprofessional nature of the jobs they perform. A technician may be offered a high wage to perform professional responsibilities, but professional librarians may only be offered technician level wages unless they can prove their professional value to the parent organization. Sometimes, professional librarians may be hired to set up a library, but once this is done, they may be replaced by less expensive personnel. Thus, unless the special library becomes very important to its parent body, finances may strongly dictate a library's staff size and services.

In spite of such factors, staff members in special libraries usually enjoy being part of the larger organization. They enjoy working closely with company or organization personnel and take pride in contributing to the accomplishments or profits of the parent body. Since the special libraries are small and require small staffs, each member can usually work in many areas of library services rather than being limited to one area. For many staff members, this flexibility and feeling of importance may be what draws them to this type of library.

LIBRARY COOPERATION

And yet, not only have special librarians joined associations based on a subject or media form, they have also become active members of the Special Libraries Association. This association has very strong local chapters, primarily in metropolitan areas, where special librarians from all kinds of libraries can informally share their problems, improve their knowledge, and sharpen their strengths. They have found that the common characteristics which make their libraries "special" provide a common bond with other special libraries. That is why local chapters have been very active in developing and supporting workshops, institutes, and publications for the Special Libraries Association. Over 10,000 members of SLA have evidently found that such an association can satisfy their needs.

Special librarians have also felt a tremendous need for access to information. That this need has not always been met can be seen in the growth of a new type of librarian to provide this information, the information broker. The information broker is an independent librarian or firm who will search out and provide information on a profit-making basis. Special librarians have found them very useful in providing information that is outside the realm or depth of their libraries' collections. Sometimes, business or industrial firms will use information brokers to establish or organize their special libraries. The services provided by the information broker (some of them prefer to be called information specialists or free-lance librarians) range from searches of computerized data bases to translations to market surveys. Their ability to specialize and produce results in a short span of time have made them invaluable additions to the information resources available to the special library.

In searching for quick and efficient ways to gain access to information, special librarians have participated for many years in informal library cooperation and are now investigating formal library cooperation, resource sharing, and networking with other major types of libraries. Many librarians have recognized that without such cooperation, they might never be able to afford access to the bibliographic online data bases that would support their companies' or organizations' needs. Also, as special libraries must produce more services and information with smaller budgets, librarians see networking as an efficient means for solving this dilemma. Special libraries and the SLA are taking an active part in developing guidelines for special library participation in such networking. They recognize that provisions must be made for protecting private corporate or product information, but they also realize that special libraries may gain more than they give by participating in such networks.

Special library participation in these networks is seen by many librarians as the best way they can solve their problems in the coming decade. Business and industry are entering the eighties with threats of recession hanging over their corporate heads; institutions and organizations are facing reduced funding and tightened budgets; and all publicly supported agencies are feeling the results of taxpayer revolts at the high cost of government. Even libraries financed by endowments have had to recognize their funds are not inexhaustible and that information is being developed and published faster than they can assimilate it. The hope of the 1980s for special libraries, as it is for all libraries, is that automation and networking will enable them to build a strong enough dam to stem the tide before they are awash in a sea of information from which they cannot extricate themselves.

REVIEW QUESTIONS

1. Identify the major objectives of special libraries.

2. Identify the characteristics most common to special libraries.

3. Describe the scopes and services of the three U.S. national libraries.

4. Describe the kinds of materials usually included in business library collections.

5. List the many kinds of special libraries.

6. Visit one or two special libraries and compare their objectives, services, and collections to those discussed in this chapter.

7. Identify some of the duties of the LMTA in the above special libraries.

SELECTED READINGS

Bailey, Martha. *The Special Librarian as a Supervisor or Middle Manager.* New York: Special Libraries Association, 1977.

Christenson, Elin. *New Special Libraries: A Summary of Research.* New York: Special Libraries Association, 1980.

Cole, John Y. "The Library of Congress in American Life." In *Advances in Librarianship, Vol. 8.* New York: Academic Press, 1978, pp. 55-79.

Echelman, Shirley. "Toward the New Special Library," *Library Journal*, January 1, 1976, pp. 91-94.

Johns, Ada Winifred. *Special Libraries: Development of the Concept, Their Organization and Their Service*. Metuchen, NJ: Scarecrow, 1968.

"Library of Congress." 16mm film. Chicago: Encyclopaedia Britannica Educational Corp., 1968.

Special Libraries: A Guide for Management. 2nd ed. New York: Special Libraries Association, 1980.

Strauss, Lucille J. *Scientific and Technical Libraries: Their Organization and Administration*. New York: Interscience, c1969.

Survey of Federal Libraries, 1972. Washington, DC: GPO, 1975.

NOTES

[1]William Burlington, "To Enlarge the Sphere of Human Knowledge: The Role of the Independent Research Library," in *Libraries for Teaching, Libraries for Research* (Chicago: American Library Association, 1977), p. 174.

[2]*Survey of Federal Libraries, 1972* (Washington, DC: GPO, 1975), pp. 1, 3, and 21.

[3]Mildred Benton, *Federal Library Resources: A User's Guide to Research Collections* (New York: Science Associations, 1973), p. iii.

[4]John Y. Cole, "The Library of Congress in American Life," in *Advances in Librarianship, Vol. 8* (New York: Academic Press, 1978), p. 56.

[5]William P. Koughan, "Hospital Library Standards: An Administrator's View," *Special Libraries*, December 1975, pp. 588-91.

9
RECENT DEVELOPMENTS IN LIBRARY SERVICES

Library resources and services have been transformed in the 1960s and the 1970s by technological developments. Not only have libraries added the multitude of audiovisual media to their collections, but they have also been revolutionized by the introduction of computer and electronic technologies. These developing technologies, along with micrographics and telecommunications, have enabled libraries to develop automated library systems and services and to expand their resources beyond the wildest imagination of librarians in the 1940s and 1950s. More importantly, libraries of all sizes and types have been transformed by technological developments which only seemed feasible for large libraries a decade ago.

What factors enabled libraries to take advantage of these developments? Primarily, the phenomenal growth and development in the computer and electronics fields made it possible to process information at an extremely high speed for an affordable price. Secondly, libraries found they could join together in cooperatives or networks to share the cost of developing and operating automated computer systems. Finally, libraries found that these automated computer systems could be used to automate many library operations to provide better accuracy, access, and service for their patrons. Such automated library operations as circulation systems, cataloging, and retrieval of bibliographic information became commonplace in libraries in the late 1970s.

AUTOMATION

In order to understand the advantages the computer brought to library operations, it is important to understand how the computer works. Although many people often talk about the computer as if it were a human being capable of thinking on its own, a computer is only a machine — although it is a very complex and sophisticated one. It is made up of electronic components which operate on the principle of an electronic impulse's being either on or off as an electric light is either on or off. Computer technology has developed this simple principle to such an advanced state that the electronic impulses can be manipulated to represent characters or numbers and letters (as in Morse code) at an unbelievable speed. The computer can also take in and store instructions so that it can move, compare, and relate characters; make simple yes-no decisions; and add characters. The computer cannot think, and it can only perform these functions by switching its electronic impulses on or off. If the human operating the computer provides confusing instructions or incorrect characters, the electronic components in the computer cannot process the instruction or compare the characters correctly. Thus, errors in computer operations are almost always human error in encoding the information for the computer. The computer can only do what it is told to do!

When a person is first introduced into the world of computers, the language spoken by the "computer people" seems to be a foreign language. Terms such as "online," "offline," "batch mode," "real time," "down time," etc. can be as confusing as library terms can be to the library novice. The majority of computer terms refer to the machine known as the computer. Actually, the computer is seldom one machine but is made up of a group of machines that perform integrated functions which are referred to as computer operations. In recent years, mini-computers and microprocessor computers have been developed which are single computer machines that perform fewer functions than larger computers do. The term "hardware" is used to refer to any computer equipment.

In order to operate the hardware, individuals called programmers or systems analysts write programs called "software" which are encoded instructions for the computer equipment. A person "inputs" these instructions into the computer by using a "terminal," usually a typewriter-like keyboard. The terminal may have a TV-type screen attached to it (CRT — Cathode Ray Tube) so that the programmer can see what he or she has typed on the terminal (*see* Fig. 9-1, page 124). If the terminal is attached by cable to the computer so that responses can be received from the computer, it is called "online." If the terminal punches a tape or cards which must later be fed into the computer equipment, it is called "offline" or "batch processing." Very recent computer technology has introduced the microprocessor computer based on a microchip or microscopic electronic circuit. These microprocessors are stand-alone computer units and have the advantage that they can be programmed by anyone with a basic knowledge of a program language.

Because computer equipment is expensive to operate and can be run 24 hours a day, computer operations were developed which were based on "real time" and "time sharing." "Real time" refers to the exact time the computer is working on a process or an operation. "Time sharing" refers to the sharing or simultaneous use of a computer for several different processes or operations. Thus, computer users are usually charged for real time computer use but may share a computer with many other users. Performance of these computer processes and operations is generally referred to as "data processing," "automated data processing" (ADP), or "electronic data processing" (EDP). However, because of the complexity of these operations and the combination of scientific and business disciplines involved, this area has evolved into its own science—"information science."

LIBRARY APPLICATIONS OF AUTOMATION

With new generations of computers being developed about every 5-7 years, computer technology has developed at an unbelievable rate since its inception. It is often impossible for the layperson to comprehend the computer's capacity for storing information and the speed with which a computer can process this information. However, laypersons can recognize that these capabilities can be used to perform calculations, routines, and procedures which would be arduous or even impossible to perform in any other way. Librarians have also recognized that these capabilities are ideally suited for manipulating library characters and records. Since libraries have generally standardized the information or bibliographic record for each item in the library, they have found that computers

Figure 9-1
Computer keyboard and Cathode Ray Tube (CRT)
Photo courtesy of Research Libraries Group, Inc.

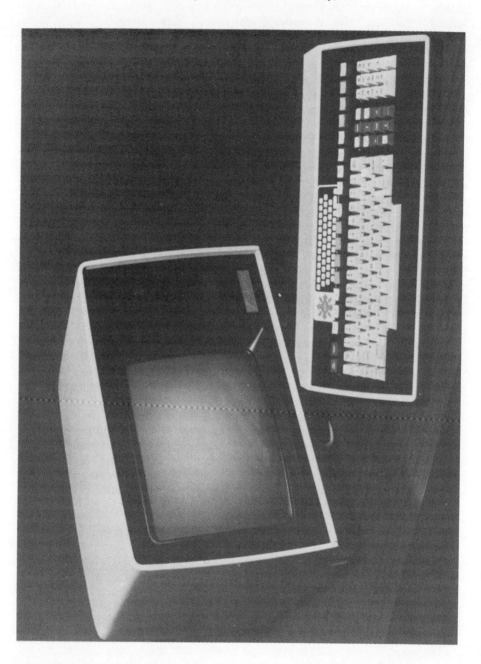

can effectively add to records for individual items, make deletions in these records, and manipulate them in a variety of ways. In fact, the principal characteristics of computers in library data processing have been their high speed in information processing, flexibility of processing, absolute accuracy, and the compatibility of different forms of output from the same computer record.

However, the computer's major contribution to library operations may not have been the actual automating of library processes but the introduction of systems thinking into libraries. Librarians were forced to look at each operation in terms of the basic objective it was to fulfill. Once this was determined, librarians were able to work with computer systems analysts to develop the best process to achieve this objective. This rethinking process enabled librarians to refine their operations and eliminate unnecessary procedures and steps. It also helped librarians to recognize that they had procedures in common with other libraries which could be automated on a cooperative basis. This realization freed librarians from reinventing the wheel by developing their own systems and allowed them to look for and purchase packaged or "turn-key" (ready for use) automated library systems.

Library systems thinking also caused librarians of the 1970s to view library automation differently from librarians in the 1950s and 1960s. In the early years of library automation, librarians expected most future libraries to have totally automated library operations and systems. These systems would be based upon a "data base" of computerized records for every item in the library (similar to a library's shelflist). When a library wanted to purchase an item, it would simply enter a bibliographic record or entry (author, title, edition, imprint, price) into the computer. The computer would compare this record with the records already in the data base and print an order for the item if the library did not already own it. When the item was received, the library would catalog it and add this information to the library record in the data base. This data base would then be used to produce book catalogs or library catalog cards. The computer would be programmed to generate accounting records such as invoices for received items or claims for items not received.

Libraries would also use this data base for automated circulation systems (*see* Figure 9-2, page 126). The location of every item in the library could be indicated for each record in the data base. When an item was charged out to a patron, the borrower and date due information could be added to this record. Thus, a library could query the computer records by using either an online terminal or a computer "printout" (printed copy of the computer records) to determine where an item was and when it was due back in the library. Libraries could also place holds or reserves on items so that when they were returned the computer would identify those items which should be held for other patrons. Again, the computer could be programmed to generate such notices as reserve notices, recall notices, overdue notices, and bills.

Computer systems would also include borrower information such as that maintained by universities and institutions or organizations. By combining the borrower records with the bibliographic data base, libraries could determine what materials a borrower had checked out or whether a borrower had any overdue materials or other library obligations. This combination of bibliographic and borrower information could be used by libraries to generate statistics they could never have access to by manual systems. The computer's ability to store information would enable libraries to retrieve statistics, such as how many times an item had been circulated in a certain time period, which classification

Figure 9-2
Automated circulation system
Photo courtesy of CLSI LIBS 100 Automated Circulation System

categories were most used, and what type of borrower used particular types of library materials. These statistics could be very useful to libraries in planning their collection development.

However, in spite of the tremendous advances library automation could bring to library operations, librarians in the 1960s began to run into several major problems in implementing such automated systems. The primary problem was that although such systems were feasible, their costs were so high that only large libraries were able to justify them. Another major problem was that very few libraries could afford their own computers dedicated solely to library operations. Thus, libraries developed computer-based systems which were shared with other departments within their institutions. As the institution demands on these computers grew, libraries found they had more and more difficulty in gaining real time access to the computer. A third major problem was that there were very few guidelines and standards to guide early libraries in developing their own software and automated library systems. Thus, these "do-it-yourself" library systems may have worked well for individual libraries, but they could not be transferred very easily to operations in other libraries. When the Library of Congress introduced its MARC program in 1966, libraries began to look to LC for leadership in solving some of these problems.

Although the Library of Congress has not emerged as the national force in automation librarians expected it to be, the MARC program was the first important factor in the development of library automation for the 1970s. MARC began as a project to provide LC cataloging data for English-language current imprints on computer-generated magnetic tapes. It was expected that libraries would purchase the MARC tapes, feed them into their own computers, and use them to provide cataloging information for their new library purchases. Instead, MARC became accepted as the worldwide standard for a computerized library bibliographic format. Rather than developing their own formats, libraries began to band together to use the MARC format to build data bases, share them with other libraries, and develop compatible automated library systems. By 1980, not only was MARC expanded by LC to include virtually all Roman alphabet language materials in many different media forms, but practically every computer library system was either based on the MARC format or compatible with it.

NATIONAL AUTOMATED SYSTEMS

The development of MARC as the standard library bibliographic format was followed by the second important factor which influenced library automation in the 1970s. Institutions and private companies became library automation vendors, making their automated library operations available to libraries on a contractual basis for a service fee libraries could afford. Libraries could avail themselves of automated systems in all areas of the library from acquisitions and book catalogs (Brodart), to circulation (CLSI), cataloging (OCLC) and reference (MEDLINE and Lockheed's DIALOG). Libraries in the 1970s did just that!

One library cooperative, OCLC, Inc., became probably the most significant development in automation since MARC. It began in 1970 as a cooperative of academic libraries in Ohio (Ohio College Library Center) and emerged in 1979 as a giant enterprise with 1,500 libraries and 22 library networks participating in its shared cataloging system. Libraries in every state from coast to coast had joined

OCLC's system because it was one of the first and best designed library automated systems available, it was well marketed, and it fulfilled a need which those libraries had for getting library cataloging quickly, easily, and at reasonable costs.

OCLC began its operations as a shared cataloging service, which meant that a cooperating library would use an online terminal in its own library to search for a cataloging record in the computer based in Columbus, Ohio. If the cataloging record was found, the library could edit the information to fit its own needs or "profile," add its location symbol to the cataloging record, and instruct the computer to print library catalog cards for this item which would arrive in about a week. If the cataloging record were not found, the library itself had to catalog the item and enter this cataloging record into the OCLC data base. Because many large libraries were adding thousands of volumes to their collections and thousands of records to this data base every year, OCLC soon developed a very large data base. In addition, many libraries received permission to do retrospective searching for cataloging records for volumes already in their collections. This two-pronged approach to building the data base enabled libraries which joined OCLC to experience "hits" or locate records for 85-95% of their cataloging needs. Not only were libraries satisfied with this success rate, they were also happy that much of the cataloging on OCLC terminals could be accessed by trained paraprofessionals and subprofessionals. Many libraries found they no longer needed to develop large professional cataloging staffs.

As OCLC developed into a national resource-sharing data base, it began to expand in other ways. It expanded its governing body to allow for input by its many customers in libraries outside of Ohio. It also encouraged libraries to join through library networks rather than as individual members. Networks such as PALINET and SOLINET provided instruction to and control over the libraries which joined OCLC in their areas. OCLC also expanded its operations into other resource-sharing areas besides cataloging. The OCLC data base was used as a union catalog, and interlibrary loan programs were developed so that libraries could use their OCLC terminals to request loans from other libraries. A serials data base was developed, and other communication systems were planned. By 1978, OCLC had become the national leader in library automation which many people had expected the Library of Congress to become.

This national leadership was challenged by the development in the late 1970s of several other viable automation networks. Stanford University's well-designed BALLOTS system joined with the Research Libraries Group to form the RLIN (Research Libraries Information Network). This system combined the powerful and versatile technical system of BALLOTS with the data bases of the RLG (*see* chapter 8). It challenged OCLC's preeminence by attracting many research and academic libraries to RLIN. The Washington Library Network (WLN) emerged in the late 1970s as another successful network. Not only did it become a regional network for many libraries, but its sophisticated software packages were transferred successfully to other library systems (even in Australia) to support shared cataloging and acquisitions as well as library processes. These two automation networks, RLIN and WLN, joined hands in 1979 to share their systems and data bases. Whether OCLC will join them in the 1980s or compete with them for library members remains to be seen.

None of the automation networks developed in the 1970s was able to provide the totally automated library operations and systems dreamed of in the 1960s. In developing their operations, most designers had to make economic decisions that limited their systems. OCLC developed a tremendous network for providing cataloging and catalog cards, but many libraries were beginning to look toward book or COM catalogs as vehicles that better served their needs. Also, OCLC had no subject access so that it could not be used for subject bibliographic searches. BALLOTS had subject access but did not have OCLC's strength in cataloging or as a union catalog, and neither network had developed feasible circulation capabilities. To fill this gap, several commercial vendors had stepped in and developed automated circulation systems.

Attempts were finally made in the late 1970s to remedy this automation fragmentation. The WLN and RLIN cooperation was one example, and another example was the connection of the ILLINET (Illinois State Library Network) data base with CLSI's automated circulation systems. These attempts were further enhanced by the development of minicomputers which made such projects economically feasible. In fact, the 1980s will probably see more use of mini-computers by networks of libraries to automate operations and systems on a regional basis. Large- and medium-sized libraries may even be able to afford in-house or in-library mini-computers to handle local library operations and procedures. Thus, by using a variety of sources for library automation, libraries may eventually achieve the automated library operations and systems dreamed of in the 1960s.

DATA BASES

No overview of library automation would be complete without discussing the contributions to library services and resources which have been made by "online" commercial, governmental, and subject data bases. These data bases enable libraries to search large bodies of literature in almost every subject area in a very short span of time. Originally, most of them were developed as by-products of commercial or governmental indexing and abstracting services when their bibliographic records were converted to machine-readable form. Thus, such familiar services as Public Affairs Information Service, Education Index, and Chemical Abstracts as well as many others are available in machine-readable form. However, it is not the form or format of the information which is important for libraries, but that these data bases allow rapid access to this information.

Data bases provide information in practically every subject area — whether it is a scientific, technical, or medical field, or an area of the social sciences or the humanities. These data bases provide comprehensive subject access to information contained in such materials as periodicals, governmental and technical reports, dissertations, newspapers, and books, and even to citation references in other articles. The information they provide may vary from a short bibliographic entry, to an entry with subject headings or descriptors, to an entry that includes a detailed abstract or summary. Some data bases even enable libraries to order printed copies of the desired text. However, this document delivery system was still in the infant stages in the 1970s. The 1980s or 1990s may make it economically feasible for libraries to provide telefacsimiles (copies transmitted over the computer telephone or telegraph wires) or access to documents via the CRT. Until this develops, libraries will take advantage of the tremendous bibliographic resources the data bases themselves have provided.

Because of the variety of data bases offered by so many different companies using bibliographic formats other than MARC, libraries usually gained access to them by purchasing computer time from commercial information processing centers. Two of the first major information processing centers were the National Library of Medicine and Lockheed Corp. NLM's MEDLINE was a single subject data base for comprehensive medical information. Lockheed's DIALOG combined many scientific and technical data bases into one data base for easier access by libraries. These centers, along with others such as Systems Dynamic Corp. (SDC) and Bibliographic Retrieval Services (BRS), provided access to over 125 data bases. Of these data bases, there were over 25 for the social sciences and related subjects, 60-70 life science data bases, and even data bases for AV materials. Because purchasing computer time from these information centers was still rather costly, many libraries joined library networks which would share such access with them. The National Library of Medicine even identified regional medical libraries which provided searches of data bases at nominal costs for libraries and their patrons.

There are several different types of searches which libraries can provide through these data bases. They can provide Selective Dissemination of Information (SDI) searches of current literature tailored to an individual's or group's specific needs or profile. They can also provide retrospective searches which search all the information on a subject published in a specific time period. Usually librarians will interview the patron to determine what specific type of search or information is desired. Next, the librarian will often consult a thesaurus of subject descriptors (similar to a subject heading authority) to determine what subject headings the computer will accept as instructions. Finally, the librarian will usually connect the terminal to the information center's computer via a dedicated telephone line. The library will be charged for the real time in which the terminal is interacting with the computer, and this charge is most often passed on to the patron or user. Many libraries would prefer to absorb the cost for these searches, but since the average cost was $30-40 per search in 1978 1979, most libraries could not afford to do so. However, libraries recognize that no matter what the cost, providing access to these data bases might be the only possible way they can provide access to the wealth of knowledge which will be gathered and disseminated in the coming decades.

OTHER TECHNOLOGIES

Computer automation was not the only technology which affected libraries in the 1970s, but it strongly influenced the development of other library technologies. The electronics and telecommunications technologies which were used to develop mini-computers and to connect computers from coast-to-coast were also able to be used in many other ways. Telephone and telegraph lines were not only used by libraries to transmit interlibrary loan requests and to search data bases, but they could also be used to deliver telefacsimiles or copies of documents. Electronics made it possible for written material to be transmitted to television screens either in libraries or in a person's own home. In fact, electronics also made "dial-access" to computers possible. With dial access, a person could dial a number, similar to a phone number, which would activate a computer program to display information on a TV or audiovisual equipment. This capability was combined with the computer to develop many sophisticated programmed instruction systems. Television itself became an important technology for libraries. Cable television stations, which connected homes by underground cables to the TV studio, were required to make programming available to public service agencies. Libraries not only used cable TV to produce library programs, but also looked forward to being able to transmit books economically via TV. Although these and other electronic and telecommunication capabilities are available in 1981, it will probably be 1990 before libraries can economically include them on any kind of regular basis.

In contrast, micrographics technology had become thoroughly ensconced in many libraries by 1980. Micrographics is the science of reducing an image to such a small size that it must be reproduced on magnifying equipment in order for a person to use it. These microimages were produced on film of various sizes and had been used by businesses and libraries since 1938. Libraries had primarily used microforms in place of serials to save space and theft of magazines. In the 1970s, the advances in computer technology were combined with micrographics so that microforms could be generated by the computer. This development of Computer Output Microform (COM) meant that information stored in the computer could be reproduced on microfiche or microfilm as well as on paper. COM capability enabled libraries and businesses to make reports, records, and inventories more readily available and to update them easily and quickly. Special libraries began to add COM technical reports and company archives to their collections. Public, academic, and special libraries began to produce COM catalogs from their computer data bases rather than relying solely upon book catalogs or card catalogs. The late 1970s saw several large libraries adopting COM catalogs for public use, and the trend will probably continue in the 1980s. This coming decade will also probably see the use of COM for in-process lists such as circulation printouts, acquisition lists, and other bibliographic products.

The only major drawback to the widespread adoption of COM products in place of printed library records may come from the library staffs and users themselves. Although many library users did not seem to mind using COM catalogs, some users, particularly scholars, objected to using microforms in place of the printed document. Also, many staff members had found it psychologically frustrating and physically exasperating to use microform materials and equipment. Although the 1970s have seen the growth of efficient and effective microform materials and equipment, it may take another decade for these negative attitudes toward their adoption to subside.

NETWORKING—INTERTYPE LIBRARY COOPERATION

Although computers influenced the development of other technologies, perhaps the greatest influence computer technology had on the development of libraries was its influence on libraries working together. Libraries had worked cooperatively for many years, but the capabilities and expense of computer systems made it advantageous for libraries to join together in cooperatives or networks to utilize these capabilities and share these expenses. This development was also encouraged by the Library Services and Construction Act (1966) which encouraged states to provide funding for intertype library cooperative ventures. These cooperative ventures developed and flourished in the 1970s because librarians realized they could best serve their patrons' needs by sharing their budgets and resources and by developing cooperative library operations and services.

These library cooperative efforts were identified by many different names. Consortia, councils, cooperatives, networks, intertype, and multitype were some of the designations used to identify cooperative efforts within a geographic area by all types of libraries. By 1979, over 340 organizations of this type were in existence. If these cooperative efforts were organized in an informal structure, they were often called consortia or councils; if the organizational structure was formal with a constitution and board of directors, they were usually called networks. However, no matter what their titles were, their goals were the same – to share resources, to exchange information, and to use computer and communications technologies to foster joint projects which would reduce needless duplication of effort and resources.

The rapid growth of networks in the 1970s and the variety of their activities attest to the fact that networks met some previously unserved library needs. They enabled all types of libraries in a geographic area to join together to mobilize the total library resources of an area to meet all of their users' needs. Public, academic, school, and special libraries in both the private and public sectors recognized they could not economically satisfy all of their user demands by themselves. Through networks, they would be able to develop new and creative ways of sharing resources and services and would be able to develop a network greater than the sum of its parts.

Networks initiated many new and creative services that had not been possible before the development of intertype library cooperation. Most networks developed resource sharing projects of one type or another, and many instituted "INFOPASS" programs which allowed patrons from one library to visit another library to use its resources. This innovation made many special library collections available on a supervised basis to members of the public who had never been able to use them before. Some networks developed reciprocal borrowing programs so that patrons from one library could check out materials from another network library. These programs were successful because they were supervised by the networks so that large libraries or special collections would not be overused or undercompensated by other libraries.

In order to facilitate resource sharing, many networks developed union catalogs and union lists of serials (which indicated the holdings of many libraries) and expanded their interlibrary loan (ILL) programs. Union catalogs and union lists of serials not only identified the location of library materials in many libraries, they often uncovered subject strengths or unusual items in unexpected libraries. These catalogs and lists were then used by libraries to request materials from other libraries (interlibrary loans). In order to speed this process, networks often used the computer or telecommunications systems such as TWX to transmit or receive requests. For the same reason, many libraries also developed same-day or overnight delivery services for ILL items. Most networks expanded their ILL programs so that besides delivering the actual books and periodicals, they could deliver photocopies, microforms (often microfiche), and telefacsimiles. However, this latter practice has raised the question of how copyright owners could be paid for such copies or protected from blatant violations of the copyright laws. This question will probably be resolved in the coming decade.

Union catalogs and lists also helped libraries establish hierarchical systems for interlibrary loan and reference requests. Libraries would first request information or materials from local libraries, then from regional libraries, and finally from state libraries or designated resource libraries. Such hierarchical systems have been developed in Illinois and New York. Illinois' statewide network, ILLINET, uses the Chicago Public Library, Illinois State Library, and the University of Illinois and Southern Illinois University libraries as back-up resource and reference libraries and the University of Chicago, Northwestern University and John Crerar Libraries as Special Resource Centers. New York established NYSILL (New York State Interlibrary Loan Network), which is made up of three referral libraries (Brooklyn, Rochester, and Buffalo-Erie County Public Libraries) and nine subject referral libraries to back-up nine regional "3Rs" systems (Reference and Research Library Resources) Systems. These 3Rs systems provide interlibrary loans, document delivery service, and reciprocal borrowing privileges. Hierarchical systems such as those in New York and Illinois have proven that networks can mobilize total library resources within an area for the benefit of all the citizens in that area.

Besides resource sharing, networks also developed many other operations and services. Many networks joined OCLC or provided automated services such as circulation systems or access to bibliographic data bases. Some networks such as the Colorado Organization for Library Acquisitions (COLA) developed cooperative library acquisitions and collection development programs so that unnecessary and costly duplications could be eliminated. Some networks developed cooperative periodicals centers or cooperative storage facilities for little used items. Other networks developed strong continuing education programs which offer workshops and institutes for the education of their members. Some networks such as the Washington Library Network were designed to be full-service networks providing automated cataloging and circulation systems which would be coordinated with resource sharing, collection building, and interlibrary loans. Other networks were designed as single function networks, as NELINET (the New England Library Information Network) was designed as a computerized technical processing center. Most of these network services and programs were developed to fit the local needs of their member libraries. In fact, it was this variety in providing programs and services and the flexibility in meeting their members' needs that made many networks so successful.

Networks were also successful for several other basic reasons. Besides being able to respond quickly to local needs and issues, they built on the strength of their members in responding to these needs. Network organizers and administrators realized that the network could only be as strong as its weakest link. Therefore, the structure of the networks ensured that the autonomy of each member library would be maintained and that larger libraries would neither dominate the other libraries nor be exploited by them. Most networks developed constitutions, bylaws, and elected boards of directors. Even informal cooperative library organizations usually had bylaws and a controlling body. Governing authorities of the networks were elected by member libraries and represented a balance among the major types of libraries in the network. They usually operated under participatory democracy. Thus, all libraries had representation in the types of services and programs which would be developed and funded.

Many networks often had network staffs which conducted their everyday operations. These staffs could range from very large (over 20) to very small (one full or part-time professional). Successful networks found they could best satisfy the networks' needs by supplementing these paid staffs with volunteer help. This help came in the form of donated facilities, materials, or staff time. Library staffs who donated their time (both on and off the job) contributed to the development of strong networks because people who worked on network projects developed deeper commitments to them. This same sense of commitment came when member libraries had to pay membership fees to support the network. Although these fees were seldom large enough to support the total budget of the network, they were effective in emphasizing a library's commitment to the network concept.

Financial support for networks usually came from a variety of sources. Membership fees were psychologically necessary but seldom enough to support the total function of the network. Most networks obtained their funds from state and federal sources. Some networks generated revenues by selling library and automated services, publishing library materials, charging fees for network programs or institutes, and passing on the costs of fee-based services (such as the use of automated data bases) to the user library. With the economic crises of the late 1970s and the early 1980s, this "soft-funding," or money which is dependent on political and variable circumstances has worried many network members and protagonists. Many persons believe the major task facing networks in the 1980s will be to develop solid funding for network operations.

Two other major problems will have to be faced by library networks in the 1980s. Although one problem is organizational and the other is psychological, they are often intertwined. The first issue has to do with governance of networks. Although most networks had governing authorities, they did not usually have any legal basis for their existence. Sometimes, networks found it difficult to work with the many different governing bodies of their member libraries when the network had no legal basis from which to operate. Sometimes joint cooperation and good will could only go so far. In the same vein, many politicians, administrators, and librarians feared they might lose their local authority or control if they joined library networks. Some administrators objected to donating volunteer time and staff to such quasi-legal entities as networks. Some librarians felt threatened because they did not understand the needs of other types of libraries which differed from their own, and they were not willing to try to understand these needs. In some networks, librarians felt that the networks were not responsive enough to their own library's needs. Often, these psychological and governance problems came to a head as networks began to cooperate and join with other networks. Although OCLC expanded its governing board in 1979 to include representation of its non-Ohio customers, librarians wonder if it will continue to be responsive in the future or if RLIN, for instance, will listen to its members. These are all major issues which will have to be resolved by networks in the near future if they are to continue growing and meeting libraries' needs.

In spite of the problems networks will face in the 1980s, they have provided a remarkable beginning for the development of national library services. By developing from local or regional networks, to state and multi-state networks, they have provided a basis for cooperative library services and resource-sharing from coast to coast, which librarians have dreamed about but never really dared to hope for. Having begun at the local or regional level to meet grass-roots library needs, networks have developed a level of sophistication which utilizes the latest developments in computer and telecommunications technologies to provide effective library services.

What makes this whole development most remarkable is that these networks have grown without national standards and without national direction. The Library of Congress and NCLIS (National Council on Library and Information

Science) almost seemed to be "Johnny-come-latelies" as they began in the late 1970s to provide leadership in developing library and information guidelines. Proponents of these guidelines, however, did recognize that the Library of Congress would probably not become the master center for national library services but instead would become a link in a national library network. However, the interest and leadership at the national level, and the interest in resource sharing which was expressed at the 1979 White House Conference on Library and Information Services, should help networks move forward in the 1980s toward the next natural step in library development — national library resource sharing. By 1990, or at least by the year 2000, we should see the development of interconnecting links between regional, state and multi-state library networks, the national automated systems and data bases, and the national libraries to provide every individual with access to the nation's library and information resources.

LIBRARY BUILDINGS

If a library's resources and services have been influenced by computers, technology, and networking, their buildings have been influenced even more so. These influences will probably cause libraries of the future to differ drastically from the libraries of the 1960s and the 1970s. In fact, libraries built in the 1970s are already being expanded and changed to include such new developments as computer centers, television studios, and media centers. However, in redesigning old buildings or in designing new ones, librarians must realize that what may be the latest technology of this decade may be out of date in the next decade. Thus, library buildings must be designed and redesigned with a flexibility and capacity for change that will enable them both to grow with the coming technologies and to support any innovative developments in library services.

In order to design well-functioning library buildings with flexibility and capacity, librarians must plan carefully and follow several basic library building principles. First, a planning team should be assembled which includes the library director, library board members or administrators, representatives of the library staff and its community (citizens, members, or faculty and students), and a library building consultant. This building consultant will assist the team in developing a workable building or remodeling program statement, ensuring that all important issues are considered, and, hopefully, preventing errors and mistakes in planning and building. At a later date, an architect may also be added to this planning team.

Once the planning team has been chosen, all of its members should recognize that a library is not just a building that houses books and other graphic material; it is a building that satisfies the objectives, purposes, and functions of the library system it serves. Thus, everyone involved in the building process must understand the objectives of the library and the objectives of any institution to which it belongs. Once the objectives are determined, the planning team should study the community that will be served to identify its needs, its makeup, and any changes that may occur in the community which could affect the library's services. These objectives and needs of the community should then be used to identify services, programs, resources, and needs which the future library building project should satisfy. In determining these needs, members of the planning team will find it useful to visit other libraries to see what is being provided elsewhere. Only after all of these steps have been taken and all of these factors considered, should the building or remodeling program statement be written.

The library building or remodeling program statement is the heart and soul of any library building or restructuring project. It is a blueprint for future services, staffing needs, facilities design, and any restrictions or innovations that should be considered. This program statement should identify the ideals, goals and dreams the planning team expects the project to satisfy. It should include not only plans for the present library but also definite plans for future services and expansion. Although this statement may have to be pared down at a later date, libraries that do not "dream big" may find they have built too timidly and conservatively and designed a building that does not suit their future needs.

In developing this program statement, the planning team should examine the library's activities and design the building to function around them. Traffic patterns should be designed to fit library needs and not an architect's plan. Too many times, a beautiful library was designed first and the activities forced to function—poorly—within the building. (That is why the architect should be brought to the planning team after this statement is developed.) As these library activities are examined, it should be remembered that they may change in the future and that *flexibility* is the watchword. For this reason, many libraries have used current quantitative library standards as guidelines rather than as requirements which they should meet. Also, many libraries found that by adding new technologies or by joining networks they did not necessarily eliminate any library spaces but just changed the kinds of spaces which were needed. For example, with the development of computer cataloging systems, most libraries found that they no longer needed large offices for cataloging staff but instead needed climate controlled rooms to house the computer terminal equipment.

Libraries have also found that societal changes such as population shifts or environmental changes may affect the future functions of their libraries. Expected population changes may convince public library planners to provide smaller areas for children and larger areas for elderly and handicapped persons. Changing study patterns of students may persuade academic libraries to provide many different study environments ranging from formal areas with tables and chairs to individual study carrels to informal lounge-type areas. School media centers and even public libraries will need to include areas for audiovisual materials which will adapt to future developments in media materials and their equipment. All of these developments, as well as others, should be possible to accommodate if the building program statement is carefully designed.

Once the activities have been planned, the program statement adopted, and an architect added to the planning team, the business of designing or redesigning a library can begin. This physical building should follow two architectural maxims. The first is that "Form should follow function," and the second is that "Form should follow imagination, form should follow the future." By following these two principles, the architect should be able to develop an aesthetically pleasing architectural form which will satisfy the library's needs. It is in this stage that the planning team must give the architect full rein, because it is the architect who will be responsible for the beauty and character of the building. However, once the building is designed, the planning team should critique it and adapt it to be sure that the planned building will truly satisfy their needs.

In designing a library, the architect should also follow several principles of library design. Most importantly, the architect should base the library upon a modular design. This would mean that all units would meet standard dimensions and that the major portion of the library would be based upon open spaces separated by columns set apart at standard distances. Although custom designed structures are often beautiful, they are also very costly to maintain or replace. Library inner walls should be movable rather than permanent and movable offices have been used successfully in libraries. Lighting and windows should be designed so that the activities of the library are best served. Some libraries have rows of library stacks placed in front of walls of windows while the staff sit in windowless and cheerless inner offices!

Architects should place the engineering mechanicals such as heating, electricity, and plumbing so that they could be changed or replaced easily and also take up a minimum of a library's usable space. Some architects are able to provide 75% usable space in the same square footage where others provide only 55%. Some recent buildings have kept this loss to a minimum by actually placing the mechanicals outside the building. Provision should be made so that future audiovisual, telecommunications, or computer technologies could be included easily in the building. The building itself should be placed on the library site not only for its best location and traffic patterns but also so that future construction can be added easily and reasonably. Although these requirements seem to be rather stringent, many architects have followed them imaginatively and successfully.

Architects and librarians have also successfully introduced many new developments into library buildings. Energy-conserving features and alternate sources of heating, such as solar heating, were being used in library buildings by 1980. Barrier-free libraries to serve handicapped persons were developed to meet state and federal regulations. Not only have security conscious librarians designed libraries with single entrances and electronic security devices to control thefts, but they also designed buildings that would protect their materials and equipment from vandalism or fire. Library planners became aware of the psychological factors in library planning and designed their traffic patterns, color schemes, and use of library spaces accordingly.

Since the economic situations of the 1970s reduced the funds for new library buildings, librarians and architects began to innovate. They successfully converted such buildings as fire stations, banks, post offices, service stations, and stores into attractive and effective libraries. The West Virginia State Library Commission even experimented with a completely new type of library. It designed "instant libraries" which were prefabricated libraries that could be erected on very small sites in a few days. These octagonal libraries were only about 30x40-feet and could provide small communities with 6,000 books and a place for library programs. Similar buildings were used as information kiosks by the Washington, DC Public Library. Many libraries which had no funds to build new buildings reexamined and redesigned their existing buildings to make better utilization of the spaces available to them. Some of these libraries (and others) installed compact shelving units or developed off-site storage units for little used materials. These building innovations show that although the funds may have dwindled for library buildings, there was no dwindling of library and architectural imagination and ingenuity when it came to developing library structures to serve library needs.

LIBRARY FURNISHINGS

Library furnishings have also changed greatly in the past 20 years. No longer are most libraries quiet places painted in dull institutional colors, floored with shining marble or tile, and filled with rows of long tables and straightback chairs. Instead, librarians have discovered that environmental factors are important in setting the psychological tone for their library services and that libraries which want to attract patrons must provide environments which will interest them. That is why many libraries now have library furnishings consultants to help them design new buildings or refurbish old ones to reflect the public image they want to create.

When a patron walks into a modern library today, he or she can usually feel the mood that library wants to create. Libraries which want to create a peaceful, tranquil, and efficient mood may decorate and carpet their rooms in soft or muted colors. Such buildings have sometimes had such soothing effects on their patrons and staffs that very few arguments or disturbances have arisen there. Other libraries may want to project an active and vibrant library "where the action is"! These libraries may have brightly colored carpets and furniture and may even spread bright supergraphics across their vinyl walls. Often, buildings which have been converted from other uses such as fire stations may retain some of the original furnishings as conversation pieces. This great variety in library decor is also carried out in the variety of the library furnishings which can be found in today's libraries.

Today's library furnishings largely reflect society's interest in more relaxed and open environments. For this reason, most public areas of libraries today are often carpeted (which is easier to maintain and quieter than tile floors) and are divided visually rather than physically into separate environmental areas for separate functions such as study, lounging, and group activities. Each of these areas will often have its own type of furnishings. Quiet study areas may have large tables with comfortable chairs rather than straightback wooden ones. Lounging areas may have casual pull-up chairs or molded foam furniture and cushions. Study areas may also have individual study carrels or tables with sides so that each patron has a study cubicle. Many children's rooms have child-sized tables, chairs, and pillows to sit on or chairs made in the shape of animals or objects such as a baseball glove. Many children's rooms have story pits and some even have tree-house-like structures where children can read undisturbed by adults. Group activities are often held in meeting rooms with comfortable chairs and conference tables that are separated from the rest of the library by sound-proofed glass walls. These glass walls not only make library supervision of these activities easier but also let the other patrons see how the library is being used. Audiovisual materials have also been brought out of their small sound-proofed closet-like rooms and arranged in lounge-type areas with headsets and equipment which enable each listener or viewer to "do his or her own thing." All of these varied environments and furnishings have been designed to help patrons feel more relaxed and welcome in today's libraries.

In choosing from among these various furnishings, library planners usually look for furniture and equipment that will be functional, durable, and attractive because library furniture must not only be useful but also last a long time with a minimum of maintenance. Good furniture design should follow function and the best designs have often been simple ones with clean attractive lines that will not become dated. Library furniture and equipment should also be convenient and comfortable for the patron to use. If the study chairs do not provide enough leg room under the study table, or if the lounge chairs are too high or too low, patrons will not use them and libraries will regret their purchase. By carefully trying out furniture or equipment as the patron would use them, library planners can ensure that these are functional as well as attractive.

Many librarians have found out the hard way that library equipment, even more than library furniture, must be functional and durable rather than attractive. Until a few years ago, the only equipment most libraries had was a few manual typewriters and perhaps a 16mm film projector. However, the information explosion also inundated libraries with needs for all kinds of audiovisual and technical equipment which they were not prepared to evaluate very effectively. Maintenance problems and the non-standardization of equipment for most media formats did not make comparisons and choices among competing machines easy. In order to help solve this problem, the American Library Association publishes *Library Technology Reports*, which are in-depth evaluative reports on library equipment. These reports have become very useful for librarians faced with such choices.

The equipment found in many libraries today has grown tenfold from those few typewriters and one projector of a few years ago. Besides including all types of audiovisual equipment such as projectors, record and tape cassette players, and videotape machines, some libraries now have video recording studios. Many libraries have TWX or telecommunications devices which receive telefacsimile copies, and some even have hookups for telephone educational networks. Many libraries have large numbers of microform machines for COM catalogs as well as computerized circulation systems and online terminals for catalog or circulation searches. Some libraries also provide personal or home computers for their patrons' use as well as for other library procedures. Libraries of all types, from special to school, are installing electronic theft detection systems. Libraries that are cramped for space have installed compact shelving units which can be moved mechanically back and forth so that the need for aisle space is minimized. These shelving units enable libraries to shelve more books in the same amount of space. In the future, libraries may even use computerized shelving systems in which the books are stored in completely separate buildings and are moved to the circulation desk by keying in book codes at computer terminals. These are just a few examples of the new kinds of technological equipment that libraries have been adding to their collections. The 1980s and 1990s will probably see even greater developments in this area.

These developments in technological equipment have a great affect on the library buildings which house them. Most of the equipment mentioned above requires special engineering features such as special wiring and air conditioning for the video studios and computers, special lighting to enable patrons to use the COM catalog readers, and special telephone or cable TV hookups. Libraries that do not take these requirements into consideration when they purchase this equipment, or when they build or remodel buildings, will find that they will be unable to use this equipment effectively. Thus, the quality of the services provided by libraries will be strongly affected by the building and the facilities which have been designed to support them.

REVIEW QUESTIONS

1. Identify the major characteristics of automation which libraries can effectively take advantage of.

2. Identify the important features of these library automation terms: MARC, OCLC, RLIN, COM, online, data base.

3. Describe some of the major applications of automation in library operations.

4. Identify other technologies found in libraries and give an example of how each one is often used.

5. Describe the major advantages for a library participating in a network.

6. Identify the members of a library planning team and explain the importance for developing a building program statement.

7. Discuss the implications for libraries of the two maxims: "Form should follow function" and "Form should follow imagination, form should follow the future."

8. Identify the major characteristics which should be met by library furnishings and equipment.

SELECTED READINGS

ALA Yearbook: A Review of Library Events. Chicago: American Library Association, 1976.

Brooks, James. *Interior Designs for Libraries.* Chicago: American Library Association, 1979.

DeGennaro, Richard. "From Monopoly to Competition: The Changing Library Network Scene," *Library Journal*, June 1, 1979, pp. 1215-17.

DeGennaro, Richard. "Library Automation: Changing Patterns," *Library Journal*, January 1, 1976, pp. 175-83.

Hamilton, Beth. *Multitype Library Cooperatives.* New York: Bowker, 1977.

Markuson, Barbara. "Automated Circulation: Recent Developments," *American Libraries*, April 1978, pp. 205-211.

"Public Library Facilities for Children," *Illinois Libraries*, vol. 60, no. 10 (December 1978), entire issue.

Saffady, William. *Computer Output Microfilm: Its Library Applications.* Chicago: American Library Association, 1978.

Saffady, William. *Micrographics.* Littleton, CO: Libraries Unlimited, 1978.

Schell, Hal B. *Reader on the Library Building.* [n.p.] Microcard Books, 1975.

10
AUXILIARY LIBRARY SERVICES

The library world has probably been one of the few areas of society which has successfully brought together the user, provider, governing authority, and supplier to work toward one common goal — better library services for all. The library patron, librarian and administrator, library trustee, book publisher, and library supplier have worked cooperatively for many years to serve the welfare of libraries rather than the betterment of their own interests. Only recently have divergent interests developed, such as those of publishers and librarians, which may alter the complexion of this cooperation. Otherwise, such organizations as the American Library Association, Friends of the Library, American Library Trustee Association, American Association of Publishers, and Library Binding Institute have been affiliated with each other since their inception and have combined their efforts in the interest of quality library services.

LIBRARY ORGANIZATIONS

Librarians recognized long ago that they could benefit their libraries by joining together in professional associations to provide mutual encouragement and growth, to exchange information, and to promote libraries in society at large. They believed that their calling was a true profession because it was based on a service orientation and upon highly specialized knowledge and skills. As a profession, librarianship needed an association that would promote library services and librarianship, set library standards, and encourage excellence among its members. Toward these ends, the first major library organization, the American Library Association (ALA), was founded in 1876. Within a century, ALA was able to achieve many of these goals.

The American Library Association achieved many of its goals because of its unique organizational structure. Besides having individual professionals as members, as do other professional associations, ALA has also allowed libraries to join as institutional members. Thus, the interests of both the employee and the employer were represented in one organization. ALA's individual members also differed from members of other professional associations, because ALA allowed anyone interested in promoting quality library services to join the organization rather than restricting membership to professionally trained librarians. This membership policy brought interested citizens or "Friends," trustees, library professional and nonprofessional employees, library supervisors, and library directors into the same organization. Although many librarians through the years have objected to this melting-pot approach, it has provided librarians with a much stronger voice in the marketplace and the political arena than they would have had if they had stood alone.

This strident voice of the American Library Association has been heard on many issues in the last 100 years. ALA has been an active proponent of intellectual freedom, actively opposing censorship and supporting the freedom of individuals to read. It has also worked for the development of nationwide library services by publicizing the plight of the nation's libraries and lobbying in Washington and the state capitols for federal and state funds to support such services. In the late 1970s, ALA pushed for a national library policy and was the guiding light behind the White House Conference on Library and Information Services held in November 1979. Internationally, ALA has cooperated with other national library organizations to develop international standards for cataloging and other areas of common interest. Through its efforts in these many areas, ALA has helped promote library services.

ALA has also helped to promote library services within the libraries themselves. It encouraged the education of library personnel by setting personnel guidelines (*see* chapter 2) and by establishing guidelines for Library/Media Technical Assistant Programs and accrediting procedures for graduate library school programs. ALA has also encouraged the development of library services by setting standards through the years for all types of libraries. It has encouraged the development of services in specialized areas such as services to children and adult education, and has established a comprehensive awards program to recognize and publicize outstanding achievements in the library field. For many years ALA has been strongly involved in the development of quality library collections, authorizing and publishing bibliographies and review magazines (most notably *Booklist* and *Choice*). All of these endeavors, and more, have been supported by a prolific publications program which has not only disseminated library information and promoted library development but has also been very profitable for ALA (*see* Fig. 10-2, page 144).

The American Library Association has been able to accomplish so much in 100 years because its leadership has been strong and its membership diverse and vast. In 1979, ALA had approximately 35,000 members representing all types of interests in all types of libraries. The organization itself is run by elected officers and a council of 100 members elected at large and 51 members elected by the state library association chapters. This council governs the association although its decisions can be put aside by a vote of the membership (which has occurred several times). The operations of the association are carried out by a headquarters staff under the direction of an executive secretary. However, the committees, which are appointed by the elected president, perform a large portion of the policy-making and standard-setting functions of the association. Some critics of ALA consider that this structure does not allow for full member participation in its governance because new members find it difficult to serve on committees or on the council. However, many members have made effective contributions by serving on division or round-table committees.

ALA is divided into numerous divisions, sections, and round-tables which enable members of similar interests to share their ideas and solve their problems. ALA members may join divisions based on the type of library they work in (e.g., school or public library) or the type of work they do (e.g., reference or children's work) (*see* Fig. 10-1, page 143). They may also join round-tables, which are smaller groups concerned with more specific topics, such as the Junior Members Round Table (JMRT) for new ALA members. Many of ALA's divisions are national associations in their own right and provide very dynamic programs to serve their members' needs. ALA also has chapter affiliations with library associations in every state, although members who join one association are not required to join the other. Each state association also has its own state divisions and round-tables so that members can become involved in the decision-making process if they wish to.

Figure 10-1
American Library Association – Organizations*

DIVISIONS
    American Association of School Librarians (AASL)
    American Library Trustee Association (ALTA)
    Association for Library Service to Children (ALSC)
    Association of College and Research Libraries (ACRL)
    Association of Specialized and Cooperative Library Agencies
    Library Administration and Management Association (LAMA)
    Library and Information Technology Association (LITA)
    Public Library Association (PLA)
    Reference and Adult Services Division (RASD)
    Resources and Technical Services Division (RTSD)
    Young Adult Services Division (YASD)

STANDING COMMITTEES
    Accreditation
    Disadvantaged, Office for Library Service to the
    Instruction in the Use of Libraries
    Intellectual Freedom
    International Relations
    Legislation
    Library Education
    Library Personnel Resources, Office for
    Mediation, Arbitration, and Inquiry, Staff Committee on (SCMAI)
    National Library Week
    Professional Ethics
    Program Evaluation and Support
    Publishing
    Research
    Standards
    Women in Librarianship, Status of

ROUND TABLES
    Exhibits Round Table (ERT)
    Federal Librarians Round Table (FLIRT)
    Government Documents Round Table (GODORT)
    Intellectual Freedom Round Table (IFRT)
    Junior Members Round Table (JMRT)
    Library Instruction Round Table
    Social Responsibilities Round Table (SRRT)

---

*The lists in this figure are by no means exhaustive. For names of other ALA-affiliated organizations see the *ALA Handbook of Organization, 1980/1981 and Membership Directory* (Chicago: American Library Association, 1980).

Figure 10-2
American Library Association—Publications*

ACRL Nonprint Media Publications
ALA Washington Newsletter
American Libraries (official ALA periodical)
Booklist
Choice (ACRL)
College and Research Libraries (ACRL)
College and Research Libraries News (ACRL)
Documents to the People (GODORT)
Exhibit Newsletter (ERT)
FLIRT Newsletter (FLIRT)
Friends of the Library National Notebook (LAMA)
Journal of Library Automation (LITA)
Library Resources and Technical Services (RTSD)
Library Technology Reports
Membership Directory
Newsletter on Intellectual Freedom (IF Committee)
Public Libraries (PLA)
Public Library Trustee (ALTA)
RQ (RASD)
RTSD Newsletter (RTSD)
School Media Quarterly (AASL)
SRRT Newsletter (SRRT)
Top of the News (ALSC/YASD)
Women in Libraries (SRRT)

Besides having associations affiliated with it as divisions, ALA also affiliates with many other national and international organizations. About 20 national library organizations such as the American Association of Law Libraries, American Society for Information Science, Association of Research Libraries, and the Catholic Library Association have affiliated formally with ALA as has the Council on Library Technical Assistants (COLT). COLT's primary purpose is to represent the trained LMTA's interest within the field of librarianship. COLT achieves its goals by working with ALA as well as developing its own programs.

ALA does not only send representatives to other organizations but the association itself belongs to many other educational and social organizations. ALA is an active member of the International Federation of Library Associations (IFLA) and works with the Library Association (British) and the Canadian Library Association to accomplish joint projects such as the *Anglo-American Cataloguing Rules.* Needless to say, ALA has maintained a very close relationship with the Library of Congress over the years, and units of both organizations have worked on many joint projects. Thus, the American Library Association has had a greater effect on the library world than its own membership activities would show.

*This list is by no means exhaustive. For titles of publications by other ALA-affiliated organizations see *ALA Handbook of Organization, 1980/1981 and Membership Directory* (Chicago: American Library Association, 1980).

Two other organizations ALA is affiliated with in different ways are very important to the library world. The American Library Trustee Association (ALTA) became a division of ALA in the 1970s and works closely with another division, the Public Library Association (PLA). ALTA is probably the only organization for employers which belongs to an organization controlled by its employees. Its major goal is to take full responsibility for helping trustees to carry out their roles effectively and to develop quality library service. ALTA tries to fulfill this goal by working with other divisions and state library trustee associations to educate trustees through workshops and publications.

The other association that works closely with ALA and ALTA is Friends of the Library. Members of this group are interested citizens who care about libraries and who want to help libraries provide the best possible services. They have become excellent community spokespersons for local library services. Friends groups have helped pass library referenda, have raised funds for library buildings, purchases, and services, and have generally served as library consciousness-raising groups in their local communities. They are affiliated with ALA through the Friends of Libraries Committee of the Public Relations Section of the Library Administration and Management Association, one of ALA's divisions. This division provides educational programs and publications for local Friends groups. Thus, ALA has close links with both the employers and the users of its services. It is this coalition which has helped forge a unified library world.

As much as the American Library Association has done for the library world, however, it has not truly served librarians as a professional organization. By allowing anyone to join and by including institutions as well as individuals as members, it has emphasized its purpose of promoting library services rather than the welfare of librarians. Many librarians since the 1960s have criticized ALA for not taking an active role in library employment, salaries, and working conditions. Although ALA responded through informal channels, as an organization it did not seem inclined toward following the lead of the American Nursing Association (ANA) and becoming a quasi-union for its members. To do so, ALA would have to change its organization structure and it would probably lose its tax exempt status and some of its financing. Thus, many librarians since 1960 have begun to look elsewhere for an organization that will help them improve their employment conditions.

The 1970s marked a rise in librarians' forming library unions or joining other unions and associations because of several important factors. Primarily, libraries were becoming larger, more complex, and more bureaucratic so that librarians felt excluded from the decision-making process. At the same time, the introduction of technology into libraries, combined with the loss of library revenues, brought about changes and reductions in library staffs. Finally, society's attitude toward professionals and public employees' joining unions had changed. Many laws were passed which allowed public employees to bargain collectively. Many professional associations such as the National Education Association (NEA), American Association of University Professors (AAUP), and the ANA were becoming quasi-unions and bargaining collectively for their members. In this climate, many librarians no longer felt "less professional" if they joined together in unions.

The 1970s saw a significant growth in the number of librarians and other library staff members joining union organizations. Library unions developed in large public libraries in areas where membership in unions in general was strong such as the East, the Midwest, and California. These library unions were often composed of both professional and nonprofessional library employees and negotiated with government officials or library administrators for salaries and conditions of employment. Sometimes the staffs of an individual library would form local staff associations which negotiated for salaries and conditions of employment. Some library staff members joined public service employee unions such as the American Federation of State, County and Municipal Employees (AFSCME) and the Service Employees International Union (SEIU). Librarians who worked in school and academic libraries usually joined organizations that represented the other professionals in their institution such as NEA, AFT (American Federation of Teachers), or AAUP, and special librarians often joined the Newspaper Guild.

However, in all of these organizations there did not seem to be any strong interest in developing a national library union or organization concerned solely with the welfare of professional librarians. In 1975, the National Librarians Association (NLA) was founded to fill this gap. NLA's membership was limited to professional librarians and its goals were to protect and advance the concerns of professional librarians. This organization may emerge in the 1980s as the national voice of professional librarians. However, because of the nature of cooperation among librarians, NLA will probably exist side by side with ALA rather than compete strongly with it.

PUBLISHING

Libraries have been closely allied with the publishing field for many years. At state and national library conventions, publishers have been present and active not only as library exhibitors, but as partners in library programs and the awarding of library prizes. Book publishers and librarians have cooperated in supporting intellectual freedom and the freedom to read as well as in encouraging the spread of reading and the use of libraries through the National Book Awards and National Library Week. Publishers have cooperated in establishing cataloging programs such as Cataloging-in-Publication (CIP) which includes printing Library of Congress cataloging in books as they are published. They have also worked together in developing International Standard Book and Serial Numbers (ISBN and ISSN) so that each edition or serial title can be easily identified. However, despite these cooperative ventures, publishers and librarians have often had a love-hate relationship. At times their vested interests have brought them into conflict on such subjects as library discounts, copyright laws, and fair use violations of such laws. Whether or not these latter problems will be ironed out in the 1980s will have a great effect on the future cooperation between publishers and libraries.

Publishers were originally afraid that strong library development and use would limit the purchases of their publications. However, as libraries grew, publishers found that people continued to buy books. After World War II, they also found that reading was stimulated by the increases in population, income, and leisure time, and by the increased interest in education. Contrary to expectations, book clubs founded in the 1920s and the growth of TV in the late 1950s and 1960s stimulated reading and book sales rather than diminished them. Also, the phenomenal sales of paperback books and magazines only seemed to stimulate rather than compete with traditional book sales. After Sputnik, publishers found that the availability of federal funds for libraries to purchase materials had further expanded the publishing markets. Thus, since its beginnings in the late nineteenth century, the publishing industry has grown extensively.

The publishing industry not only grew in size, but also changed in form. The mass production of paperbacks and reprints helped revolutionize book publishing. Many publishers began to publish and sell paperbacks as well as trade books, and sometimes they published a title in trade and paperback editions simultaneously. Sometimes, publishers even published books in both hard copy and microform to satisfy the growing market for microforms among libraries. By 1976, there were over 400 micropublishers publishing doctoral dissertations, serials, research reports, government documents, and books—many of which were only available in microforms.

Serials were another major type of publication which proliferated in the 1960s and 1970s. The publication of serials had increased from a few thousand titles in the 1950s to over 70,000 titles by 1976. Libraries that were hardpressed to house books and serials often turned to microform copies to solve their libraries' storage dilemmas. The result was that libraries often had subscriptions not only to the serial itself but to the microform copy of the serial volume as well. The 1970s also saw the splintering of periodicals into several publications. Some serials spawned new publications (e.g., *People* magazine from *Time*), others were divided into two serials (e.g., *Publishers' Weekly* and *Weekly Record*), and some periodicals which had ceased publication were even reinstated (e.g., *Saturday Evening Post* and *Life*). However, the bulk of the serial increases was due to the increase in scientific and technical journals and to the many specialized or "little magazines" which usually struggled for a while and then quietly folded.

The growth of publishing since 1950 has also influenced the growth of publishing firms. Most publishing companies began as private firms run by individual families which published for specific publics or published special subjects. So many of these family firms were merged with other publishers and companies in the 1960s and 1970s that many people (especially authors) became concerned about their anti-competitive implications. The purchase of such publishing firms as Praeger and Fawcett by CBS; Random House, Knopf, Pantheon and Ballantine by RCA; and R. R. Bowker by Xerox caused librarians to wonder if corporate profits might begin to replace literary expression as the guiding factor in book publishing. This seemed a strong possibility since only about 200 out of 3,000 firms were responsible for over 70% of a year's publications.

However, as a contrast to this merging of companies at the top, many specialized and small presses had developed further down the publishing ladder. Many small or little presses developed which concentrated on quality literary publications while other presses concentrated on strong subject publications such as West in law and Mosby in medicine and nursing. The two venerable library presses, R. R. Bowker and H. W. Wilson Co., were joined by newer companies such as Scarecrow Press, Shoe String Press, and Libraries Unlimited to satisfy the needs of the library community for research and bibliographic materials. University presses and professional associations which had developed strong publishing programs to produce scholarly works of the highest caliber began to expand their range to appeal to a broader readership. Finally, the U.S. Government Printing Office which prints U.S. government documents, had become the largest printer in the world, producing titles under the imprint of innumerable government agencies and organizations. For the most part, this variety of publishing companies seemed able to provide sufficient outlets for varying literary and subject publications in the 1970s rather than stifling such efforts.

A number of publishing associations enabled publishers and others to keep a watch on these developments. The American Association of Publishers (AAP), the American Booksellers Association (ABA), the Children's Book Council (CBC), the National Association of College Stores, and other associations worked together to improve the quality of publishing as well as to encourage the sale of books. The AAP, the ABA, and the CBC also formed affiliates with ALA to discuss mutual problems and issues which concerned members of all the associations. These problems and issues increased greatly as the 1970s saw tighter library budgets and inflationary rises in book and serial prices.

As publishers of all types of materials moved into the 1980s, they had some major problems to resolve. Most of these problems revolved around inflationary rises in paper and production costs which caused book and serial prices to soar. In fact, book prices have increased from 50-100% since the late 1960s, and many serial prices have risen from 100-300%. Besides price increases, the increase in production of books and serials rose so dramatically that overproduction became one problem while the inadequate distribution of these publications was yet another problem. In order to solve other problems brought on by rising postal costs, some publishers even turned to home delivery of their subscription books and serials.

All of these problems came to a head in the controversy between librarians and publishers over the new copyright law which went into effect in 1978. This law acknowledged the "fair use" principle by allowing the copying of a small number of pages or articles from a periodical or book within a specific period of time for an individual's use without paying a royalty. Libraries welcomed "fair use" as a way that they could share their library materials through Interlibrary Loan without being required to purchase every book or serial. Publishers objected to it for the same reasons—that librarians would not have to buy their own copies or to pay royalties. Publishers were so concerned that they should receive "fair compensation" that they established the Copyright Clearance Center (CCC) to handle financial transactions between the copyright holder and the user. However, as of 1979 the CCC seemed to be running into difficulties. Another solution which may develop instead to solve this copyright dilemma may involve special assessment fees or higher serial subscription prices for materials purchased by library networks or destined for resource sharing. However, no matter what the solution to the copyright problem is, the real question behind it is whether or not library resource sharing will substantially affect the future sales and publication of books and serials. As we move into the 1980s, neither librarians nor publishers know what the answer will be.

LIBRARY SUPPLIERS

Libraries and their suppliers have always enjoyed a close working relationship since the first library supply house (Library Bureau) was founded by Melvil Dewey in 1876. Library suppliers have developed library supplies, equipment, furniture, and services which met library needs and specifications and which could not be purchased locally for a reasonable price. By specializing in the library market, library suppliers have been able to cater their products and services to this special market. This has enabled many suppliers to develop new products in anticipation of or in response to changing library requirements. In fact, it has been library suppliers who have often furthered changes in the library field.

Commercial "for profit" library suppliers exist in every area of the library field. There are wholesalers or jobbers for books, serials, audiovisual materials, and microforms. There are library binders who bind materials to library specifications. There are suppliers who furnish specialized library supplies, equipment, and furniture, and there are commercial services which provide library computerized services and cataloging services. Since all of these suppliers are generally interested in making a profit, they recognize that service is often the most important product they have to offer to libraries. For this reason, many suppliers employ professional librarians on their staffs. These librarians and other trained salespersons are able to discuss problems with librarians in the field and to offer suggestions and solutions. They are often consulted by librarians when problems arise or changes are planned. It is this working partnership between libraries and library suppliers that has encouraged the development of many recent improvements in library supplies, equipment, and services.

Library wholesalers or jobbers have based their entire business on this relationship. They work on the principle of supplying libraries with books, serials, microforms, or audiovisual materials from many different publishers more reasonably or more easily than libraries could purchase these materials for themselves. Jobbers enable libraries to place one order, receive all or most of their materials from one source, and pay one invoice. Jobbers are able to perform this service because they maintain large stocks of newly published titles from many different publishers, and they can order other titles from many more. These services free librarians from ordering materials from thousands of publishers, large and small, American and foreign.

There are many different kinds of jobbers for many different materials. Book jobbers may be general jobbers supplying all book titles in all subjects, or they may be special jobbers specializing in one type of work, such as out-of-print books, or in particular subjects. Some book jobbers such as Baker & Taylor may specialize in stocking new book titles and shipping them out quickly while others such as Blackwell of North America may specialize in providing special orders such as foreign publications. In recent years, serial jobbers have tended to merge with a few large subscription jobbers or agencies such as EBSCO and F. W. Faxon. Other jobbers have developed to sell library materials such as microforms or audiovisual materials. Some of these jobbers have also specialized. Xerox University Microfilms provides microform subscriptions to periodicals and microform copies of dissertations, and Bell & Howell provides microforms of newspapers, particularly retrospective collections of such papers. A few major jobbers have also begun to sell all types of media forms from books and films to slides and tapes.

No matter what kinds of material jobbers may handle, many of them provide similar services. Many jobbers will not only provide the materials but will also provide specialized cataloging in many different forms, as well as complete material processing. Jobbers also provide preview announcements of new titles in stock or new titles librarians might want to buy. Many also provide approval plans (sending materials on approval for the librarian to review), collection development plans, and lease plans for new and popular library materials. They will assist librarians in the bidding or billing processes and will usually fit into the libraries' acquisitions routine rather than requiring special ones designed to fit the jobbers' needs. Because of all of these services, many libraries of all types will usually purchase their materials through jobbers of one type or another.

Although library binders are not true jobbers, they may sometimes function in that capacity. Many binders in the 1960s and 1970s began to purchase books from publishers and to rebind them in "library bindings" and then to sell them to libraries. This service arose as libraries found that books which were library bound, or bound according to stiff library standards, before they were circulated were more durable than trade bindings. This development was possible because the Library Binding Institute (LBI), made up of library binding firms, had worked for many years with librarians to establish binding standards for many different types of materials. These standards have become so much a part of the library world that the LBI standard for Class A library binding is generally used by libraries as a criterion in bid specifications. Besides prebinding new books, library binders also bind serials and rebind old books. Although serial binding used to make up a large portion of the binding for many firms, it has decreased as libraries have purchased serials in microform. Unfortunately, this decrease has also decreased the number of library binding firms. In order to retain as much library binding business as possible, library binders usually provide many services to help libraries meet their material preservation needs.

Library supply houses or vendors, which provide specialized library supplies, equipment, and furniture, have been working with libraries since 1876 when both the ALA and the first supply house were founded. These houses are generally mail order houses, similar to Sears, which provide specialized library supplies. The library suppliers order materials to be manufactured to library specifications, and their own specifications, and make these materials available to libraries through attractive catalogs. These catalogs usually include the basic library supplies, equipment, and furniture for circulation, cataloging, processing, etc., as well as new items which their firms hope will also become basic items in the future. Although the major houses such as Gaylord, Demco, and BroDart usually have only one distribution center, they can usually provide their items more reasonably and more quickly than local suppliers can. These houses, as well as Library Bureau, Buckstaff, and others, can also supply such items as furniture and equipment built to library specifications and, therefore, able to satisfy library needs. Besides supplying items to satisfy a library's present needs, these supply houses have been very active in developing new library materials and systems, such as circulation and theft-detection systems. Without their important influence, most libraries might still be using library supplies which were useful in 1876.

Library suppliers have changed and grown tremendously in the 1960s and the 1970s, and no where is this more evident than in the cataloging and computerizing services which are presently offered to libraries. Many firms are offering cataloging services to libraries, from catalog cards printed to fit their own needs to book and COM catalogs designed for their own collections. Cataloging services will often provide "instant libraries" or "opening day collections" of books processed and ready to place on the shelves. They may also provide professional library staff to go into a library and catalog a library collection. Many cataloging services are also using MARC tapes from the Library of Congress to produce bibliographic data banks for libraries or to provide online cataloging.

The 1970s have seen a growth of computerized services such as OCLC as well as commercial ventures such as Gaylord and CLSI (CL Systems, Inc.); the 1980s will probably bring many more. The minicomputer and the microprocessor have enabled companies to provide "turn-key" systems which libraries can plug in and use. These operations may vary from circulation systems, to acquisition systems, to inventory control systems. The 1980s will probably bring many more such systems designed specifically for library operations. They may come from commercial vendors or from quasi-profit organizations such as OCLC and the Washington Library Network, but they will come, and libraries will probably be using many of them by 1985 or 1990.

In using all of these library service companies and suppliers, the librarian and the library staff have always realized that the major purpose of these organizations is to make a profit. Librarians have, therefore, turned to these companies for advice but have not necessarily accepted that advice as the final answer to their problems. Most librarians will talk with other librarians about supplies, services, and equipment before they will make their final decisions about any purchases. They will also check ALA's Library Technology Reports which are in-depth evaluative reports on every aspect of a product or a system. Only after such thorough investigation will most librarians commit themselves to a jobber, binder, or other type of library service agency. Thus, it is by developing a healthy respect for the strengths as well as the limitations of their library suppliers that libraries have been able to work with them over the years to develop and improve library procedures and services.

REVIEW QUESTIONS

1. Describe the major purpose, the organization, and the governing structure of the American Library Association.

2. Identify the complete names of the following organizations: ALA, NLA, ALTA, COLT, NEA, AAUP, AFSCME, AASL, ABA, LBI.

3. Describe the areas of cooperation and the areas of disagreement among publishers and librarians.

4. Identify the types of jobbers which serve libraries and list the kinds of services they offer.

5. Describe the evaluation process a library should follow when choosing a library supplier, jobber, or binder.

SELECTED READINGS

ALA Handbook of Organization, 1978/1979. Chicago: American Library Association, 1978.

ALA Yearbook: A Review of Library Events. Chicago: American Library Association, 1976- .

The Copyright Dilemma: Proceedings of a Conference Held at Indiana University. April 14-15, 1977. Edited by Herbert S. White. Chicago: American Library Association, 1978.

Guyton, Theodore Lewis. *Unionization: The Viewpoint of Librarians.* Chicago: American Library Association, 1975.

Harlan, Robert H. "Trends in Modern American Book Publishing," *Library Trends*, vol. 27, no. 3 (Winter 1979), pp. 389-407.

Roth, Harold L., ed. "An Analysis and Survey of Commercial Library Supply Houses," *Library Trends*, vol. 24, no. 4 (April 1976), entire issue.

11
THE DEVELOPMENT OF
GOOD LIBRARY SERVICE

Libraries throughout the ages have developed to satisfy specific needs within their societies, and a library's importance within a society has often been determined by how well it has satisfied these needs. Libraries, such as those in Rome and in Renaissance Europe, flourished because they provided for the aesthetic, cultural, scientific, recreational, and educational needs of their patrons. They were able to provide for these needs by acquiring manuscripts and books, preserving them from harm and destruction, and making them available for patrons to use. Although today's libraries no longer follow the examples of these earlier libraries by acquiring their books through ransacking other libraries or preserving their books by chaining them to the shelves for safety, they do still make their materials available for their patrons to use.

Over the years, this concept of availability of materials has evolved into a philosophy of library service which is made up of several important elements. These elements include: access to information in all its forms, stated objectives which a library should fulfill, and policies and procedures that encourage and develop the best possible service for a library's public. How well this philosophy is being fulfilled by today's libraries, both generally and individually, will determine how important our libraries will become in tomorrow's society.

INTELLECTUAL FREEDOM

Access to information in all of its forms has been provided by American libraries in response to the basic needs of a democratic society. In contrast to other societies, a democracy is dependent upon an educated citizenry which can make informed decisions. Thus, subscription libraries, public libraries, academic libraries, and school libraries grew up over the years to satisfy this need of their citizens for education and information. Libraries became repositories of information and culture which allowed citizens to read and examine differing philosophies and theories and to make their own political decisions. From this need has evolved the principle that each individual has the right freely to obtain and to read or view materials without restriction by others. This principle has been identified as "Intellectual Freedom" and has its basis in the First Amendment to the U.S. Constitution: "Congress shall make no law abridging the freedom of speech or of the press or the right of the people peaceably to assemble and to petition the government for a redress of grievances."

Although even the U.S. Congress has enacted laws at different times which have limited these rights, the public and the courts have generally upheld the belief that a democracy can only be strengthened if its citizens have access to all viewpoints on a subject. In spite of the fears which attempted to silence opposition to governmental policies through the Sedition Act, the Espionage Act, and the paranoia of the McCarthy era, our democracy has not fallen to foreign powers. Even the opposition of citizens in the 1960s to the Vietnam War eventually resulted in open discussion of the subject which legally brought about changes in governmental policy. Thus, in the 200 years of the United States' existence, its citizens have proven that freedom of speech and freedom of the press can provide an educated citizenry capable of making informed decisions.

However, there are many would-be censors in today's society who believe they should be able to restrict this access for others. Many people believe that ideas which they disagree with or find offensive should not exist in the marketplace of ideas. Such persons are often acting upon very sincere beliefs that society will be debased or debauched if such ideas are allowed to circulate freely. They also believe that distribution of even small amounts of such ideas will be like a chink in a dike which will slowly widen to allow a whole river or ocean of ideas and speech which they believe will threaten and destroy their society. Such censors point to the relaxed morals of the 1970s and the permissive society which allows "obscene" material to appear in books, films, and on television as proof that the dike has already broken.

This attitude was given impetus by the U.S. Supreme Court decision in 1973 in which Justice Berger identified guidelines for setting community standards for obscene material in that "the work in question, taken as a whole, must appeal to prurient interest as determined by applying contemporary community standards and that the work, taken as a whole, lacks serious literary, artistic, political or scientific value."[1] ("Prurient" has been defined as being obsessively interested in "improper" matters, especially of a sexual nature.[2]) By this ruling, Justice Berger authorized local communities to determine what they considered to be of prurient interest and to be lacking in serious literary, artistic, political, or scientific value. Such a ruling is very difficult to defend in a democratic society if one considers its implications. Many of the world's greatest works of art and literature could be determined prurient by some local community. Michelangelo's statue of David would surely offend some people, and the accounts of David and Bethsheba in the Bible could just as easily offend others.

What are the kinds of ideas which the would-be censors object to and would limit others' access to? These ideas range from explicit descriptions and pictures of nudity and sexual matters, to the use of obscene language and of language which, though acceptable in most societies, some people find objectionable. Some parents of small children have objected to the concept of "vomit" in a preschool children's book, while another parent objected to pictures of the birth of a calf in a book for elementary school children. Other parents and citizens have objected to such subjects as drugs for teenagers in *Go Ask Alice*, a realistic portrayal of life in John Steinbeck's *Grapes of Wrath*, and a boy's growing up in that most censored of all books — *Catcher in the Rye*. (Still considered by many to be the modern classic in young adult reading.) For many years books on communism were censored, and in recent years books have been objected to on the grounds that they were racist or sexist. Even the government has joined the censorship ranks by censoring materials which officials felt were threatening or a danger to national security.

No one would deny anyone the right to disagree with these kinds of materials and ideas. However, many people can object to the manner in which these objections are often raised. Persons who object to "obscene" or "filthy" words and pictures usually have not read the complete book or watched the entire film. They have judged the material guilty without evaluating whether or not, "The work, taken as a whole, lacks serious literary, artistic, political or scientific value." Thus, some persons concerned with obscenity have objected to the "obscene" language of such classics as *Andersonville* or *To Kill a Mockingbird* without recognizing that the true obscenity is really man's degradation of his fellow man.

Because censors fear the ideas contained in the materials they object to, they often assume that the defender of these materials must approve of them. This is not necessarily the case. Many defenders of a book or a film may not approve of its content, particularly if it contains materials that may appeal only to prurient interests. However, defenders of a censored item realize that what is at stake is not an interest in obscene or prurient materials but the "liberty to think." They believe that if the right to protect "works of serious literary, artistic, political or scientific value" is not fought in every case, a chink will appear in the dike that will let through an ocean of restrictive censorship. Because this censorship could ultimately end in the reduction of many of our freedoms, opponents of censorship are constantly working for preserving "intellectual freedom" in all of its forms.

Libraries have moved to the forefront of the defenders of the rights of free speech and free press because they are the repositories of a society's ideas and information. No library has existed for long which only collected and made available those ideas which were approved by the ruling authority. Even the Roman Catholic Church's Vatican Library, one of the greatest libraries in the world, contains other ideas and doctrines besides those which are accepted church doctrines. Could libraries in a democratic society do any less? The answer of American libraries has generally been a resounding "no!" Throughout their history, libraries have fought censorship and restrictions on the kinds of materials they could include in their collections. In 1948, the American Library Association adopted *The Library Bill of Rights* (*see* Appendix A) which has subsequently been adopted as formal policy by many libraries. This document, "recognizes that censorship of any materials and in any guise eventually affects the library ... [it] provides libraries with principles for opposing censorship and promoting intellectual freedom, in the broadest senses."[3]

Although the basic policies expressed in *The Library Bill of Rights* are only those which a democratic society would seem to support, there have been many people over the years who have objected to them. In the 1950s, many libraries were attacked for containing books which were written about communism or by communist authors. These censors felt that such books should either be removed from the libraries' shelves, labeled as the works of communists, or purged of the offending paragraphs or pages. They even demanded that the materials be prohibited from being placed on the libraries' shelves in the first place. Other censors have objected to materials being made available to children or young people which they consider to be for "mature" audiences. Thus, there has been controversy for years over whether sex education materials should be placed on a library's open shelves for children to get as they need them.

Censorship of materials is not the only obstacle to complete service that has faced our libraries. In the South, many objected to black people entering their libraries so many libraries limited their facilities to members of the white race. (Although a few cities did develop two public library systems, one for each race.) In order to help libraries respond to such challenges, the ALA adopted the

Freedom to Read statement in 1953 and revised it in 1972 (*see* Appendix B). This statement supported the principles of the *Library Bill of Rights* by defining "the rights and responsibilities of publishers and librarians in maintaining the freedom of Americans to read what they choose."[4] Thus, it was formally recognized that the library in a democratic society should not be a watchdog of culture and a repository of "good" books but should make available materials of all views and expressions. For the first time, it was also acknowledged that publishers, library boards, and librarians do not have to approve of every idea or presentation they publish or add to their collections. Instead, they have a responsibility to encourage and publish books on all views and to resist any attempts to remove such materials from library collections.

The principles of intellectual freedom expressed in the *Library Bill of Rights* and the *Freedom to Read* statement were further expanded by interpretive statements from the ALA. These documents provided librarians and library boards with philosophical ammunition in their struggles against censorship. The Freedom to Read Foundation, founded in 1969, gave legal assistance to such struggles. ALA also encouraged libraries to adopt the *Library Bill of Rights* and to develop material selection policies based on its principles. Libraries were also urged to develop policy statements for the retention and reconsideration of library materials before the need for such policies arose. It was recommended that these policies include a complaint form for the questioner to fill out. Such forms usually ask whether or not the person is operating as an individual or as the representative of a group, whether the entire work has been read or viewed, and exactly what was being objected to. By following such principles and policies, many libraries found they were able to eliminate censorship complaints or at least to reduce or minimize their effects on the community.

That libraries would be more and more likely to have censorship problems in the future became apparent throughout the 1970s. The political mood of the country shifted toward a conservatism at the same time that religious beliefs became more fundamental. These factors caused people to look for simplistic solutions to complicated problems. American adults became disillusioned with the youth culture and with what they perceived as a "promiscuous and selfish society," while the youth looked in horror at the "materialistic society" of their elders. At the same time, the traditional middle class library patrons had difficulty relating to the literature of the lower classes which was often expressed in very raw terms. Thus, the local library, with the range of ideas in its collection, became an easy target for the arrows shot by persons of many different political and moral persuasions. Some persons objected to obscene language; others objected to the portrayal of sex. Some objected to the racism of *Little Black Sambo*; others objected to the stereotype of a policeman as a pig in *Sylvester and the Magic Pebble*. Some persons objected because their child was allowed to take out a particular title, while others objected because their child was refused a book. Not only parents, but children, teachers, administrators, school or library board members, and city officials all complained about library materials.

Sometimes librarians and their staffs have even encouraged censorship in several ways. In some instances, librarians have not challenged the removal of library materials because they did not want to fight their administrators, boards, or communities. At other times, librarians have not purchased materials they considered objectionable or feared members of the community would disapprove of. This indirect censorship may be as injurious to a library's intellectual health as all of the other censorship attempts combined.

But, if librarians cannot object to a book, does this mean that they must buy every item that is published, regardless of its merits? No, librarians will still use selection criteria which include the accuracy of the material, whether the manner in which it is presented contributes to its literary, artistic, or scientific value, and the importance of the item in light of the library's budget. However, what it does mean is that the librarians must make decisions based upon good selection techniques rather than upon personal preferences. Because a librarian, staff member, or board member does not, for instance, like to read science fiction, does not mean that he or she should keep it from the library.

Although some librarians across the nation have practiced censorship either directly or indirectly, many more have spoken up and fought for intellectual freedom. Many librarians have worked with their staffs, administrators, or governing boards to develop a climate for intellectual freedom. They have discouraged censorship in their communities by advocating freedom of access to ideas. When presented with censorship complaints, these librarians have stood firm, explained their positions well, and, sometimes, won over the opponents. In some cases, they have had to go to court or seek the assistance of ALA or the American Civil Liberties Union (ACLU), but they have often won these battles for freedom. As long as there are librarians, boards and staff members to fight these battles, the freedom of speech and freedom of the press should remain alive and well.

LIBRARY ETHICS

Intellectual freedom and the freedom of speech and of the press will not survive for long in libraries unless they become integral parts of a library's philosophy of service. Unless a library's objectives, policies, and procedures reflect these beliefs, that library will not be fulfilling the needs of a democratic society. In order to ensure these needs are met, librarians, staff members, and board members must always be on the alert to choose and review policies and procedures that will contribute to intellectual freedom. Librarians and library staff members must be particularly careful that their own personal attitudes and philosophies contribute positively to a library's philosophy of service. This positive contribution can be facilitated if the library staff understands the ethics or rules and standards governing the conduct of library personnel.

"Library ethics" refers to the personal conduct of an individual in his or her relationship with others in libraries. These ethics are well defined in the *Statement on Professional Ethics*, approved by ALA Council in 1975 (*see* Appendix C). Although this statement was written long ago for professional librarians, the ethics it describes could also be followed by all library staff and board members. Library ethics include an individual's relationship with library patrons, fellow library staff members, and library supervisors and administrators (including the governing authority). Although the ethics are prefaced with the word "library," they are really just refinements of the moral and humanitarian principles that are expected to govern any person's behavior in our society. That they are library ethics means they are further based on the library principles as adopted in *The Library Bill of Rights* and the *Freedom to Read* statement.

Besides being based on these documents, the prescribed library ethics governing the relationships with library patrons are also based upon "library etiquette" or upon commonly accepted practices of courtesy. Primarily, library staff members should treat all library patrons as fairly and impartially as possible. This would mean that, in a public library, a senior citizen and a small child would receive the same service as would a board member. It would also mean that students' needs would be given the same consideration as teachers' and administrators' needs in schools and colleges. Too many times, librarians have provided services to their patrons based upon who they are rather than upon what their needs are.

Library etiquette also would dictate that each library patron be treated as an individual. This would mean that a staff member should look at a patron when he or she is talking, address the patron by his or her name, and use correct Standard English rather than slang or library jargon. Questions should be answered pleasantly rather than begrudgingly (no matter how many times a question such as "Where is the children's room?" has been asked). Referrals to other staff members should include the staff member's name and complete directions for finding the person. Such statements as "Go see the librarian in Reference" do not communicate very much to a library patron who does not know what or where "reference" is.

Another common courtesy is also a very important library ethic. That ethic is to treat a patron's question as a private conversation between the patron and the staff member. This would prevent delicate matters from being broadcast throughout the library (e.g., a patron might not want others to know that she is going to have a baby). Also, as in private conversations, the library staff member should not repeat conversations to others unless it is necessary to satisfy the patron's library need. If such confidential information is repeated, it not only might harm the patron but might also destroy that person's faith in the library's integrity.

An added advantage to treating every question as a private matter is that it enables the library to limit a citizen's censorship complaint to the few people involved. If a library staff member does receive such a complaint, he or she should immediately turn it over to a professional librarian. The librarian should then explain the library's materials selection policy and the principles of *The Library Bill of Rights* and the *Freedom to Read* statement. A library's policy for reconsidering materials should be followed and the patron asked to fill out a complaint form. All staff members involved should remember to be courteous and to treat the complaint in an impersonal, yet polite and serious, manner. They should avoid giving any personal opinions of the material and, at all costs, they should not lose their tempers or get into arguments with patrons over the material being objected to. By handling the complaint or situation in a professional and ethical manner, the library staff will be better able to defend the work in question and to support the principle of intellectual freedom.

Besides protecting conversations with patrons, library ethics would also protect the individual person's right to read and check out materials without this information being divulged to other sources. In the name of national security, there have been attempts by the federal government to obtain such information. In Atlanta and Milwaukee, the U.S. Treasury Department demanded to review circulation records of public library patrons. Other libraries may have such attempts made by administrators or library board members. Therefore, library staff members should recognize that this is an invasion of the reader's intellectual privacy that should be fought whenever it occurs.

The second important area of library ethics concerns the relationships among all of the library staff members. Although common courtesy is important in this area, there are more specific ethics or rules and procedures which also apply. First, although library employees may become great personal friends, this is not necessary for a library to develop a friendly and harmonious atmosphere. Such an atmosphere can develop if each employee respects every other employee and the strengths which he or she brings to the job. This respect should enable employees from several different levels or backgrounds to work harmoniously in accomplishing the objectives and goals of the library. Secondly, if there are differences of opinion or problems between employees, the people involved should sit down and try to resolve them. (Complaining in the lounge to friends will only aggravate a problem.) If such a discussion does not eliminate the problem, the employee should then go to his or her immediate supervisor and explain the situation and what has been done about it. A staff member should not go to a higher supervisor or a supervisor in another department without first talking with his or her own supervisor. This procedure follows the line of supervision and is essential for keeping the communications lines open. If problems not solved at one level are taken to the next higher level, it is a good procedure to inform all of the persons involved. This practice will help staff members develop a spirit of trust and cooperation.

If a library employee is concerned with or has a question about a policy or procedure, he or she should not just criticize it but should discuss it with the supervisor. In the discussion, the employee might learn more about the background or objectives behind a policy or procedure. Only then can the employee make a valid criticism or offer possible alternatives. Although no one likes to hear chronic complaints, most supervisors will welcome suggestions that are well-reasoned and that follow these outlined steps. Since librarians are particularly charged by the *Statement on Professional Ethics* to "endeavor to change those [policies] which conflict with the spirit of the Library Bill of Rights," they should welcome suggestions by staff members along these lines.

The final important area of library ethics concerns the relationships of an employee with his or her supervisors and administrators, including the governing authority. All employees in a library should understand the lines of supervision and recognize which persons have the authority to assign duties, change schedules, approve leaves, make evaluations or reprimands, and hire and fire the library staff.

In most libraries, these duties are split among various levels of supervisors subject to final approval by a board. By understanding the authority and responsibility of each of these levels, a staff member could become a better employee. Then, he or she would better understand that a librarian might be unable to make desirable changes because the principal or library board disagreed. An employee would also realize that although he or she is a friend or relative of a board member, no special privileges should be granted by the librarian. On the other hand, board members should also understand that, for ethical reasons, they should not get personally involved in matters which the librarians and staff should be handling. If all of the persons involved in libraries, including librarians, staff members, and board members accepted these obligations to develop positive working relationships with each other, libraries might better be able to direct all of their energies into providing good library service.

Unfortunately, some library staffs, administrators, and boards seem to be at odds with each other. Some library staffs seem more interested in maintaining the status quo than in initiating new library services desired by the board. Some administrators seem more interested in establishing themselves in the library world than in directing their library operations. And some boards are more interested in cutting budgets and keeping salaries low than in providing library services. Because libraries are service-based institutions, such conflicting attitudes can severely affect the levels of library service which are given to a community. If this begins to occur in a library, all persons involved should take stock of their positions. Library staff members may find that a union will enable them to bring pressure upon a penny-pinching board. Library board members may find that working cooperatively with a staff association or union might help enlist support for new services and ideas. However, if staff members find they cannot ethically work within the objectives and philosophy being carried out by the administration and board, perhaps they should resign and work from the outside to change the system. If board members find they cannot ethically agree with board-adopted library policies or with *The Library Bill of Rights* and what it means for a library, perhaps they should also resign. Only if all of the persons connected with a library are totally committed to carrying out its policies and procedures based upon library ethics might a library be able to fulfill its philosophy of library service.

THE LMTA'S PLACE IN THE LIBRARY

In order to understand the LMTA's role in library service, it is important to know where the LMTA usually fits in a library's organizational structure. Many libraries use the LMTA effectively as a paraprofessional and assign authority and responsibilities which utilize an LMTA's training. Other libraries, such as special libraries or small school libraries, may inappropriately give professional librarian responsibilities to an LMTA. And some libraries may treat the LMTA as a high-level clerk and not assign any real authority or responsibility to this position. How each library handles the LMTA position will usually depend upon the outlook of the library administration.

Library administrators who try to build an effective library organization are usually among the first to reorganize their personnel structures to utilize the LMTA. This reorganization often evaluates the professional and nonprofessional duties of its librarians and redistributes the nonprofessional duties to other personnel. For example, until a few years ago, many libraries had circulation librarians. However, when these positions were reevaluated, it was determined that only a few of their responsibilities required professional expertise and these few responsibilities could be handled by the public services librarian. Thus, many libraries have replaced their circulation librarians with LMTA circulation supervisors.

Another typical change occurred in the technical services area. When the acquisitions librarian position was reevaluated, it was found that the professional duties (primarily selection) could be separated from this position and that an LMTA acquisition technician could handle the job just as well and more economically than a librarian could. In addition, administrators began to recognize that many other duties which had formerly been performed by beginning professionals were really technical or high-level clerical in nature. Once the trained LMTA was available to perform such tasks, administrators recognized that it was more cost effective for LMTAs than librarians to do them.

Thus, many duties in various departments of the library have been expanded to include LMTAs. In public services, LMTAs have been put in charge of reserve book collections, serial collections, pamphlet collections, and government document collections. They have also been assigned as interlibrary loan technicians, information desk assistants, and reference technicians. In technical services, LMTAs not only have been put in charge of acquisitions, but have also been put in charge of the binding area and the materials processing area. In the cataloging area, the introduction of prepared cataloging copy such as OCLC, MARC, and CIP (Cataloging-in-Publication) data have made it possible for well-trained technicians to reduce the number of professional librarians needed for original cataloging. In the audiovisual area, LMTAs have taken over film booking and rentals, production of many audiovisual materials, and the maintenance and repair of AV equipment. However, in all of these areas, the LMTA still exercised judgment within guidelines set by the librarian in charge of each department.

In one major area, that of supervising clerical and other technical personnel, LMTAs began to come into their own. This phenomenon occurred for several important reasons. First, if LMTAs were to become supervisors, such as circulation supervisors, they must be able to supervise library clerks and pages. Second, librarians had received training in professional areas which did not necessarily involve them in supervising other personnel. Librarians such as catalogers, children's librarians, and reference librarians might work years in a library before they were in positions which required them to supervise other personnel. Third, economics and other considerations encouraged library systems to put LMTAs in charge of bookmobiles, branches, or small libraries. In these positions, LMTAs were required to train and supervise library personnel and to introduce them to the concepts of library service.

THE LMTA'S ROLE IN LIBRARY SERVICE

The role of the Library Media Technical Assistant in providing library service is vital if a library is to fulfill its philosophy of library service. Although librarians set the policies and procedures which direct the operations of the library, LMTAs are often responsible for translating these policies and procedures into library service. As supervisors, LMTAs can be responsible for training the library clerks, assistants, pages, and volunteers who are under their supervision to reflect the library's philosophy of library service. Because the average patron believes that the clerk at the circulation desk is in charge of the library, the circulation LMTA must see that this clerk (usually the newest person in the library) understands the principles of library ethics and *The Library Bill of Rights.* The LMTA should also be sure that each new employee is informed of the library's stated objectives and understands how these objectives relate to the employee's job.

Once the LMTA has trained a new employee, he or she should supervise and direct the employee in developing a philosophy of "service to the patrons." This should include recognizing that the public's needs should come before the convenience of the staff when procedures are being set up or policies revised. It also should include an awareness of common library etiquette as discussed in the section on library ethics. Many library patrons have forsaken libraries forever because of the curtness or rudeness of a few library staff members. The LMTA supervisor should also remind staff members that the library is still considered to be a place for quiet study by many of its patrons. All too often, the library staff members are the noisiest persons in the library! Therefore, staff members should remember to hold conversations in quieter tones (preferably outside the studying space of their patrons).

LMTAs have another important function in library services. They may be in charge of areas such as the circulation desk or the processing of materials in which library procedures are involved. If so, they should be on the alert for new procedures, new techniques, and new ways in which their own libraries could improve upon their procedures or services. LMTAs may see a new technique at a nearby library or a new process at a library convention which could affect their area and which could be useful in their own libraries. If this occurs, the LMTA should investigate everything about the "new idea," including the costs and any problems others have encountered. The LMTA could then present a written proposal to the librarian with the possible pros and cons for adopting the "new idea." The librarian could review and evaluate this information and make an informed decision regarding the proposal. Thus, the LMTA can support the librarian by providing background information on procedures or areas in which the librarian is not directly involved. After all, Butler did say in 1933 that the technician level should be concerned with the internal institutional efficiency of the library. By following these procedures, the LMTA can take his or her rightful place as a member of the library team providing good library service.

GOOD LIBRARY SERVICE

Good library service does not just happen, it is consciously developed by all members of the library team working together to achieve a common goal. This service does not necessarily depend upon a library's ability to provide the most up-to-date equipment and materials. Instead, good library service depends more upon the concern, imagination, and interest of all those involved – be they staff members, librarians, administrators, board members, or patrons – in developing services which are tailor-made to satisfy the needs of each library community. Thus, although libraries may differ from each other in their materials, objectives, and services, successful libraries will share the following elements of library service:

- A library should follow its stated objectives.

- A library should support and defend the principles of *The Library Bill of Rights*.

- A library should practice a philosophy of service to its public.

- All library activities and services should encourage and provide the best possible service to its public.

- This library service should include:

   1. determining the needs of the library's public

   2. providing materials, programs, and services to satisfy these needs and to support the library's objectives

   3. presenting materials which represent all points of view and not removing materials because of partisan or doctrinal disapproval

   4. providing the right information to the right person at the right time

   5. choosing routines and procedures that facilitate rather than hinder the individual's use of the library

   6. updating these procedures and services to reflect current needs of the public

   7. making the resources and services of the library known to its potential users

   8. providing enough trained staff to give personal attention to patrons' problems and needs

   9. being polite and courteous to patrons

   10. treating every patron as fairly and impartially as possible

   11. maintaining the confidence of the library public

   12. showing respect for library employees and working with a spirit of courteous cooperation

   13. making only constructive criticisms and channeling these to the proper authority

REVIEW QUESTIONS

1. Define "intellectual freedom."

2. Discuss the relationship of *The Library Bill of Rights* and the *Freedom to Read* statement to the materials that should be included in a library's collection.

3. Identify the basic elements of library ethics and etiquette as they relate to library patrons, fellow staff members, and those in higher authority.

4. Describe the procedures a staff member should follow when confronted by an irate patron with a censorship complaint. Describe the procedures that should be followed if the librarian is not available.

5. Develop a statement of a personal philosophy of library service based on the elements of good library service.

SELECTED READINGS

ALA Yearbook: A Review of Library Events. Chicago: American Library Association, 1976- . Articles on "Intellectual Freedom"; "Ethics."

American Library Association. Office for Intellectual Freedom. *Intellectual Freedom Manual.* Chicago: ALA, 1974.

Busha, Charles H. *Intellectual Freedom Primer.* Littleton, CO: Libraries Unlimited, 1977.

"Code of Ethics for Librarians" (adopted by American Library Association, 1938). Chicago: American Library Association, 1938.

Illinois Libraries, vol. 60, no. 2 (February 1978). Four articles on intellectual freedom, pp. 112-24: "Librarians and the Cause of Freedom," by George Anastapio; "Threats to the First Amendment," by Gilda Parrella; "Restricting Pornography While Protecting First Amendment Rights," by Dick Simpson; "How Free Is Our Freedom," by Lawrence Golden.

NOTES

[1]U.S. Supreme Court. *Miller v. California.* 37 L Ed 2nd 419.

[2]*American Heritage Dictionary of the English Language* (Boston: Houghton Mifflin, 1969), p. 1054.

[3]Office for Intellectual Freedom, American Library Association, *Intellectual Freedom Manual* (Chicago: American Library Association, 1974), p. 10.

[4]Office for Intellectual Freedom, *Intellectual Freedom Manual*, p. 10.

12
ENTERING THE LIBRARY WORLD

The library/media world today offers a great variety of opportunities. In addition to choosing the occupational level at which one wants to, or can, work, each person can choose from within a range of jobs in a great number of different types of libraries. Once these choices have been made, he or she can begin the search for a library position that fits his or her own needs and desires. Although this process might seem to be endless and unrewarding at times, the guidelines presented in this chapter may help each person conduct a search which is productive in locating and procuring the position he or she truly wants.

WHAT KIND OF WORK DO YOU WANT?

The hardest part about choosing a new job is first determining what type of work you truly want to do. Many times, people have accepted what seemed to be ideal jobs only to find out within a short time that they had made disastrous choices. Others have accepted positions and been very happy with them even though their friends and associates thought surely they would be unhappy in such jobs. These discrepancies between a person's expectations and the reality of a situation are influenced by many intangible variables. These variables can be emotional, physical, psychological, or economic, and their importance at any one time can affect a person's satisfaction with his or her job.

In order to minimize these variables, you should first ask yourself "What makes me tick?" As a prospective employee, you should evaluate your personal, physical, and psychological strengths and weaknesses. For example, do you prefer working in a quiet area by yourself or do you like to work near other people? One library technician took a position as the only full-time employee in the library of a local historical society. Within a month she was ready to quit the library field because she could not stand being alone so much of the time. After she moved to a busy public library she was very happy. Another technician accepted a position in a high school library and then found out that she did not enjoy working with the ninth and tenth grade students. By taking the time to evaluate your own personality needs, you may be able to avoid similar situations.

A good place to begin is by evaluating your physical strengths and weaknesses. Do you have the dexterity or talent, in addition to the interest, for working with media equipment and materials? Or, on the other hand, are you too overwhelmed by mechanical objects to relax and allow yourself to become familiar with them? Do you prefer jobs in which you sit still most of the day or do you like jobs where you can stand up and move around? Would you like to type or use a computer terminal for much of the day, or would you rather work at a circulation desk? Once you have considered questions such as these, it will be easier for you to understand what kind of job might interest you.

Besides all of these personal traits and characteristics, many people also have personal interest preferences which may influence their choices. Some people may want to work in college libraries in order to get free tuition and continue their formal education. Other people may want to move to a particular geographic location and be willing to accept any number of positions in order to be in that location. Some may want to work in a particular type of library, such as a special library, and might turn down other jobs until what they want comes along. Such personal preferences as these may seem strange to others, but if the person making the decisions is happy with them, that person will more than likely be very happy with a job that satisfies such preferences.

Finally, there may be outside considerations that may affect a person's job choices. To some persons, a well-paying position is most important, while to others having a flexible schedule with summers off is most important. Some persons cannot relocate or commute to a job because of family responsibilities, and other persons might prefer to do just that because of their family responsibilities. In all of these considerations, the primary point to understand is that you alone must decide which considerations and variables, both personal and external, are most important to you and which ones will determine your choices as you begin to look for a job in the library world.

WHERE DO YOU WANT TO WORK?

Once you have taken an inventory of your own preferences and needs, it is useful to compare them with the kinds of library positions and library opportunities available to you. First, think about the library courses you thought were most interesting. Then, analyze them to see what you liked about them. More often than not, there will be some particular areas or subjects which will indicate a library area that will most interest you. For example, if you enjoyed story hours or children's literature, you might like to work in a school library or in children's work in a public library. If you preferred bibliographic searches and verifying, you might enjoy either interlibrary loan work or acquisitions searching in a library's order department. If you like to meet people and enjoy variety, jobs in the circulation areas (particularly in public libraries) might appeal to you most of all. Thus, by analyzing library jobs in the light of your own needs, you should be able to identify a range of jobs which would interest you.

Next, if you have not observed persons working in such jobs, it might be worth your while to do so. Volunteer to help out in a library department for a few days to see if you really do like the work. If libraries do not want volunteers (and some of them may not), ask if you can observe their library operations for several hours. Unless you have observed or worked in a school library media center, it is very difficult to understand the chaos which erupts when the bell rings. This first-hand experience will not only help you learn more about the library, but it also will let librarians and staff members know that you are available and are willing to work.

WHERE ARE THE JOBS?

Once you have decided on the type of work you would like to do, you should begin looking for a place of employment. Although libraries obviously spring to mind, you should explore all types of libraries including public, school (both public and private), all academic, and any special libraries in your area. You should also compile a list of all of the possible industries, businesses, and organizations which might need someone to perform these particular job duties. You should realize that libraries are not the only places where materials must be organized and distributed. Too often, prospective library employees have bemoaned the lack of library opportunities because the local libraries or schools are "not hiring." Do not be misled into thinking that only a library will hire you.

Businesses, industries, institutions, governmental agencies, private organizations, and national associations often provide job opportunities for those persons who investigate these possibilities (*see* Fig. 12-1, page 168). An example of such opportunities exists in practically every hospital in the United States. Because hospital accrediting associations encourage hospitals to staff their medical libraries, hospitals are excellent places to look for a job. Similarly, law offices and county law libraries may be able to use the talents of someone interested in filing and searching. Companies which show signs of growth or strong economic bases may have expanded to the point that they are ready to have someone organize their company records. These are just a few examples of the kinds of library-related jobs which may be available in non-library environments.

Probably the most frequent question asked of someone who gets a new job is "How did you find out about it?" So many people believe that jobs appear as if by magic or because of "Who you know," that they cannot believe anyone obtained a job through his or her own tenacity and perseverence. It is less romantic, but much more realistic, to recognize that finding a job you want may take lots of time and energy. A good definition to remember is that "luck is opportunity meeting preparation."

One of the first places you will probably look for a job will be at the nearest library which has the kind of job you want. However, you should not only contact the most obvious library but also contact all possible nearby libraries. If you know someone who works in the library, you can ask that person if there are any job openings coming up. However, in addition, you should go to the library or institution and ask for an application form. (Applying for a job will be discussed in a later section.) Do not be discouraged if your friends or the library indicate that there are no job openings at the present time. Often there are unexpected turnovers in the staff so that an opening may appear without warning.

After you have applied to the local libraries, you can begin job-hunting in earnest by looking through the want-ads of all available newspapers. Do not prejudge any paper because you think it is too small or too large to cover the area you are interested in. This perusal of newspaper ads can begin many months before you will be available for a job. Not only is this an excellent way for you to keep abreast of the jobs which are available but it also ensures that you won't miss an opportunity. One LMTA student found the job of her dreams by doing just that, even though she had another year to finish before she graduated. By following up a local ad for the national headquarters of a barbershop quartet singing society, she was able to combine her library interests with her love of vocal music.

Another good source of information about jobs can be the people you know. You should not be bashful about letting those around you know you are looking for a job. Friends, relatives, teachers, fellow students, and friendly librarians may have heard about job opportunities and be happy to tell you about them. If this happens, you should treat each lead as a valid job opportunity and follow it up. Although some of the leads might be false ones, others could be very important ones. Also, the fact that you did follow the leads will encourage these friends as well as others to tell you about other opportunities as they hear about them.

Figure 12-1
Sample want-ads for library positions

ASSISTANT MEDICAL LIBRARIAN
One of Chicago's most modern health care facilities has an immed. opening for an Asst. Medical Librarian. Duties include: handling circulation & interlibrary loans, technical processing, assisting patrons with reference inquiries and audio-visual equipment. Hours: M,T,Th,F 12:30 PM-9 PM. & W 8 AM-4:30 PM.

The qualified individual should have at least several hours credit in basic Library Science or equivalent library work experience. Good typing skills are required.

Interested candidates should send their resume to Jane Jones at: St. Mary of Bethlehem Hospital Center, 3322 N. Halsted St., Chicago, IL 60622.

Library   CLERK TYPIST
Detail oriented individual required to check in journals for association library. Some library experience preferred. Light typing. Pleasant, near north location. Call 450-3563. American Doctors Assoc.

LIBRARIAN/TYPIST
Immediate opening, no degree required just brains, memory and good organizational skills to clip, file, maintain data for our business library. Occasional phone research. Salary leverage for super typing skills. Reply to: 150A, 2520 N. Jefferson, Chicago, 60614.

LIBRARY ASSISTANT
Full time, to perform clerical routines at circulation desk. Hours include 2 eves. per week, every other Sat, and 1 Sunday out of 4. $8,915 annually. Applications obtained at Park Summit Library, 45 N. Oakton, Park Summit, IL. Deadline for applications is Aug. 12, 1981. Civil service exam to be held Aug. 22, 9:30 AM at the library.

LIBRARY CLERK
Technical services (OCLC, typing, filing, ordering and receiving). Lib. exp. or 1 year college pref.; will train you, 37½ hrs. per wk. flex time, ½ tuition for NTC courses. Salary $9,000. Send resume to: Library Personnel Office, National Technical College, 1725 Sheridan Rd, Chicago, IL. No phone calls please.

PART-TIME LIBRARY TECHNICIAN
sought for the Youth Services Dept. of the Public Library, 320 Juniper Lane, Prairie Meadows, IL. The Associate degree in library science or a BA is required. This position involves planning and executing programs for children (aged 3-14) & reader's advisory in this group. The Position is 15 hrs. per week, $5.90 per hour. Contact Jean Arnold, Youth Services Librarian, 295-5230.

School placement offices and government employment agencies are also useful places to learn about job opportunities. These offices not only have current job listings, but they will also let you register or file an application for future job openings. At government employment agencies, you can often register for a particular geographic location and category of personnel. The agency will then notify you about job openings which fit your choices. The federal and state governments and some city governments all have civil service employment systems. (For further information about federal library jobs write the U.S. Office of Personnel Management, 1900 E Street, NW, Washington, DC 20415.) These systems are designed to ensure that every applicant has an equal opportunity for being hired for a job. Thus, each applicant must usually successfully pass a civil service test or pass it with a very high score before he or she is even interviewed for a job. When you apply to a placement office or employment office it might be very useful for you to attach a copy of your resume to your application form. This can later be copied or detached by the office and forwarded with an application or civil service test score to the prospective employing librarian.

A final way to locate information about job openings is by "letting your fingers do the walking." As you do in the telephone yellow pages, look up information about libraries and companies in professional or trade directories. The *American Library Directory* can be found in many libraries. This directory lists libraries geographically by state and then by city (a particularly useful feature if you are planning to relocate). Under each city, the names and statistical data are given for every library, including the director's name, size of the staff and names of the department heads, annual budget, the total staff salaries, size of the collection, and other useful information such as any special collections. Other professional and trade directories may provide similar information about any companies that interest you. Also, your local library may have annual reports on local businesses, industries, or hospitals. By reviewing all of this information, you may be able to choose several libraries, institutions, or businesses which could make use of your talents and abilities. You could then write letters to individuals at each company inquiring about any job opportunities and enclosing a copy of your resume. (*See* the section below on Letters of Application.)

HOW TO GET THE JOB YOU WANT

Before you write any letters or fill in any application forms, you should first evaluate and identify your strengths and weaknesses. Every person has particular talents or abilities which would be important to a prospective employer if he or she only knew about them. Therefore, it is up to you to identify these in the job application process. This does not mean that you should be a braggart, but it does mean that you owe it to yourself to present the information in as favorable a light as is possible. You can record any awards or honors you have received or list any special courses or programs you have taken or participated in. If you can indicate that you have directed or organized any special programs, the better your resume will look.

Because library employers are looking for staff members with specific qualities, they may be looking at your life experience as a whole rather than just at your academic credentials. To an employer, students who are active in LMTA or school activities indicate an interest in others and a willingness to work. Adults who have spent years of volunteering their time for parent-teacher associations, scout work, and church work have also indicated that they can work with groups, help organize activities, and direct others. Therefore, if you have experiences such as these in your background, you should certainly include them in your resume and refer to them at the appropriate time in your interviews.

RESUMES

A resume is a concise summary of your personal data, educational background, and occupational information. It usually consists of 1-3 pages and contains all of the pertinent data a prospective employer would want to know when considering you for employment. The purpose of the resume is to present the vital information about you in an easy-to-read format. Thus, you should present your information simply, legibly, and accurately. The information should be selected with care and should indicate your activities and employment from high school up to, and including, the present time. The resume should serve as a thumbnail sketch of your life which can then be expanded upon in an interview (*see* Fig. 12-2).

A resume is usually divided into four or five basic sections. The first section gives personal data such as your full name, address, and phone number. It may also include other data which could be of interest to a prospective employer. For example, a statement that you have three children would subtly explain a ten-year absence from the work force. Although employers may not legally ask such personal questions anymore, they will usually greatly appreciate your volunteering such information.

Other sections of the resume cover your educational background, occupational experience, and any activities or honors. It is useful to write down all of this information once, keep it up to date, and use it in the future as a guide for filling in application forms. Your educational data should indicate the names and location of the schools you attended, the years you attended, when you graduated (if you did), and any degrees you received. Also you can indicate your major courses of study and can even list any library and occupational courses if they might be important. Since many employers might not be familiar with the LMTA degree or courses, you also might attach a list of the courses you took and include a short description from the school catalog for each course.

The occupational section should list all of your major places of employment in reverse order beginning with your present job. You should include the name of the library or company, the dates employed (in whole years) and your job titles. You do not need to list your reasons for leaving your job or give the names of your supervisors. If an employer wants this kind of information, it will be included on the application form. Also, you probably should not indicate any information about salaries you have earned or may want unless it is very important to you. Salaries in libraries may vary greatly depending upon many factors, and you would not want to eliminate yourself from consideration because the salary you asked for is more than a professional librarian makes. However, if you include brief descriptions of your duties in each of your jobs, you will help the employer form a mental picture of your abilities and capabilities.

This mental picture can be further enhanced by the section which lists your skills, activities, and honors. Here you can indicate any skills or special areas of knowledge you have which may be useful to a future employer. For example,

Figure 12-2

Sample resume

NAME: JANE ELLEN (DOE) BROWN
ADDRESS: 1234 Green St.
                           Milwaukee, WI 53201
PHONE: (414) 443-2610
BIRTHDATE: February 3, 1951
BIRTHPLACE: Milwaukee, WI
MARITAL STATUS: Married, 3 children

EDUCATION

East High School, Milwaukee, WI, 1966-1969 (Business Diploma, 1969)

Business College of Wisconsin, Milwaukee, 1969-1970 (Secretarial Certificate, 1970)
     100 WPM Typing Award.

Gateway Technical Institute, Kenosha, WI 1979-1981 (Associate of Applied Science
     Degree, 1981. Library/Media Technical Assistant major.)
     A list of Library/Media Technology courses is attached.

OCCUPATIONAL EXPERIENCE

Kearney and Trecker Co., West Allis, WI, 1970-72. Clerk-typist.
     File clerk and typist for four engineers.

COMMUNITY ACTIVITIES

Congregational Church Cooperative Preschool (President, 1976)
Parent-Teachers Association (Secretary, 1978)
Brownie Scout Troop Leader and Cookie Sale Chairperson
L/MTA Club, Gateway Technical Institute.

REFERENCES

Ms. Barbara Chernik, Instructor LMTA courses, Gateway Technical Institute, Kenosha,
     WI 53140
Mr. Norbert Link, Instructor media courses, Gateway Technical Institute, Kenosha, WI
     53140
Mrs. Connie Jones, Executive Director, Milwaukee Area Girl Scout Council, Milwaukee,
     WI 53201.

---

working on the school newspaper or doing volunteer hospital work may indicate an ability in public relations or a strong interest in working with people. Sometimes these outside activities can be just as important as a person's occupational experiences when the final hiring decisions are being made.

The final section of your resume is very important to the library world. This section should indicate the names of several "references" or persons who would recommend you for employment. These references should be acquainted with your work capabilities rather than serve as character witnesses. They should not be relatives or close personal friends because these people often cannot be completely objective about your abilities. Also, you should ask each person if you might use his or her name as a reference before you do so. References are very important in the library world because librarians cooperate so closely with each other. More often than you will realize, a prospective employer may know your former employer or supervisor and ask him or her about you anyway. Therefore, examples of good references to choose would be former library teachers, supervisors, librarians, and library staff that you might have worked with.

Once you have compiled your resume information, the most important thing to remember in preparing your resume is that it introduces you to the prospective employer. If it is clear, concise, legible, and accurate, it will give a good impression of you. If it is sloppy, illegible, and incomplete, it will be an indictment against you. Therefore, take time to prepare this document well and be prepared to pay to have it commercially copied or duplicated.

LETTERS OF APPLICATION

Once the resume has been prepared and duplicated, you can begin writing letters of application to send out as cover letters with the resume. These letters should be written individually to each employer and should be geared to that individual employer's needs. Such information can be gleaned from the *American Library Directory* and other business sources. You may also mention where you heard about a job opening—from an ad, a friend, or just that their library's reputation has drawn your interest. You should write your letter from the employer's point of view and keep the "I's" to a minimum. There are a number of books available which provide information on writing such letters. Basically, you should try to interest the employer enough to ask you for an interview. Thus, your letter can touch on your abilities or qualifications for a job, and refer the reader to the enclosed resume for more information. The letter should also indicate your interest in an interview (or in receiving an application) and give an address and phone number where you can be reached.

You can send out these letters of application in response to ads, in response to a lead from a friend, or as blind letters to libraries or institutions you have chosen from the library or business directories. In each case, your letter should follow the guidelines described above, and you should write to each institution as if it were the only one you are writing to. Although your resume may be printed, each letter should be an original letter which is legibly and accurately typed. It should be addressed (correctly!) to a specific individual, preferably the head of the library or the personnel manager. The care you take to find out such information should favorably impress the receiver of the letter. Your letter should be written in correct letter-writing form and be accompanied by a copy of your resume. For future reference, you should be sure to keep a copy of every letter you send.

Because many large institutions, including libraries, may have personnel offices, it might be wise to send two letters and resumes to such institutions. One set would be sent to the Personnel Office and another set to the person in charge of the library itself. Thus, in a school system, the second letter might go to a school librarian or principal and in a company it might go to the special librarian or the director of research. This duplication can be very worthwhile, especially in institutions that have many employees and centralized personnel departments.

In addition to sending out letters of application to libraries, it might be worth your while to write letters answering several newspaper ads even if you are not entirely interested in the jobs. The experience of answering an ad and interviewing for a job will help you perfect your job-hunting skills. This experience will also help you develop your strengths, minimize your weaknesses, and learn to relax. One important thing to remember in answering ads, however, is that many other people will also be answering the same ads. In order to ensure that your letter will be reviewed, you should follow several guidelines. First, your response letter to the ad should mention the ad in your first paragraph. Do not make the reader guess which newspaper you saw the ad in. Next, you should be sure to include all of the information which the ad asks for. Finally, your response should be clearly stated, legibly typed, and include a copy of your resume. Unless these conditions are met, your response might never make it past the first screening process.

APPLICATION FORMS

The second screening process usually involves filling out an application form. This form may be a general purpose personnel application form for an entire institution or it may be an application form geared specifically to one library. In any case, you should provide all of the requested information to the best of your knowledge. At this time, your resume can be very useful in providing names and dates you might otherwise have forgotten. It is very important that you provide accurate information because an employer can fire you for knowingly giving false information on an application form.

If any questions are asked which might cause you some problems, you should be as truthful as possible. For example, if you have a medical condition such as epilepsy or heart problems, you could state this but also indicate that your condition is controlled by medicine. Also, if you were fired from your last job, you could state that you had a difference of opinion with your supervisor or that you are looking for more challenging work. If a job application asks for an expected salary level, you should indicate a salary which would give credit for your education and employment. It would be useful for you to determine what comparable positions are paying before you fill in this blank. Too often, employees have asked for and been given a salary which they considered to be high only to find out later that they were getting paid less than other employees for similar work.

A final word of caution about applications is that you should take your time in filling them out. A messy application form may be interpreted to mean that you are either a careless person or not interested in the job. Above all, take your time to be accurate in your grammar and spelling. You do not want to misspell such words as "library" or to make a freudian slip of the pen. To reduce such chances, be sure to proofread the application before you sign it.

INTERVIEWS

Once your resume and application have been reviewed, you may be invited to interview for the job. If so, you should take the time to find out all you can about the library or the institution beforehand. On the day of the interview, you should dress for the business world in a suit and tie or a dress and heels. Also, be sure that your personal cleanliness is above reproach. You should arrive for your interview early enough so that you can tour the library or just sit and relax if you are in a personnel office. Although you may be nervous, it is not a good idea to smoke or chew gum. By paying attention to these external details, you can help yourself to relax and gain a measure of inner confidence.

When you meet the interviewer or interviewers, you should learn their names and titles. This will not only impress them, but it will also give you some indication of the areas they will probably be interested in. As you answer any questions, you should give the impression that you want to work at *this* library more than at any other place of employment. You can indicate this by asking questions about the library and about the job you are interviewing for. If you are asked about salary, you can indicate your education and experience and ask to be placed on the salary schedule accordingly. Interviewers will expect you to have some questions about insurance and leave benefits and work schedules, but you should not limit yourself to such questions. Also, you should not get sidetracked onto personal or non-library related topics. Do not talk negatively about your present or former jobs because it is very likely that the interviewers may be very good friends with your employers. Finally, if you are given the opportunity to make a final statement, it would be useful for you to review your qualifications and describe how and why you could perform the job very well.

Some libraries and personnel departments have expanded the interview process to include an assessment center concept. Such a center may provide simulated library situations for you to take part in. These situations might be face-to-face encounters or written problems and exercises for you to respond to. They enable interviewers to observe your reactions and decision-making abilities in situations similar to those you would encounter on the job. If you are interviewed through such a process, you should remain calm, try to forget the observers, and respond as normally as possible to the situations presented to you.

After the interview, you might want to write a brief thank you note to the interviewer. Such a note could highlight your qualifications for the job and would indicate that you are still interested in the position. However, unless you have been told to do so, you should not phone the interviewer and ask if you got the job. Such a response might not be perceived very well by the interviewer.

If you are offered the job, you should weigh all of the factors surrounding it before you say yes or no. Besides considering the salary offer, you should review the benefits which are included. These benefits are taxfree and can sometimes represent a monetary value equal to ¼ to ⅓ of your salary. You should also consider any opportunities for advancement if this is important to you. If you will need to commute to the job, will the expenses of commuting be offset by the advantages of the job? Above all, will this particular job satisfy your emotional and psychological, as well as economic, needs? If it does not, it would not be fair to either you or the employer for you to take a job which you do not expect to enjoy or to stay in for a minimum of two years. After you have considered all of these factors, you should be able to make a decision about the job which you will be happy with. Then, you should write to the employer informing him or her of your decision.

BEGINNING THE JOB

Once you have accepted the job offer, you can begin to prepare for the job. You should find out what your work schedule will be and exactly what day and time you are to begin work. You should learn the name and title of your immediate supervisor and stop in to meet him or her if you have not already met. This supervisor will usually introduce you to others in the department and you might be given an insider's tour. At this time, it would be useful to find out about such employee practices as which door to come in (especially if you begin work before the library opens) and where the staff members eat their lunches. You may also observe how the other employees are dressed so that you can do the same. Although these matters may seem inconsequential, your attention to them may save you some embarrassing moments as well as indicate to the staff that you are willing to learn. This attention to detail will also help you feel more at ease on your first day of work.

When you start your first day you should arrive at your desk on time or even a little early. Usually, your supervisor will help orient you to your job or assign someone else to do so. In either case, you should ask if there are any policy or procedures manuals you could read to familiarize yourself with library operations. Since such manuals will more often than not be out of date, it would be wise for you to take notes for the first few days or weeks. This will help you remember instructions and ask intelligent questions about those areas you do not understand. Your supervisor and fellow employees will usually appreciate this quality because they often find it so frustrating to train a new employee.

For the first few weeks, it would be politic for you to observe and record what you are instructed to do rather than to question or challenge. After you have reviewed your notes, you can ask how and why a certain operation is done. You should wait a few months before you offer suggestions for changes unless that is an expected part of your job. However, even then you should suggest changes objectively and diplomatically. Otherwise, you might inadvertently antagonize someone because you have questioned his or her pet project. You also should try to avoid being drawn into office politics by listening to one staff member complain about another. If you maintain a pleasant manner toward everyone and are conscientious in learning your job, you will find that most library staffs are very congenial and willing to accept new members.

REVIEW QUESTIONS

1. Review your own personal needs and preferences and make a list of those needs which are most important to you in searching for a job.

2. Review the types of work available in libraries and identify the type of work you would most like to do.

3. Look through the local newspaper ads for two weeks and make a list of those which interest you.

4. Write a resume for yourself following the guidelines identified in this chapter.

5. Select a job which interests you from Figure 12-1 and write a letter of application for this job. (Or, write a letter of application for the person whose resume is shown in Figure 12-2.)

6.   Visit a nearby library which interests you and ask for an application form to fill out. Fill out this application form.

SELECTED READINGS

American Library Directory. annual. New York: Bowker, 1908- .

Bolles, Richard. *What Color Is Your Parachute?* 5th ed. Berkeley, CA: Ten Speed Press, 1979.

Corwen, Leonard. *Your Resume: Key to a Better Job.* New York: Arco, 1977.

Donaho, M. *How to Get the Job You Want: A Guide to Resumes, Interviews and Job Hunting Strategy.* Englewood Cliffs, NJ: Prentice-Hall, 1976.

Estabrook, Leigh. "Job Seekers in the Buyer's Market: How Library Employers Judge Candidates," *Library Journal*, February 1, 1973, pp. 385-87.

Josey, E. J. *Opportunities for Minorities in Librarianship.* Metuchen, NJ: Scarecrow, 1977.

McDonald, Joseph. "How I Got My Library Job Good," *Library Journal*, February 1, 1973, pp. 388-90.

Montgomery, Gerald. *The Selling of You: A Practical Guide to Job Hunting.* Seattle, WA: Montgomery Communications, 1980.

Myers, Alpha. *Your Future in Library Careers.* New York: Arco, 1976.

Resumes That Get Jobs. 2nd ed. New York: Arco, 1976.

Rudman, Jack. *Library Assistant.* Syosset, NY: National Learning, n.d.

Rudman, Jack. *Library Clerk.* Syosset, NY: National Learning, n.d.

Rudman, Jack. *Senior Library Clerk.* Syosset, NY: National Learning, n.d.

Sellan, Betty-Carol. *What Else Can You Do with a Library Degree?* Hamden, CT: Gaylord Professional Publications, n.d.

Strohmenger. *How to Complete Job Application Forms.* Falls Church, VA: American Personnel, 1975.

Sullivan, Peggy. *Opportunities in Library and Information Science.* Skokie, IL: National Textbook, 1977.

Writing That Successful Application Letter. New York: Counseling Career Plan, 1979.

You Can Pack Your Own Chute. (16mm film) Newport Beach, CA: Ramic Productions, 1972.

APPENDIX A

Library Bill of Rights

The American Library Association affirms that all libraries are forums for information and ideas, and that the following basic policies should guide their services.

1. Books and other library resources should be provided for the interest, information, and enlightenment of all people of the community the library serves. Materials should not be excluded because of the origin, background, or views of those contributing to their creation.

2. Libraries should provide materials and information presenting all points of view on current and historical issues. Materials should not be proscribed or removed because of partisan or doctrinal disapproval.

3. Libraries should challenge censorship in the fulfillment of their responsibility to provide information and enlightenment.

4. Libraries should cooperate with all persons and groups concerned with resisting abridgment of free expression and free access to ideas.

5. A person's right to use a library should not be denied or abridged because of origin, age, background, or views.

6. Libraries which make exhibit spaces and meeting rooms available to the public they serve should make such facilities available on an equitable basis, regardless of the beliefs or affiliations of individuals or groups requesting their use.

Adopted June 18, 1948.
Amended February 2, 1961, June 27, 1967, and January 23, 1980,
by the ALA Council.

Reproduced by permission of the American Library Association.

APPENDIX B

FREEDOM TO READ STATEMENT

We therefore affirm these propositions:

1. It is in the public interest for publishers and librarians to make available the widest diversity of views and expressions, including those which are unorthodox or unpopular with the majority.

    Creative thought is by definition new, and what is new is different. The bearer of every new thought is a rebel until his idea is refined and tested. Totalitarian systems attempt to maintain themselves in power by the ruthless suppression of any concept which challenges the established orthodoxy. The power of a democratic system to adapt to change is vastly strengthened by the freedom of its citizens to choose widely from among conflicting opinions offered freely to them. To stifle every nonconformist idea at birth would mark the end of the democratic process. Furthermore, only through the constant activity of weighing and selecting can the democratic mind attain the strength demanded by times like these. We need to know not only what we believe but why we believe it.

2. Publishers and librarians do not need to endorse every idea or presentation contained in the books they make available. It would conflict with the public interest for them to establish their own political, moral, or aesthetic views as the sole standard for determining what books should be published or circulated.

    Publishers and librarians serve the educational process by helping to make available knowledge and ideas required for the growth of the mind and the increase of learning. They do not foster education by imposing as mentors the patterns of their own thought. The people should have the freedom to read and consider a broader range of ideas than those that may be held by any single librarian or publisher or government or church. It is wrong that what one man can read should be confined to what another thinks proper.

3. It is contrary to the public interest for publishers or librarians to determine the acceptability of a book solely on the basis of the personal history or political affiliations of the author.

    A book should be judged as a book. No art or literature can flourish if it is to be measured by the political views or private lives of its creators. No society of free men can flourish which draws up lists of writers to whom it will not listen, whatever they may have to say.

Adopted June 25, 1953 by Council of the American Library Association. Reprinted by permission of the American Library Association.

4. The present laws dealing with obscenity should be vigorously enforced. Beyond that, there is no place in our society for extra-legal efforts to coerce the taste of others, to confine adults to the reading matter deemed suitable for adolescents, or to inhibit the efforts of writers to achieve artistic expression.

    To some, much of modern literature is shocking. But is not much of life itself shocking? We cut off literature at the source if we prevent serious artists from dealing with the stuff of life. Parents and teachers have a responsibility to prepare the young to meet the diversity of experiences in life to which they will be exposed, as they have a responsibility to help them learn to think critically for themselves. These are affirmative responsibilities, not to be discharged simply by preventing them from reading works for which they are not yet prepared. In these matters taste differs, and taste cannot be legislated; nor can machinery be devised which will suit the demands of one group without limiting the freedom of others. We deplore the catering to the immature, the retarded, or the maladjusted taste. But those concerned with freedom have the responsibility of seeing to it that each individual book or publication, whatever its contents, price or method of distribution, is dealt with in accordance with due process of law.

5. It is not in the public interest to force a reader to accept with any book the prejudgment of a label characterizing the book or author as subversive or dangerous.

    The idea of labeling presupposes the existence of individuals or groups with wisdom to determine by authority what is good or bad for the citizen. It presupposes that each individual must be directed in making up his mind about the ideas he examines. But Americans do not need others to do their thinking for them.

6. It is the responsibility of publishers and librarians, as guardians of the people's freedom to read, to contest encroachments upon that freedom by individuals or groups seeking to impose their own standards or tastes upon the community at large.

    It is inevitable in the give and take of the democratic process that the political, the moral, or the aesthetic concepts of an individual or group will occasionally collide with those of another individual or group. In a free society each individual is free to determine for himself what he wishes to read, and each group is free to determine what it will recommend to its freely associated members. But no group has the right to take the law into its own hands, and to impose its own concept of politics or morality upon other members of a democratic society. Freedom is no freedom if it is accorded only to the accepted and the inoffensive.

7. It is the responsibility of publishers and librarians to give full meaning to the freedom to read by providing books that enrich the quality of thought and expression. By the exercise of this affirmative responsibility, bookmen can demonstrate that the answer to a bad book is a good one, the answer to a bad idea is a good one.

    The freedom to read is of little consequence when expended on the trivial; it is frustrated when the reader cannot obtain matter fit for his purpose. What is needed is not only the absence of restraint, but the positive provision of opportunity for the people to read the best that has been thought and said. Books are the major channel by which the intellectual inheritance is handed down, and the principal means of its testing and growth. The defense of their freedom and integrity, and the enlargement of their service to society, requires of all bookmen the utmost of their faculties, and deserves of all citizens the fullest of their support.

We state these propositions neither lightly nor as easy generalizations. We here stake out a lofty claim for the value of books. We do so because we believe that they are good, possessed of enormous variety and usefulness, worthy of cherishing and keeping free. We realize that the application of these propositions may mean the dissemination of ideas and manners of expression that are repugnant to many persons. We do not state these propositions in the comfortable belief that what people read is unimportant. We believe rather that what people read is deeply important; that ideas can be dangerous; but that the suppression of ideas is fatal to a democratic society. Freedom itself is a dangerous way of life, but it is ours.

APPENDIX C

STATEMENT ON PROFESSIONAL ETHICS

Approved by ALA Council, January, 1975

INTRODUCTION

The American Library Association has a special concern for the free flow of information and ideas. Its views have been set forth in such policy statements as the Library Bill of Rights and the Freedom to Read Statement where it has said clearly that in addition to the generally accepted legal and ethical principles and the respect for intellectual freedom which should guide the action of every citizen, membership in the library profession carries with it special obligations and responsibilities.

Every citizen has the right as an individual to take part in public debate or to engage in social and political activity. The only restrictions on these activities are those imposed by specific and well-publicized laws and regulations which are generally applicable. However, since personal views and activities may be interpreted as representative of the institution in which a librarian is employed, proper precaution should be taken to distinguish between private actions and those one is authorized to take in the name of an institution.

The statement which follows sets forth certain ethical norms which, while not exclusive to, are basic to librarianship. *It will be augmented by explanatory interpretations and additional statements as they may be needed.*

STATEMENT

A librarian

* has a special responsibility to maintain the principles of the Library Bill of Rights.

* should learn and faithfully execute the policies of the institution of which one is a part and should endeavor to change those which conflict with the spirit of the Library Bill of Rights.

* must protect the essential confidential relationship which exists between a library user and the library.

Reprinted by permission of the American Library Association.

- must avoid any possibility of personal financial gain at the expense of the employing institution.

- has an obligation to insure equality of opportunity and fair judgment of competence in actions dealing with staff appointments, retentions, and promotions.

- has an obligation when making appraisals of the qualifications of any individual to report the facts clearly, accurately, and without prejudice, according to generally accepted guidelines concerning the disclosing of personal information.

INDEX